Spatializing Culture

This book demonstrates the value of ethnographic theory and methods for understanding space and place. It considers how ethnographically based spatial analyses can yield insight into prejudices, inequalities and social exclusion, as well as offering people the means for understanding the places where they live, work, shop, and socialize. In developing the concept of spatializing culture, Setha Low draws on over twenty years of research to examine social production, social construction, embodied, discursive, emotive, affective, and translocal approaches. A global range of fieldwork examples are employed throughout the text to highlight not only the theoretical development of the idea of spatializing culture but also how it can be used in undertaking ethnographies of space and place. The volume will be valuable for all scholars interested in the study of culture through the lens of space and place.

Setha Low is Professor of Anthropology, Earth and Environmental Sciences (Geography), Environmental Psychology, and Women's Studies at the Graduate Center, City University of New York, USA. She is the former President of the American Anthropological Association and served as Deputy Chair of the World Council of Anthropological Associations.

Praise for this book:

"Setha Low has taken an incredibly useful and conceptually comprehensive look at anthropological understandings of 'social production' and 'social construction' in the context of engagements with bodies, language, affect, translocality and their impact on how we navigate space/place. The chapters bring these ideas to life in ways that work both for students in a classroom and for general readers . . . Low's work demonstrates anthropology's singular contribution to theories of space, place and power today."

John L. Jackson, Jr., *University of Pennsylvania, USA*

"Setha Low brings together in this wonderful volume the great extent of her knowledge of cities and her urban scholarship, the delicacy and richness of a visually inclined ethnography, and the conceptual sophistication of a deep historical and contemporary knowledge of theories of place and space."

Caroline Knowles, *Goldsmiths, UK*

"Drawing theoretical inspiration from across the social sciences, *Spatializing Culture* presents state of the art analysis of contemporary social relations and cultural settings. Setha Low demonstrates the power of ethnography as both method and textual craft to examine how meanings, representations and material effects are felt and embodied in the rough and smooth of peoples' everyday lives."

Gareth A. Jones, *London School of Economics and Political Science, UK*

Spatializing Culture

The ethnography of space and place

Setha Low

Routledge
Taylor & Francis Group
LONDON AND NEW YORK

First published 2017
by Routledge
2 Park Square, Milton Park, Abingdon, Oxon OX14 4RN

and by Routledge
711 Third Avenue, New York, NY 10017

Routledge is an imprint of the Taylor & Francis Group, an informa business

British Library Cataloguing-in-Publication Data
A catalogue record for this book is available from the British Library

Library of Congress Cataloging-in-Publication Data
Names: Low, Setha M., author.
Title: Spatializing culture : the ethnography of space and place /
    Setha Low.
Description: New York, NY : Routledge, 2016. | Includes
    bibliographical references and index.
Identifiers: LCCN 2016003615 | ISBN 9781138945609
    (hardback : alk. paper) | ISBN 9781138945616
    (pbk. : alk. paper) | ISBN 9781315671277 (ebk)
Subjects: LCSH: Human geography. | Population geography. |
    Spatial analysis (Statistics) | Place (Philosophy) | Social
    sciences—Research—Methodology.
Classification: LCC GF50 .L68 2016 | DDC 304.2—dc23
LC record available at https://lccn.loc.gov/2016003615

ISBN: 978-1-138-94560-9 (hbk)
ISBN: 978-1-138-94561-6 (pbk)
ISBN: 978-1-315-67127-7 (ebk)

Typeset in Sabon
by Apex CoVantage, LLC

For the future: Alexander, Max and Skye

Contents

Illustrations

Figures

Photographs

Acknowledgments

This book began as a series of conversations with Dolores Hayden, Sally Merry and the late Neil Smith in response to their searching questions about fieldwork methods, forms of evidence and theory building for the study of space and place. Deborah Pellow, Theodore Bestor, Matthew Cooper, Robert Rotenberg and Margaret Rodman offered important insights through their publications and our dinners at the American Anthropological Association annual meeting. Denise Lawrence-Zuñiga contributed directly to this book by sharing materials that we have talked about and written together. During the writing phase of this project, Jeff Maskovsky, Ida Susser, Galey Modan, Kristin Monroe, Rebio Diaz, Babette Audant, Claire Panetta, Eva Tessza Udvarhelyi, Vesna Vučinić, Chihsin Chiu, Aseel Sawalha, Jessica Winegar, Farha Ghannam, Sarah Hankins, Sandra Weil, Stephane Tonnelat, Suzanne Scheld and Vaiva Aglinskas came to the rescue by reading chapters and offering suggestions and constructive criticism. I am deeply indebted to these colleagues for their intellectual, emotional and substantive support of this project.

While co-teaching landscape architecture and urban planning studios with Laurie Olin and the late Robert Hanna at the University of Pennsylvania, I learned that site surveys, circulation plans, social activity programs and schematic designs are crucial components of imagining and creating space and place. In planning and design studios and on design consulting projects, they encouraged the use of ethnographic methods to produce better understandings of the role of the social and cultural as well as the architectural in creating places of opportunity rather than inequality. Recently, my colleagues at Pratt Institute, Ron Shiffman and David Burney, highlighted the importance of ethnographic understandings in the creation of a Placemaking program. I want to thank these dedicated colleagues for providing the opportunity to explore how ethnographic methods can make a difference in the analysis and design of the built environment.

The ethnographic examples presented in this book depended on the funding and teamwork of many people. I particularly would like to thank the National Park Service, and especially Doris Fanelli at Independence National Historical Park; Richard Wells at Ellis Island; William Garrett at Jacob Riis

Park; the late Muriel Crespi, past director of the National Park Service Applied Anthropology Program located in Washington, DC; and Rebecca Joseph and Chuck Smythe, past East Coast regional directors of the ethnography program for their support. I would also like to thank the Graduate Center of the City University of New York and the Center for Human Environments for their assistance. Without Susan Saegert's encouragement and Jared Becker's expertise, these research projects would have been much more difficult.

Numerous foundations and granting agencies provided the financial support for my ethnographic fieldwork. The research on the history and ethnography of the plaza in San José, Costa Rica, was funded by a research grant from the Wenner-Gren Foundation for Anthropological Research, a National Endowment for the Humanities Fellowship, a Fulbright Research Fellowship and a John Simon Guggenheim Memorial Foundation Fellowship. Wenner-Gren Foundation for Anthropological Research and the Research Foundation of the City University of New York funded the gated community research. The Moore Street Market study was part of a project undertaken by the Project for Public Spaces in New York City. The Russell Sage Foundation funded a pilot study of Battery Park City community change post-9/11, and the Social Sciences and Humanities Research Council of Canada funded the condominium project as a comparative component to Randy Lippert's study in Toronto. I would like to thank the many foundations that made these projects possible. I would also like to thank the University of Pennsylvania and the Graduate Center of the City University of New York for funding sabbatical leaves so that I could complete the fieldwork and write up the findings.

A long list of graduate students at the Graduate Center of CUNY collected the data for the National Park Service projects, many of whom are now professors in their own right and include Suzanne Scheld, Dana Taplin, Tracy Fisher, Larissa Honey, Charles Price, Bea Vidacs, Marilyn Diggs-Thompson, Ana Aparicio, Raymond Codrington, Carlotta Pasquali, Carmen Vidal, Kate Brower and Nancy Schwartz. Research teams that are a part of the Public Space Research Group undertook many of the ethnographic projects. The Battery Park City project included Mike Lamb and Dana Taplin, who I continue to work with. The gated community co-researchers – Elena Danaila, Andrew Kirby, Lynmari Benitez and Mariana Diaz-Wionczek – were graduate students at the time and collected many of the New York City interviews. Gregory Donovan, Jen Gieseking, Jessica Miller, Owen Toews and Hillary Caldwell made up the two cooperative housing research teams, and Jennifer Ortiz, Helen Panagiotopoulos and Shelly Buchbinder contributed to the condominium project. I am grateful to these young scholars who made the research process fun and intellectually compelling. Their ideas, enthusiasm and hard work kept projects going, even when faced with adversity and setbacks. I could not have completed this work without them.

Moreover, I would like to thank the following colleagues for the use of their photographs: Petar Dekić for the Smederevska Palanka *corso* photographs, Gregory Donovan for the photograph of Union Square, Babette Audent for photographs of the Moore Street Market, Jessica Miller for the photograph of a large co-op building and Joel Lefkowitz who contributed many photographs. The National Park Service, Bree Kressler, Chihsin Chiu, Claire Panetta and Deen Sharp contributed figures that Erin Lilli expertly redrew and developed. Erin is an architect and my graduate student research assistant. She transformed and created figures to illustrate each chapter. I am very appreciative of her beautiful work.

Many colleagues gave me permission to cite their work extensively to provide a broader range of ethnographic illustrations. I would like to thank Chihsin Chiu for permission to use his work on Shilin Market in Taipei, Taiwan; Babette Audant, Rodrigo Corchado, Amanda Matles and Bree Kressler for their field notes on the Moore Street Market; Doris Fanelli, Dana Taplin, Suzanne Scheld and Tracy Fisher for field notes and publications on Independence National Historical Park; Jessica Winegar and Farha Ghannam for their publications on Tahrir Square during the protests in Cairo, Egypt; Aseel Sawalha for her work on Beirut, Lebanon; Sarah Hankins for her work on the New Central Bus Station in Tel Aviv, Israel; and Galey Modan for her publications and insights into her Mt. Pleasant, Washington, DC, housing cooperative. I asked each of these authors to read what I have written about their work, and they graciously agreed. The errors that remain are my own.

My editor, Katherine Ong, has been encouraging throughout the writing and publication process by finding excellent reviewers who also helped make the manuscript better. I would like to thank her along with her effective and careful editorial assistant, Lola Harre. During Katherine Ong's leave, her replacement, Louisa Vahtrick, continued to offer help and advice. Project manager Autumn Spalding was able to produce the book efficiently and in record time with the help of the production editor, Ruth Berry.

And, finally, I would like to thank my partner in life, Joel Lefkowitz, for his love and support throughout the research and writing process. It has been a long journey, and he was essential to the completion of this book by reading drafts, editing and encouraging me to keep going. Joel is an academic but also a professional photographer who accompanied me to the field and took many of the photographs found in the book. His faith in the importance of this book and his willingness to do everything from cooking dinner to scanning, faxing, and finding lost sources to allow it to be completed was crucial. I am grateful for his humor and good sense.

Chapter 1

Introduction

The importance of and approaches to the ethnography of space and place

Introduction

The ethnographic study of space and place is critical to understanding the everyday lives of people whose homes and homelands are disrupted by globalization, uneven development, violence and social inequality. These dislocating processes encourage and, in many cases, force people to leave the communities and the neighborhoods where they grew up and to search for other meaningful places to live and place-based identities. There is a sense of urgency that the spatial effects of crises of poverty, neoliberal restructuring and global capitalism be recognized in north/south population shifts, refugee camps, urban gentrification, privatization of public spaces and profit-driven planning and redevelopment. The impact of competing claims to space and place and the ensuing territorial and cultural conflicts are transforming social relations among ethnic and religious groups, social classes, regions, states and neighborhoods. Contemporary world problems such as human-made disasters, civil wars, terrorist attacks, climate change and other environmental concerns are inextricable from the material, symbolic and ideological aspects of space and place.

Interest in the ethnography of space and place is also growing as a result of research in environmental studies, geographic information systems, urban studies, global systems analysis, migration studies, build/design technologies and other fields concerned with space, place and territory. In the field of medicine, the significance of space and place is gaining attention in response to the findings of three researchers awarded the 2014 Nobel Prize for their work on the brain's "inner GPS" that enables rats as well as humans to navigate their surroundings. Dr. John O'Keefe, in 1971, located what he calls "place cells" and "showed that these cells registered not only what they saw but also what they did not see, by building inner maps in different environments" (Altman 2014). In 2005 Drs. Edvard and May-Britt Moser discovered another component of the brain's positioning system by identifying nerve cells that permit coordination and positioning, calling them "grid cells" (Altman 2014). These studies postulate a biological basis for wayfinding and greater focus on human space and place experience. Even in the field of architecture where built form and spatial relationships often are determined by formal design principles disconnected from user experience and preferences, there has been a renaissance of thinking about space from a cultural point of view while place concerns are reflected in the emergence of "place-making" courses and programs in architecture and design schools (Weir 2013).

An awareness of the importance of ethnography as a methodology for addressing sociospatial problems and public policy is also gaining ground. Within the social sciences, there have been appeals for a more engaged ethnographic practice and commitment to social justice objectives (Low 2011, Low and Merry 2010), the development of a public anthropology committed to uncovering racial bias and racism (Mullings 2015) and a public sociology that reaches beyond traditional quantitative policies studies (Burawoy 2005). Didier Fassin argues that "ethnography is particularly relevant in the understudied regions of society" and "illuminates the unknown" while it "interrogates the obvious" (2013: 642). Ethnographic research is becoming respected even within the international justice system through its use in tracking human rights violations and documenting an escalating sense of world insecurity (Goldstein 2012, Merry et al. 2015). The ability of ethnography to produce precise descriptions and nuanced analyses from multiple perspectives provides the flexibility and creativity to address the complexity of contemporary social relations and cultural settings. The ethnography of space and place as a subset of these methodologies contains all of these attributes as well as the ability to integrate the materiality and meaning of actions and practices at local, translocal and global scales.

Overview of Union Square, New York City

One way to appreciate what the ethnography of space and place offers is to consider an existing site and the kinds of research questions and intriguing interconnections that emerge. For example, what captures your attention when looking at this photograph of Union Square in New York City (Photo 1.1 Union Square)? Do you see an urban square surrounded by high-rise buildings designed by major architects, broad sidewalks lined with trendy stores and streets filled with automobiles? Or do you focus on the people gathered there and their many activities? Are you intrigued by the variety of textures and furnishings – some areas are lined with trees and grass and others defined by monuments, kiosks, vendor stalls, tents and different kinds of paving and steps – or are you more interested in the boundaries of the space, the infrastructure of the existing physical systems or whether there are Internet hot spots and video surveillance cameras? Are you reminded of an experience in a similar place at another time and location, or do you wonder what it would feel like to be sitting there now? How would you start to explore, examine or reimagine this public space?

Photo 1.1 Union Square (Gregory T. Donovan)

There are many ethnographic approaches to answering these questions. Are you particularly interested in the history of the place and want to know when it was built and under what circumstances? Did you perhaps reflect on the politics involved in financing and designing it and whether it was publicly or privately funded and maintained? These types of questions constitute a social production approach to its analysis.

What if, instead, you are intrigued by why so many people are congregated at some locations rather than others and you want to learn who these people are and what they are doing and thinking? Or are you more interested in knowing what this urban square means to those using it and to others who live nearby or even in the suburbs? Are some people comfortable in the space while others feel excluded? Questions about groups of people, their social activities and everyday meanings make up a social constructivist approach to its understanding.

There are other kinds of questions that illuminate how a place transforms a visitor's experience. Does this square feel different to local residents, tourists or youth of color? Does what people say about the square alter their perception of it? How does meandering through versus walking purposefully in one direction influence the experience of the place? How does physical space become part of the social world and, at the same time, how does its sociality become material? Affective, discursive, embodied and translocal approaches to the study of space and place address these kinds of questions.

This book offers multiple ways to answer these questions that draw on various genealogies, theoretical perspectives and ethnographic projects. These ways of thinking about space start with two well-established approaches: the social production of space and the built environment, and the social construction of space and place-making. But the book goes beyond these approaches by also examining space through theories of embodiment, discourse, translocality and affect. A basic assumption is that space is socially constructed as well as material and embodied, and the aim is to develop a conceptual framework – spatializing culture – that brings these ideas together.

The book draws on the premise that ethnographers have an advantage with regard to understanding space and place because they begin their studies in the field. Regardless of whether it is a long-term study or rapid ethnographic assessment of a place, a multisited analysis of a region or a comparison of circuits of mobility and movement, there is an engagement with the inherent materiality and human subjectivity of fieldwork. Conceptualizations of space and place that emerge from the sediment of ethnographic research draw on the strengths of studying people *in situ*, producing rich and nuanced sociospatial understandings. While disagreements over epistemology, what constitutes data and forms of representation sometimes magnify differences in conceptual positions, it is no small matter to recognize that the common experience of fieldwork and its grounded imperative pervades ethnographic research.

Within this general framework, a sociocultural perspective on space and place is employed that draws upon social science and design profession understandings and definitions, but retains some definitional boundaries. It privileges a fluid and context-dependent concept of culture, the use of ethnography as a foundational methodology, and a preference for grounded theory that emerges from the data in dialogue with dominant conceptual frameworks. Although the book offers a complex array of theories of space and place, there are threads that hold this body of work together. Articulating these threads and predispositions offers opportunities for expanding the way one can look at and frame questions about space and place that distinguish ethnographic research from that of our interlocutors who face different challenges. For example, David Harvey in *Spaces of Global Capitalism* struggles to define space by positing that it has such a complicated set of meanings that we risk "losing ourselves in some labyrinth" (Harvey 2006: 119). Harvey's challenge is moving from Marxist concepts of abstract space to relational concepts – theoretical articulations that are often difficult to resolve. Dolores Hayden wrestles with defining place as "one of the trickiest words in the English language, a suitcase so overfilled one can never shut the lid" (1995: 15). She probes the social, historical and architectural properties of place by employing methods that emphasize the evolution of building techniques, planning strategies and the politics of design to understand its meaning.

Ethnographers are situated in between these intellectual traditions and able to draw fruitfully from both. They are equally facile at grappling with the political economic forces of Marxist approaches that produce physical space, as with historical accounts of the built environment and the lived experience of individuals that result in place-based meaning. While the analysis of space and place is not a simple task and is complicated by ongoing disagreements about the prioritization of space or place and the nature of their relationship, ethnographers are nonetheless uniquely anchored in fieldwork in a way that is particularly useful. Without empirical grounding, it is easy to get lost or end up with a full suitcase that cannot be closed. The goal of this book, therefore, is to demonstrate how ethnographic research and methodology have been deployed to understand space and place and to argue that ethnography offers a unique and valuable approach to this interdisciplinary endeavor.

Space as a location of culture was important to early ethnographers who wrote descriptions of the built environment such as H. L. Morgan's (1881) ethnography *Houses and House Life of the American Aborigines*. Studies of spatial forms and settlement patterns also were included in comparative inventories of material culture as part of cross-cultural research compilations, including the *Ethnographic Atlas: A Summary* (Murdock 1967). As a manifestation of culture, indigenous architecture, village spatial organization and house design were considered part of a complex of material traits that enabled adaptation to the physical environment (Rapoport 1969).

Space was also part of the ethnographic foundations of anthropology and sociology from the perspective of Durkheim (1965) and Mauss (Mauss and Beauchat 1979 [1906]) that considered the built environment as integral to social life (Lawrence and Low 1990). The salvage ethnography of Boas (1964 [1888]) and his students, for example, Spier (1933) and Kroeber (1939), provided extensive documentation of the use and meaning of spatial arrangements. These spatial descriptions were seen as a backdrop to daily activities providing data for culture-area theories linking cultural traits through symbolism, geographical locale and pathways of migration.

One reason for the hesitancy that some contemporary ethnographers initially felt about using spatial concepts was an assumed indexicality of people and place, making it difficult to discuss space or place in a way that did not confine the inhabitants. Arjun Appadurai (1988) and Margaret Rodman (1985, 1992) correctly criticized ethnographic depictions of place and space that provided taken-for-granted settings to locate their descriptions or reduced the ethnographic to a locale that "imprisoned" natives. As pointed out by Alberto Corsín Jiménez, "'natives' who stay put in a particular area move as much as people who are displaced or migrate" (2003: 140), and he has criticized the implied indexical relationship of a cultural group and its geographic location. Instead, contemporary ethnographers require a flexible and mobile conception of space, one that speaks to how space is produced historically and physically, as well as how bodies in motion, dreams and desires, social interaction and environment interrelations create it. While early ethnographies relegated space to the description of the material setting, a contemporary ethnography of space and place is process-oriented; person, object and community-based; and allows for multiple forms of agency and political possibilities.

One solution is to acknowledge that place and space are always embodied. Their materiality can be metaphoric and discursive, as well as physically located and thus carried about. Introducing embodiment "in which the body is the subjective source or intersubjective ground of experience" (Csordas 1999: 143) into spatial analysis problematizes space and place in a way that allows for exploration at various scales. It is through embodied space that the global is integrated into the inscribed spaces of everyday life. Moving toward a conceptualization of space and place that identifies the embodied spaces of individuals and groups as sites of translocal and transnational spatial flows, as well as of personal experience, place-making and perception solves some of the misplaced rootedness found in earlier anthropological and sociological thought.

This discussion of the concepts of space and place necessarily draws upon the work of philosophers, social theorists, geographers, environmental psychologists, architects and anthropologists who have considered these questions and offer thought-provoking analyses reviewed in Chapter 2. But much of this writing is abstract and, although suggestive, does not always accommodate ethnographic and other forms of empirical investigation. Thus the prerequisite that the ethnography of space and place provide methodological and practical guidance for field researchers is also a concern.

At the same time, ethnographers and field-workers often are not included in theoretical discussions of space and place because their ethnographic and ethnoarchaeological accounts are not easily incorporated into macro theories of spatial analysis. Nuanced and fine-grained ethnographic data is considered tangential rather than central to the development of theory. This book challenges this assumption by articulating the ways in which ethnographers spatialize culture to reveal its theoretical and methodological potential.

Spatializing culture

These considerations – further developing a conceptual framework for an ethnographic approach to space and place and incorporating an embodied space perspective that is both material and experiential – form the scaffolding of this book. They are accomplished through an in-depth analysis of "spatializing culture," an idea that grew out of my work on the Latin

American plaza (Low 2000) and Deborah Pellow's (2002) ethnography of West African sociospatial organization and institutions. Through subsequent research and theory building, "spatializing culture" has evolved into a multidimensional framework that includes social production, social construction, embodied, discursive, emotive and affective, as well as translocal approaches to space and place. By "spatialize" I mean to produce and locate – physically, historically, affectively and discursively – social relations, institutions, representations and practices in space. "Culture" in this context refers to the multiple and contingent forms of knowledge, power and symbolism that comprise human and nonhuman interactions; material and technological processes; and cognitive processes, including thoughts, beliefs, imaginings and perceptions.

Spatializing culture is useful not only as a conceptual framework but also provides a powerful tool for uncovering social injustice and forms of exclusion. Further, as the ethnographic examples in this book illustrate, it can facilitate public engagement because spatial analyses offer people and their communities the means for understanding the everyday places where they live, work, shop and socialize. Spatializing culture is not only a scholarly endeavor but also offers a basis for neighborhood activism such as opposing or modifying architectural, planning and design interventions that have the ability to destroy the architectural centers of social life, erase cultural meanings from the landscape and restrict local participation in the built environment.

At its core, spatializing culture is a dialogic process that links the social production of space and nature and the social development of the built environment (King 1980, Lefebvre 1991, Low 1996, Smith 1984) with the social construction of space and place meanings (Kuper 1972, Lawrence and Low 1990, Rodman 1992, Rotenberg and McDonogh 1993, Pellow 1996, 2002). It brings together the social, economic, ideological and technological aspects of the creation of the material setting with phenomenological and symbolic experience as mediated by social processes such as exchange, conflict and control. The materialist emphasis of social production is useful in defining the historical emergence and political economic formation of urban space, while social construction refers to the transformation of space through language, social interaction, memory, representation, behavior and use into scenes and actions that convey meaning. Both are contested and fought over for economic, political and ideological reasons (Low 1996, 2000).

This initial formulation, however, neglected the ways in which human and nonhuman bodies also produce, reproduce, shape and assemble space and place (Amin 2014, Amin and Thrift 2002, Butler 1993, Simone 2006). An embodied approach that conceives of bodies as mobile spatial fields made up of spatiotemporal units with feelings, thoughts, preferences and intentions as well as out-of-awareness cultural beliefs and practices opens up the spatializing culture framework. Humans and nonhumans create space through their bodies and the mobility of those bodies, giving meaning, form and, ultimately, patterning of everyday movements and trajectories that result in place and landscape (Massey 2005, Munn 1996, Pred 1984, Rockefeller 2009.)

The addition of a language and discourse approach that focuses on how space is categorized and represented linguistically further expands spatializing culture by examining how talk and media are deployed to transform spaces and spatial practices (Duranti 1992, Hall 1968, Modan 2007). Emotion and affect similarly play central roles in transforming space and place through preconscious, unconscious and conscious processes that color and influence behavior and practices and transmit and circulate feelings (Anderson 2009, Ramos-Zayas 2012, Thrift 2008).

A final modification to the dialogic model is a rethinking of space and place through the bifocal optics of global and local perspectives. Globalization has done more than restructure economies and nation-states through time-space compression and rapidly accelerating circuits of capital, labor and people. It is also producing new kinds of space, including special economic and tax-free zones as self-contained and self-governed spatial locations (Looser 2012). At the same time, transnational and virtual networks enlivened by instantaneous communication technologies and social media are creating forms of translocal space where people experience and live in multiple sites simultaneously. The addition of a translocal approach as transcending geographical location and imagining human and nonhuman materiality in the context of time-space compression gives spatializing culture greater potential for addressing future global realities.

Selecting the best characterization to represent this overall framework has been problematic, as any number of terms – perspectives, approaches, dimensions or domains – could be used to denote the various facets of spatializing culture. For example, the term domain seems too fixed, as if ways of exploring space and place had clear, non-overlapping boundaries, and dimension suggests the possibility of ordinal measurement or a continuum that does not yet exist. Perspectives or approaches seem needlessly vague. Instead, the metaphor of a conceptual frame or lens indicates that these are focused areas of inquiry and ways of encountering, structuring or viewing the research question. A conceptual lens is open-ended with permeable boundaries, but also directs the researcher to concentrate on a particular aspect of phenomena and thus acts as a guide to the complex terrain of space and place studies. Each conceptual frame offers a different approach to describing, explaining and applying findings and implies the use of specific ethnographic methods and techniques.

Thus this book is organized around spatializing culture as a framework made up of various conceptual frames. Each is examined with three objectives in mind. The first is to trace its scholarly development and discuss its strengths and limitations. Each offers a particular lens on the study of space and the built environment with epistemological concerns and methods that, while not mutually exclusive, emphasize different theoretical conventions and techniques of knowledge production.

The second objective is to demonstrate how ethnography can elucidate each and provide insights into a range of places and problems. This is accomplished through the inclusion of ethnographic examples that illustrate the ideas presented and address two methodological questions that arise when studying space and place: (1) How does a conceptual frame shape a particular research project? (2) How does ethnographic research help to clarify and enhance the utility of the approach?

Exploring each conceptual frame provides a foundation for the third objective, which is to show how the different conceptual frames overlap and intersect. For example, the conceptual frame of embodied space integrates the material/biological and sensing body with perceptions, thoughts, intentions and feelings that are shaped and resisted through both sociocultural habits/practices and the local/global environment. In this way, the embodied space frame articulates with the conceptual frames of social production and construction, affect and translocality. This book takes a first step in developing such models and methodologies of space and place, especially with regard to their application in ethnographic research and political activism.

As in any book of this considerable scope, decisions were made as to what and what not to include. The genealogies of space and place presented in Chapter 2 outline the intellectual traditions that inform the use of the concepts of space and place in this work. Drawing upon my own ethnographic experience enables readers interested in grounded theory building to ascertain how ideas and methods evolve within a field of study as reflected in a career of long-term fieldwork as well as applied research projects. The addition of other ethnographic examples drawn from the published work of colleagues working across the globe enables exploration of how culture is spatialized in very different ethnographic contexts. The six approaches (social production, social construction, embodiment, language and discourse, emotion and affect and translocality) and multiple environments included (plazas, parks, housing, memorials, neighborhoods, city centers, markets and train and bus stations) are those that have facilitated my research and teaching. Because much of my fieldwork has focused on the Americas, the literature and examples reflect this limitation.

Organization of the book

When studying space and place, social science researchers often begin with a social constructionist perspective that highlights the role played by social interaction, symbols and language in giving form and meaning to physical space. While this perspective has been particularly generative of research on place-making and the social meaning of space, it also has drawbacks. Social construction does not address the materiality that is foundational in political, economic and historical approaches, such as the social development of the built environment (King 1980), Marxist historical materialism (Harvey 1976, Smith 1984) and the social production of space (Lefebvre 1991).

Scholars and researchers, especially those who espouse Marxist, materialist and historical perspectives, are more likely to start with the political economy and history of a space for their analyses. The social production perspective emphasizes the history and political economy of the built environment and landscape, providing insights into how and why they came into existence, who (governments or people) or what (earthquakes or earthmovers) were involved in their emergence and when this took place. It provides a materialist rendering of how space and place are conceived, built and created. Social production approaches do not necessarily exclude social constructivist understandings since the material environment is given meaning through representational and symbolic processes. But it posits that materiality is of primary importance and shapes social construction processes through specific power dynamics, hegemonic practices, economic strategies and political and military control.

Both the social construction and social production conceptual frames are commonly employed in the ethnographic study of space and place and make up the bulk of the research. The other perspectives presented in these pages are less well established and more speculative, such as those based on embodied space and place-making, language and discursive analyses of space and place, emotional and affective aspects of space and environments and the impact of time/space compression on transnational and translocal places. Some of the conceptual frames, especially embodied space and translocal space, integrate the experiential, social and material dimensions of space and place in intriguing ways. They are discussed further in the conclusion as part of the layered methodology that constitutes the ethnography of space and place.

Chapter 2

Genealogies

The concepts of space and place

Introduction

Tracing the history of the ideas of space and place is a first step to elucidating their ethnographic significance within an interdisciplinary field made up of scholarly traditions that employ the terms in distinctive ways. It is difficult to examine their contemporary meanings or to consider their potential for generating new insights without reviewing previous conventions and disciplinary practices. Familiarity with different definitions and usage is indispensable because these complex concepts have a long and often ambiguous history in philosophy, social sciences and architecture and design.

A thorough analysis of the disciplinary bases of space and place, however, constitutes its own project (see Hubbard and Kitchin 2011 and Cresswell 2015 for geography, Casey 1998 for philosophy, Hayden 1995 and Forty 2000 for architecture, Low and Lawrence-Zuñiga 2003 and Lawrence and Low 1990 for anthropology). This chapter offers an overview of how these terms are used and how my usage draws upon and differs from others. Denise Lawrence-Zuñiga and I (Lawrence and Low 1990, Low and Lawrence Zuñiga 2003) have published reviews of space and place within the field of anthropology that are not repeated here. Instead, this discussion concentrates on the formulations and definitions that have been most generative of current thinking and ethnographic research.

The chapter is structured as a series of loosely organized genealogies. Rather than a history of ideas, the term "genealogy," in the sense of Foucault's exposition, is utilized to depict an assemblage of ideas that have resemblances and influence one another rather than a strict historiography. In "Nietsche, Genealogy, History," Foucault argues, "genealogy is gray, meticulous, and patiently documentary. It operates on a field of entangled and confused parchments, on documents that have been scratched over and recopied many times" (Foucault 1977: 139–140). In the same sense the theoretical and research references do not necessarily fit neatly together, but provide insights into ongoing intellectual debates. The chapter juxtaposes definitions employed and disputes about their utility by philosophers, social theorists, geographers, anthropologists, environmental psychologists and architects. The intention is to present a rough outline of the authors, articles and treatises that underlie, inform and influence the assumptions and conceptualizations discussed in the remaining chapters.

There has been considerable semantic confusion within and across disciplines that has led to disagreements about the conceptual relationship of space and place. Some scholars argue these constructs are redundant and cover the same domain, while others distinguish between the two and see them as overlapping or contained within one another. The differentiation or lack of differentiation is usually attributed to the theoretical framing of the research problem and the specific aspects of this framing, such as scale, epistemology or disciplinary meaning. To clarify this ambiguity, it seems helpful to consider the connections and disconnections between the two.

One conceptualization is that they are separate constructs with no overlap, or that only one, either space or place, is primary and theoretically relevant. For example, phenomenological theories and epistemologies underlie humanist geographers', Heideggerian philosophers' and environmental psychologists' use of place as the predominant construct. Marxism, neo-Marxism, mathematics, geometry and historical materialism, on the other hand, are the theoretical foundations of those who use space as the all-encompassing construct. Thus at the extreme ends of the continuum are two epistemologically discrete positions that can be found in many of the genealogies.

A second less common theoretical position is that space and place are separate constructs, but overlap such that, at least conceptually, there is an area where they intersect and come together. This point of contact can be thought of as an integration of the two or a merging of some of their properties that link the otherwise disparate constructs. Examples of this configuration are presented in Chapter 8 in a discussion of how translocal spaces are produced through embodied space, space-time compression and communication technologies. Translocal space can be thought of as a moment when material spaces formed by circuits of migration and other transnational processes intersect with the places of migrants' everyday lives.

Another conceptual configuration reflects the most common way that social scientists think about space and place. In this case, space is the more encompassing construct, while place retains its relevance and meaning but only as a subset of space. Place is defined as lived space made up of spatial practices and is phenomenologically experienced, such as the culturally meaningful space of home.

The reverse relationship of space and place also occurs in the literature with place being the larger category encompassing a conceptually limited and more narrowly defined construct of space. While not a common conceptualization, it captures aspects of "placenessless" (Relph 1976) in which place is the dominant ontological category of human life, but can be stripped of its personal and cultural meanings by ongoing social and economic forces. Through the processes of modernization, industrialization and globalization, place can become abstract space, thereby losing its cultural intimacy and affective qualities.

The final conceptualization used most frequently by the general public and nonspecialists is that space and place represent the same domain and therefore are redundant. While casually using the terms interchangeably is common in everyday conversation, in this book, these distinctions are made quite purposely.

A series of five Venn diagrams illustrate these conceptual relationships. Figure 2.1 (Separation of space and place) is made up of two separate circles, the constructs of space and place. Conceptually they can both exist independently or only one exists to the exclusion of the other. In Figure 2.2 (Overlapping of space and place), the space and place constructs overlap, creating a third area of space/place that has the potential of bringing together aspects of both constructs into a new synthesis. Figure 2.3 (Place contained within space) represents space as the dominant construct with the concept of place located inside of space, a subcategory or special kind of space. Alternatively, Figure 2.4 (Space contained within place) reverses space and place, indicating that place is ontologically significant and space is a subset, or, as I suggest, a place stripped of meaning. Finally, Figure 2.5 (Space and place coterminous) is simply one circle titled space/place, suggesting that these

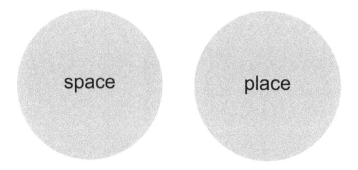

Figure 2.1 Separation of space and place (Setha Low)

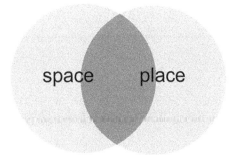

Figure 2.2 Overlapping of space and place (Setha Low)

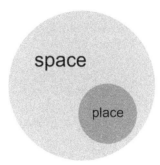

Figure 2.3 Place contained within space (Setha Low)

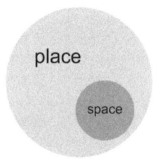

Figure 2.4 Space contained within place (Setha Low)

Figure 2.5 Space and place coterminous (Setha Low)

two constructs are entirely overlapping – i.e., conceptually redundant as is assumed in everyday speaking and writing.

The conceptual relationships of space and place are included to guide the reader's journey through the sometimes circuitous discussions that follow. The diagrams provide visual templates for the ongoing arguments and frames of reference of the many disciplinary paths and theoretical orientations. The conclusion of this chapter returns to this discussion to identify the definition and space/place relationship that is used in this book.

Genealogies of space and place

Philosophical and mathematical genealogy

Philosophical treatises by Newton, Leibniz, Kant and Einstein, as well as others, provide the basis for many definitions of space. Their understandings of the concept of space revolve around two alternative notions: a definition of space as something that is absolute and real, thus a "thing" that allows us to position our bodies, or a relational concept in which space does not exist except in relation to time, experience, thought, objects and events.

Philosophical discussions usually begin with the Newtonian view that space is absolute and real in the sense of Euclidean geometry – an entity that is independent from whatever occupies it. Absolute space is fixed and empty, a void waiting to be filled or a grid that can be measured. It is the container of or stage for human activity:

> Absolute space, in its own nature, without regard to anything external . . . remains always similar and immovable. Relative space is some movable dimension or measure of the absolute space which our senses determine by its position to bodies.
>
> (Newton 1846 [1687]: 77)

John Agnew (2005) suggests that since Newton is a transitional figure in the development of a modernist view of space, he endorsed a medieval thing-like concept that, in accordance with previous generations, he saw as concrete and real.

With the advent of the work of Leibniz, the founder of the modernist view of space, space is conceived of as relational and not independent of objects and events, but made up of the relations among them (Agnew 2005). Leibniz, in his 1695 *Specimen Dynamicum* (Ariew and Garber 1989), objected to Newton's absolute view that made it seem that God was in command of spatiotemporal experience. Instead, the relational view posits that there is no space or time outside of the processes that define them:

> [Space] is that order which renders bodies capable of being situated, and by which they have a situation among themselves when they exist together.
>
> (Leibniz 1715–1716 *Letter to Samuel Clark* cited in Alexander 1956: 25–26)

David Harvey clarifies this further in his discussion of the philosophical foundations of relative space: "Processes do not occur *in* space but define their own spatial frame. The concept of space is embedded in or internal to process" (Harvey 2006: 123).

Kant, who in his early writings agrees with Leibniz and his concept of relational space, however, concludes his article on "regions of space" (1768) by moving closer to the Newtonian position, undergirding his argument with Euclidian geometry. He posits

> Up to now it has been assumed that all our cognition must conform to the objects; but all attempts to find out something about them *a priori* through concepts that would extend our cognition have, on this pre-supposition, come to nothing. Hence let us once try whether we do not get further with the problem of metaphysics by assuming that the objects must conform to our cognition, which would agree better with the requested possibility of an *a priori* cognition of them, which is to establish something about objects before they are given to us. This would be just like the first thought of Copernicus, who, when he did not make good progress in the explanation of the celestial motions if he assumed that the entire celestial host revolves around the observer, tried to see if it might not have greater success if he made the observer revolve and left the stars at rest.
>
> (Kant 1781: 295–296)

Kant asserts that space is a subjective condition that the individual intuitively possesses, and it is required in order to perceive spatial and temporal representations. He tries to reconcile Leibniz and Newton by not eliminating the notion of a real objective space, but argues that without this predisposition or sensible intuition, space and time cannot be experienced.

The relative notion of space associated with Einstein and non-Euclidean geometries first emerged in the nineteenth century. It was developed by Gauss and Euler and then mathematically formalized by Einstein (Harvey 2006). Einstein (1922) pointed out that measurement depends on the frame of reference of the observer, thus it is impossible to understand space independent of time, shifting formulations to those of spatiotemporal analyses. Einstein's general theory of relativity provided the possibility of recombining space and matter and empirical evidence for a materialist approach to the concept of space.

While many social scientists utilize concepts of space based on these philosophical and mathematical foundations, others argue that space should not be given the primacy accorded it and draw upon another philosophical tradition based on place. Cresswell, for example, argues that a philosophy of place first emerges in the work of Plato and Aristotle, "both of whom gave place a particularly powerful position in the lexicon of ideas" (2015: 25). In Greek, two words mean "place," *topos* and *chora*. The first connotes place in the abstract sense of cartography and mapping, and the second is place in a more existential sense (Berque 2010). Cresswell (2015, also see Casey 1998) suggests that Plato employs *chora* as a container with content, while Aristotle uses *chora* as the larger region (as in chorology[1]) and *topos* to refer to a smaller place.

Edward Casey (1996, 1998) begins his analysis of place with Greek philosophy, but also draws heavily on the work of the phenomenologists Edmund Husserl and Maurice Merleau-Ponty. He argues that space is a modern concept preceded by the premodern notion of place. Place is primary and the universal form of all human existence. He "defines his own agenda as an extended philogical treatment of place that explicitly takes into account the experiential and agential basis of place" (Casey 1993: xv). Thus place is general and includes space, while space is particular and derived from it (Casey 1996). From Casey's work emerges a definition of place as intimate and encompassing all experience and meaning in life.

Martin Heidegger's (2001) notion of "dwelling" is also employed as a philosophical point of departure for grappling with the existential immediacies of place in ethnographic and phenomenological work (Boatright 2015). For example, in *Building, Dwelling, Thinking*, Heidegger argues that dwelling is a spatial process that involves both building and thinking and that the act of dwelling creates place through the intentional modification of environment (Boatright 2015, Heidegger 2001). Dwelling is the basis of place-making activity and reflects the entanglement of human beings' relationship with the world (Heidegger 2010). Dwelling, in the Heideggerian sense, thus provides another philosophical foundation for asserting that place, rather than space, is the basis of human ontology. The ongoing debate of the ontological significance and primacy of place versus space reoccurs many times in the following discussions of geographical, anthropological, environmental psychological and architectural theories.

French social theory genealogy

French social theorists generally focus on relative space and develop the concept by decoding spatial practice as an aspect of the social analysis of power and its deployment. These scholars are concerned with how physical space and spatial relations subjugate or liberate groups and individuals from the state and other sources of power and knowledge rather than categorizing the concept of space as absolute or relational. Bourdieu (1977 [1972]), Lefebvre (1991 [1974]), Foucault (1977 [1975]), de Certeau (1984 [1980]), and Deleuze and Guattari (1987 [1980]), also address the movement and manipulation of the body as a dimension of spatial and political control, providing a basis for embodied spatial arguments.

Of all the French social theorists, Henri Lefebvre (1974, 1991) is the most intrigued by the capacity of space and spatial relations to produce and reproduce social life positing, "space is never empty: it always embodies a meaning" (1991: 154). Lefebvre rethinks space, moving away from a Cartesian separation of space and its ideological ends, and instead proposes a single, unitary theory that brings its different modalities together (Merrifield 2002). He views space as a social product that masks the contradictions of its own production and deconstructs this "illusion of transparency" by explicating how social space is made up of a conceptual triad of spatial practices, representations of space and representational spaces (Lefebvre 1974, 1991). This tripartite dialectical model creates a framework for uncovering the ways that space is produced and exposing the social contradictions inherent in these forms of production. Although he is unclear about their precise interaction and how they work empirically, he claims 1) spatial practices, e.g., spaces created through lived practices; 2) representations of space, e.g., maps and theories of planning; and 3) spatial representations, e.g., art, spatial experiments and underground spatial practices can be analyzed to reveal the hidden means of spatial production and thus lead to revolutionary action (Lefebvre 1991, Shields 1991, Merrifield 2002). Lefebvre provides a theory of space that includes embodied spatial practices and emphasizes the role the human body plays in producing and not just conceiving space. His theory of space underpins the perspective of social production discussed in Chapter 3.

In an effort to link human agents and spatial domination, Pierre Bourdieu (1972, 1977) focuses on the spatialization of everyday behavior and how the sociospatial order is translated into bodily experience and practice. He proposes the key concept of "habitus," a generative and structuring principle of collective strategies and social practices that produce existing structures. In his early work (Bourdieu 1973), the Kabyle house becomes the setting in which body space and cosmic space are integrated through metaphor and homologous structures. Thus it is through the experience of living in the spatial symbolism of the home that social structure becomes embodied and naturalized in everyday practice. Since the concept of habitus spatially links social structure to the human body and spatial practices, the possibility of resistance to these practices becomes more apparent. His influence on embodied space is discussed in Chapter 5 and later in this introduction under anthropological genealogies.

Michel Foucault, in his seminal work on the prison (1975, 1977) and in a series of interviews and lectures on space (Foucault and Rabinow 1984), takes a historical approach through an analysis of the human body, spatial arrangements and architecture. He examines the relationship of power and space by positing architecture as a political technology for working out the concerns of government – that is, control and power over individuals – through the spatial "canalization" of everyday life. The aim of such a technology is to create a "docile body" (Foucault 1977: 136) through enclosure and the organization of individuals in space. Foucault theorizes how spatial relations and architecture contribute to the maintenance of power of one group over another at a level that includes both the control of the movement and the surveillance of the body in space. His work on social control and spatial governmentality is discussed in Chapter 3.

Michel de Certeau (1984), on the other hand, sets out to show how peoples' "ways of operating" constitute the means by which users reappropriate space organized by techniques of sociocultural production (1984: xiv). These practices are articulated in the details of everyday life and used by groups or individuals "already caught in the nets of 'discipline'" (de Certeau 1984: xiv–xv). By tracing the operations of walking, naming, narrating and remembering the city, he develops a theory of lived space in which spatial practices elude the discipline of urban planning and government controls. The pedestrian's walking, as the *flâneur* of Walter Benjamin (1999), is the spatial acting out of place, creating and representing public space rather than being subject to it.

For de Certeau (1984) power is embedded in space through territory and boundaries in which the weapons of the strong are classification, delineation and division – what he calls "strategies" – while the weak use furtive movement, short cuts and routes – so-called "tactics" – to contest spatial domination. Tactics never rely on the existence of a place for power or identity, instead they are a form of consumption and "never produce proper places, but are always using and manipulating these places" (Cresswell 1997: 363). Thus the spatial tactics of the weak are mobility and detachment from the rationalized spaces of power. In this sense, the pedestrian is not the same as the migrant or traveler who upon arrival at a destination takes on its identity and comes under state control.

Gilles Deleuze and Felix Guattari (1987) are also concerned with how people resist spatial discipline and the state. They distinguish between the ordered and hierarchical machinations of the state and the war machine of the nomad, who moves by lines of flight or by points and nodes instead of place to place (Deleuze and Guattari 1986). Deleuze separates himself from Foucault in this regard by saying:

> What surprised Foucault was that faced with all these powers, all of their deviousness and hypocrisy, we can resist. My surprise is the opposite. It is flowing everywhere and governments are able to block it. We approached the problem from opposite directions. You are right to say that society is a fluid, or even worse, a gas. For Foucault it is an architecture.
>
> (2006: 280)

In Deleuze and Guattari's (1986) spatial analysis, the nomad escapes the state by never becoming reterritorialized, slipping through the striated spaces of power, and remains undisciplined and a metaphor for the forces that resist state control. This spatial mobility based on a horizontal vista of mobile meanings, shifting connections and temporary encounters (Chambers 1986; Hannam, Sheller and Urry 2006) is characteristic of the propinquity of encounters in the city or spontaneous street theater and political action (Copjec and Sorkin 1999, Amin and Thrift 2002, Merrifield 2013). It is also found in the world of the international airport with its shopping malls, restaurants, banks, post offices, phones, bars, video games, television chairs and security guards – a simulated metropolis inhabited by a community of modern nomads (Augé 1995, Chambers 1990). Within the miniaturized world of the airport, the metaphor of the nomad becomes emblematic of definitions of post-modern space (Augé 1995, Looser 2012).

Geographical genealogy

Geographers write about space or place depending on their philosophical lineage. Marxist geographers Harvey (1990, 2006) and N. Smith (1984, 2008) argue for the primacy of space, whether absolute or relative, and an analysis of spatial production and reproduction similar to Lefebvre (1974, 1991). Humanist geographers and phenomenologists such as Relph (1976), Tuan (1977), Seamon (1979), Buttimer (Buttimer and Seamon 1980) and Cresswell (1997, 2015) begin their analyses with the experience of place. These two schools of geographical thought are developed with seemingly parallel, but at times intersecting, trajectories.

From David Harvey's (1973, 1990, 2006) earliest work, he has been concerned with the concept of space as a way to understand urban processes under capitalism. His response to the question "What is space?" is replaced by "How is it that different human practices create and make use of different conceptualizations of space?" (Harvey 1973: 13). In order to characterize these different conceptualizations, he develops the now familiar tripartite division of absolute, relative and relational space and emphasizes that the three aspects are in constant interaction:

> If we regard space as absolute it becomes a "thing in itself" with an existence independent of matter. It then possesses a structure which we can use to pigeon-hole or individuate phenomena. The view of relative space proposes that it be understood as a relationship between objects which exists only because objects exist and relate to each other. There is another sense in which space can be viewed as relative, and I choose to call this relational space – space regarded in the manner of Leibniz, as being contained in objects in the sense that an object can be said to exist only insofar as it contains and represents within itself relationships to other objects.
>
> (2006: 121)

For Harvey, property relationships create absolute spaces, while the movement of goods, people and services take place in relative space "because it takes money, time, energy, and the like to overcome the friction of distance" (1973: 13). Parcels of land also contain relationships with other parcels of land in the form of relational space and are an important aspect of human social practice (1973). Relational processes focus on the dialectics of understanding space, and Harvey argues cogently that people are inexorably situated in all three frameworks simultaneously, but not necessarily equally. He points out, however, that while this dialectical tension is exciting and innovative, it is hard to apply in any easy empiricist or positivist sense (Harvey 2006).

Neil Smith (1984), a student of Harvey's, cautions that the concept of space is often taken for granted and needs to be critically examined to uncover its contradictory meanings. He focuses on geographical space or, more generally, "the space of human activity, from architectural space at a lower scale up to the scale of the entire surface of the earth" (Smith 1990: 66). He distinguishes geographical space from absolute and relative space and reintroduces social space, linking it to Marxist-inspired theoretical traditions through an analysis of its material production. To accomplish this task, he traces three strands of inquiry that are important to the development of a post-positivist geographic theory – that is, 1) humanist geography that proposes the importance of subjective modes of knowing; 2) a radical political tradition that simultaneously explains space as objective and a product of social forces; and 3) the conception of the production of space, such that "geographical space is viewed as a social product" (Smith 1990: 77).

Humanist geographers analyze place rather than space, drawing upon Heidegger's (1971, 2001) notion of dwelling and the individual's situatedness in the world. Place is defined as space made cultural and intimate with an emphasis on inhabiting and feeling at home. Humanist geographers use phenomenological methods to study place and assume that there is a natural relationship when people and place are connected through time or genealogy (Seamon 2014). Relph (1976) goes so far as to argue that placelessness occurs when the three components of place – physical setting, activities and meaning – are disrupted, while Agnew (2005) posits that the authenticity of preindustrial places is lost with the sameness of modernity. Meaning and authenticity are also the central concern of Tuan (1977), Seamon (1979, 2014) and Relph (1981) in their analyses of how places are destroyed by contemporary architecture and planning. Casey (1993) strengthens Relph's position by claiming life is so "place-oriented" that the notion of placelessness causes deep anxiety.

John Agnew's (2005) definition of place as "location, locale and sense of place" creates a continuum from generalized to particularistic notions:

> The first is place as location or a site in space where an activity or object is located and which relates to other sites or locations because of interaction and movement between them. A city or other settlement is thought of in this way. Somewhere in between, and second, is the view

of place as locale or setting where everyday-life activities take place. Here the location is no mere address but the where of social life and environmental transformation. Examples would be such settings from everyday life as workplaces, homes, shopping malls, churches, etc. The third is place as sense of place or identification with place as a unique community, landscape, and moral order. In this construction, every place is particular, and thus, singular.

(Agnew 2005: 2)

Agnew's three-part definition operates well as a set of categories for description and offers a clear definition of place. He makes an important point in his insistence that the space/place dichotomy is effectively a continuum of scales from experience-near to experience-far positions and perceptions.

The geographer Michel Lussault (2007) develops a different grammar of space employing a vocabulary of scale in which place is the smallest, indivisible unit marked by limits and contiguity and space an area or territory that is similar but divisible, connected to a network that is vast, open and not marked by limits. He posits that the space in which an individual lives

turns out on closer inspection to be a *composite:* a mixture that is indissociable, on the one hand, from physical forms and structures on various scales . . . to a highly diverse set of idealities, from the least reflexive to the most objectifiable, from the most singular to the most general, from mental images and representations that are associated more or less directly with sensory experience to the most abstract ideas, wholly or in part detached from a precise spatial referent.

(Lussault 2011: 1–2)

His spatial analysis emphasizes the performative roles of images, stories and language in the production of the space of everyday lives (Lussault 2007, 2011).

Edward Soja is also concerned with geographical scale, but in relation to the space of the body. He theorizes space as "a multi-layered geography of socially created and differentiated nodal regions nesting at many different scales around the mobile personal spaces of the human body and the more fixed communal locales of settlements" (1989: 8). This model of ontological spatiality locates the human subject within the formation of geography. Although in *Seeking Spatial Justice*, Soja (2010) privileges the concept of space as primary, in his theory of Thirdspace, he asserts instead

everything comes together in Thirdspace: subjectivity and objectivity, the abstract and the concrete, the real and the imagined, the knowable and the unimaginable, the repetitive and the differential, structure and

agency, mind and body, consciousness and the unconscious, the disciplined and the transdisciplinary, everyday life and unending history.

(1996: 56–7)

With Thirdspace, Soja moves away from contingent definitions of space and
place and seeks to understand human spatiality in a way that allows for
social change.

Doreen Massey (2005), on the other hand, views space as contingent on
who inhabits it: it is an open interactional system where connections offer the
possibility of social and political relationships among a multiplicity of people.
Her propositions weave together some of the concerns of the humanists in
which place is based solely on human experience and Marxist geographers in
which space is the product of power relations and political struggle.

These integrated perspectives characterize the use of space and place
within geography today. Many of these formulations are the basis of the
conceptualizations of space and place in architectural theory, environmental
psychology and anthropology.

Architectural genealogy

Architectural theorists and historians have been more preoccupied with form
and processes of form giving than with space and place. There was some interest in the concept of space between 1890 and 1970, but it declined at the same
moment that the spatial turn became popular within the social sciences (Üngür
2011). In *Words and Buildings: A Vocabulary of Modern Architecture*, Adrian
Forty (2000) traces the use of form and its relationship space to Kant (1781),
while attributing the idea of space in architecture to a genealogy of German
philosophers, especially Gottfried Semper, et al. (2004 [1860]). Semper "proposed that the first impulse of architecture was the enclosing of space" (Üngür
2011: 132) and the material and form of the building were secondary.

A few architects consider the concept of space as foundational to modernism. Sigfried Giedion's (1941) *Space, Time and Architecture: The Growth
of a New Tradition* began what was to become a "cult of abstract space"
during the 1950s and 1960s (Sabatino 2007). Bruno Zevi's *Architecture
as Space: How to Look at Architecture* (1957 [1948]) contributes to this
modernist vision through a history of architecture that identifies space as
defining, animating and illuminating architectural creations so that their
beauty – or indifference – is exposed. Bernard Tschumi (1987) argues
that while architecture was once an art of measurement and proportion
that allowed people to measure space and time, with the "deregulation of
architecture," that is, the rupture in the relationship of the signified and
the signifier that occurs with modernism, architecture became more of a
scaffolding for light and materials. Buckminister Fuller explores this new
relationship of space and light through his experiments with the geodesic

dome and prefabricated forms (Filler 2013). Space also appears in the writing of Rem Koolhaas (2001) in his essay on junk-space, the residue and litter that humans leave behind that pollutes the planet and universe with the remains of modernism. These works suggest that space has a role to play in architectural thinking, but remains secondary to architectural form, materials and design.

Place as a concept in architecture has been relatively neglected with the exception of the work of urban historian and architect Dolores Hayden (1995), architectural historian Dell Upton (2008) and the architects Charles Moore (1966) and Arijit Sen (Sen and Silverman 2014). In Charles Moore's (1966) essay, *Creating of Place*, he sets out to move architectural debate away from formalistic notions of space and to focus on the ordinary and the vernacular (Sabatino 2007).

> In order to try to throw out our standard notions about shape and the making of it and about space and its importance, I have employed the perhaps vaguer notion of place, the ordering of the whole environment that members of a civilization stand in the middle of, the making of sense, the projection of the image of the civilization onto the environment.
>
> (Moore 1966: 20)

Moore, along with his colleagues Donlyn Lyndon and Gerald Allen, develop this notion of place by exploring the qualities of small town places in *The Place of Houses* (1974). In his plan for Kresge College at the University of California at Santa Cruz, Moore designed a college campus with places for personal encounters; later he built housing in New Haven organized around *piazzas* as areas for social interaction (Sabatino 2007). The concept of place in his work references vernacular forms and traditional architecture reinterpreted in a modern guise.

Dell Upton is equally committed to the revitalization of American vernacular architecture and writes extensively about place as "the scene" (1997: 174). Upton (1997) argues that the way places accommodate human activities is connected to their symbolic meaning and the unseen processes of their production. Arijit Sen draws upon Upton, but is also influenced by performance artists and designers who "explore visceral engagements with the environment and make place by performing, building, and acting" (Sen and Silverman 2014: 5).

The most important contribution to an architectural and urban historical definition of place is found in the work of Dolores Hayden, whose concern with its multiple definitions is cited in Chapter 1. In *The Power of Place*, Hayden explores how the many meanings and ways of knowing place make it "powerful as a source of memory, as a weave where one strand ties in another" (1995: 18) and argues that place should be at the center of any urban landscape history. She illustrates this contention through the historical photographs, personal narratives, interviews and archival documentation

that she uses to reconstitute and celebrate the forgotten and misplaced workers' and women's histories in downtown Los Angeles. Place, for Hayden, is
not just a scholarly construct but a representation and evidence of peoples'
local histories, thus offering a potential site for political resistance and community activism.

Another conceptualization of place in architecture is the application of
assemblage theory. Assemblage theory developed from the work of Deleuze
and Guattari (1987) and DeLanda (2006) and has been applied by Kim
Dovey (2010) to the study of place. Dovey (2010) argues that it is the connection between physical elements such as houses, signs, goods and people
that make a place or, in Dovey's analysis, "a place assemblage" (2010: 16).
He uses this definition to provide a more dynamic accounting that captures
the change and movement of the momentary coming together of things.
Assemblage theory provides a way to understand the experiential, material and representational dimensions of place without the essentialized and
closed meanings of other theories (Dovey 2010).

While space and place have not drawn the attention in architectural theory
that they have in philosophy, French social theory and geography, it is often
through architectural interventions that space and place are created, erased
or reconstituted. The field of environmental psychology has responded to
architecture's lack of theorization of human-environment relationships and
the importance of place to people, while at the same time critiquing the invis-
ibility of the physical context in psychological theory.

Environmental psychology genealogy

In environmental psychology, place is used to reference a broad range of
meanings, including spatial location, sense of place and a constellation of
material things with specific sets of meanings and affordances. Environmental psychologists emphasize the relationship between people and the material
world through the realm of experience and emotion. They are particularly
interested in notions such as place attachment and place identity that conceptualize lived experience as embedded in a person's sense of self and group
identity (Low and Altman 1992, Low 1992, Duyvendak 2011, Manzo and
Devine-Wright 2014). The objective of understanding human-environment
interactions through experience has its roots in geographer Yi-Fu Tuan's
concern with place as a unique and complex environment rooted in the past
and draws upon his proposition that

> place incarnates the experiences and aspirations of a people. Place is not
> only a fact to be explained in the broader frame of space, but it is also a
> reality to be clarified and understood from the perspectives of the people
> who have given it meaning.
>
> (1979: 387)

Most empirical analyses of human-environment interaction and human-behavior studies utilize Tuan's humanistic understanding of place employing a variety of qualitative and quantitative methodologies, including ethnography.

Environmental psychology distinguishes itself from the rest of psychology by its focus on the person as embedded in and inseparable from the environment. For example, Harold M. Proshansky, one of the founders of the field, uses the concept of place identity to reflect his position that the physical properties and dimensions of the urban setting are also social, cultural and psychological in nature. His goal is not to establish a new kind of ecological determinism or a kind of architectural determinism, but rather to move the lens of analysis from social context to the often ignored physical context (1978). According to Proshansky,

> the urban environment is essentially a built environment, a built environment that not only expresses human behavior and experience but also shapes and influences this behavior and experience. For the environmental psychologist the place-identity of the individual, because it both determines and is modified by this person-environment influence process, becomes a key analytical tool. Furthermore, since there is no physical setting, built or otherwise, that is not also a psychological, social, and cultural environment, place-identity is a theoretical construct quite necessary for understanding the development and expression of the other subidentities of the individual, e.g., sex, occupation.
>
> (1978: 156)

Droseltis and Vignoles further develop Proshansky's conceptualization by distinguishing "three dimensions of place identification: attachment/self-extension, environmental fit, and place-self congruity" (2010: 23). They include both place identity and place bonds as a single model, while other theorists argue that affective attachment and place identity are distinct constructs (Hernández, Martin, Ruiz and Hidalgo 2010), that affective attachment to place subsumes place identity (Hinds and Sparks 2008; Kyle, Graefe and Manning, 2005) or that both place identity and affective attachment to place are subsumed by another construct such as sense of place (Jorgensen and Stedman, 2001).

Place attachment, another frequently studied aspect of the experience of place, brings attention to the difference between abstract space and meaningful place (Lewicka 2011). The concept of place attachment remains viable even with globalization because of the increasing political importance of place, defined as local community, in a turbulent world. The uncritical use of the concept of place in place attachment, however, highlights the

> tensions between the disciplines interested in 1) the socio-cultural dimensions of place, such as community attachment; 2) the biophysical

dimensions of place, with emphasis on the 'setting or container,' and; 3) the integration of both socio-cultural and natural setting dynamics within place attachment research.

(Raymond, Brown, and Weber 2010: 422)

What is noteworthy about this work is its continuing focus on the person rather than place characteristics. So much so that Scannell and Gifford worry that when the "attachment is directed toward others who live in the place rather than to aspects of the place itself, it is considered to be a socially based place bond" (2010: 4). Other researchers suggest that attachment can reside in the physical features and materiality of the place. Stokols and Shumaker (1981) and Low, Taplin and Scheld (2005) identify physical features, elements of material culture and geographical markers as components of place attachment, especially when they offer affordances, that is, amenities or resources to support people and their social and psychological goals. Manzo and Devine-Wright's (2014) volume on place attachment presents a broad range of settings, from built environments to natural environments, as well as a wide array of methods and applications. They illustrate that, notwithstanding these advances in theory and method, the concept retains the basic idea that people are always embodied and embedded in place.

Environmental psychologists define place as a result or mediator of human-environment interaction and do not distinguish between space and place. Only recently has space been identified as a prominent concept in the field (Gieseking, Mangold, Katz, Low and Saegert 2014). Place within environmental psychology still retains elements of its humanistic beginnings with Tuan (1979) and others who employ images and imaginings of place that are synonymous with the location of meaningful community and local culture. Anthropologists also struggle with this assumption, but have been more successful in developing theories and methods that escape this limitation.

Anthropological genealogy

Many anthropological conceptualizations of space derive from French social theorist Pierre Bourdieu's point of view that space can have no meaning apart from practice. For example, Bourdieu's theory of practice provides the point of departure for Henrietta Moore's (1986) understanding of how space takes on gendered meanings among the Endo of Marakwet in Kenya. In her ethnography, space only acquires meaning when actors invoke it in practice, but she goes further and asks why meanings that are advantageous to men dominate these interpretations. For instance, Endo women are identified with the house, but the meanings invoked when using the domestic sphere privilege men's economic and social position. For Moore, spaces are subject to multiple interpretations, and she rejects the idea that dominant and muted groups, men and women, respectively, have different cultural models that produce distinct interpretations of space. Rather, men and women share the same conceptual structure, but enter into it in different positions and therefore subject it to different interpretations (Moore 1986). The notion that spaces are polysemic enables these creative interpretations.

Margaret Rodman (1992) agrees with Moore that spaces have unique realities for each inhabitant, and while meanings may be shared with others, their views are often competing and contested. She employs the concept of place rather than space to reference these sites of personal and cultural meaning, suggesting that anthropologists should empower place by returning control of meaning to the rightful producers and empower anthropological analyses of place by attending to the multiplicity of inhabitants' voices (Rodman 1992). To accomplish this task, she proposes the concept of multilocality to describe considerations of place(s) affected by influences of modernity, imperial history and contemporary contexts. In addition to accommodating polysemic meanings, multilocality seeks to understand multiple, non-Western and Eurocentric viewpoints in the construction of place, enabling a more decentered analysis. Multilocality is also useful for understanding the network of connections among places, as well as the reflexive qualities of identity formation and the construction of place as people increasingly move around the globe (Rodman 1992).

Rodman's multivocal approach urges listening to voices infrequently heard such as indigenous peoples who employ autochthonous imagery of rootedness to reference that they are inseparable from place or assert primordial connections of oneness with the land. She prioritizes place as the lived space of an individual's experience in the world and focuses her attention on "how different actors construct, contest and ground experience in place" (1992: 652).

Tim Ingold (2007, 2010, Ingold and Vergunst 2008) is also disenchanted with the concept of space as too abstract and as a reification of what he thinks should be a study of human and nonhuman practices. Drawing upon Mauss (1950) and Bourdieu (1977), he understands place in terms of the movement of the human body, such as walking and other everyday activities. Similar to the humanist geographers and environmental psychologists, his approach centers on dwelling and landscape, but is distinctive in that he includes human and nonhuman lives in his rendering of the environment. Ingold's concern with "the skills and practices by which people perceive and understand their immediate surroundings and so make themselves at home as they go about making the world" (Lorimer 2011: 251) pervades his ethnographic pursuits and is returned to in the discussion of embodied space in Chapter 5.

Some anthropologists conceptualize space and place through narratives that reflect how local populations construct perceptions of and experience place (Feld and Basso 1996). Most of this work focuses on local theories of dwelling that draw upon sensory and language-based approaches discussed in Chapters 5 and 6. One example is Keith Basso's long-term fieldwork among Native American Western Apache that uncovers the interaction of land and the self as reflective of moral relationships. Stories about places and place names, the vehicles of ancestral authority, are "symbolic reference points for the moral imagination and its practical bearings on the actualities of lives" (1988: 102). The Western Apache use the landscape as a mnemonic for self-reflexive activity, a necessary action for acquiring wisdom. Wisdom, or the capacity for prescient thinking, is learned from elders whose knowledge is enacted by visiting places, naming and recounting traditional stories (Basso 1996). By thinking of narratives set in place and the ancestors who originated them, Apaches inhabit their landscape and are inhabited by it in an enduring reciprocal relationship. Place is understood through habitation and self-identification with the land.

Although Australian Aboriginal peoples, like the Apache, tell stories about their ancestors situated in geographical locations, their narratives have a different character and function (Myers 1991, Morphy 1995). Fred Myers argues that among the Pintupi, the relationship between place and family is linked to the concept of "the Dreaming" – narratives about the mythological past in which totemic ancestors travel from place to place and finally became part of the land (1991). The Dreaming includes the means by which Pintupi selves are formed and identity is known, by which an individual owns a place and obtains the right to live in an area and the sacred knowledge associated with it. The Dreaming is contrasted with the immediate and visible world by constituting an invisible but primary reality that is unchanging and timeless. Myers suggests the Pintupi transform the landscape into narrative by invoking the Dreaming in their interactions with it and by using each place as a mnemonic for telling and reenacting the story of their whole "country" (1991: 66).

The inscription of place with meaning is not limited, however, to telling stories, but includes a complex set of sound, smell, touch and other sense-based perceptions or sensorium, which is discussed in Chapter 5 (Feld 1990, 1996; Roseman 1998; Weiner 1991; Peterson 2010). An example of this sensory and spatial ethnography is Marina Roseman's description of how the Temiar use songs to map their historical relationship with the rain forest, claim rights to its resources and translate the forest into culture by releasing forest spirits in song to sing in dreams and rituals (1998).

Alberto Corsín Jiménez (2003) offers a different critique by retaining the concept of space but insisting that it is a socially constituted notion. In his account, anthropology is influenced by the Durkheimian legacy that views space as a way to classify otherwise homogeneous territories, although this legacy is challenged by the theories of practice of Bourdieu (1977) and Giddens (1984). Nonetheless, Jiménez argues that anthropological notions of place and landscape still retain this *a priori* territorial meaning expressed as a concern with the "siting" of culture. Jiménez (2003) insists that "space is no longer a category of fixed and ontological attributes, but a becoming, an emergent property of social relationships. Social relationships are inherently spatial, and space an instrument and dimension of space's sociality" (2003: 140). Thus space is a condition or faculty, a capacity of social relationships; it is what people do, not what they are. In his analysis, the material landscape recedes as space becomes a dimension of social life and form of agency.

Thus there are disagreements between those who use place and theories of dwelling to conceptualize people's relationship to the environment and those who privilege the social construction of space to understand cultural meaning. For instance, Fred Myers (2002) criticizes Casey (1996) and Ingold (1996) for going too far in their rejection of culture and social construction. Myers instead argues for a reinsertion of practices and an analysis of the social and political processes by which places are invested with meaning and value. He suggests that Casey's and Ingold's ontology of dwelling and their rejection of the "culturalization of space" does not allow for the kind of subjectivity and orientation of Australian Aboriginal social practices. "People do not simply 'experience' the world; they are taught – indeed disciplined–to signify their experiences in distinctive ways" (Myers 2002: 103). Myers is also concerned that while the notion of "dwelling" correctly suggests the incorporation of landscape features into a pattern of everyday activities to create home, it also reasserts Heidegger's primitivism and distinction between modern and premodern. He agrees with Ingold's concern that there not be "a dichotomy between the material and mental, between ecological interactions in nature and cultural construction of nature" (1996: 144), but he conceptualizes the social mediation of place as a dialectical model of construction. This dispute continues to influence the different ways that space and place are understood in anthropology today.

Archaeological genealogy

The active engagement of human beings through practices and ongoing social relations has also been endorsed by archaeologists searching for conceptualizations that include agency in the study of historic and prehistoric sites. Wendy Ashmore (2008) contends that all places have meaning and that meaning is attached to a place because of the past and present experiences of people. Further, similar to Rodman (2001), any site may have alternative meanings, or "biographies," that can be established at different times and locations. Ashmore's concern centers on how archaeologists can appreciate diversity within ancient society by recognizing the multiple meanings that are embodied in the process of creating places. For her, material structures record meanings and practices that inscribe them in social memory (Ashmore 2008).

Christopher Tilley's (1994) discussion of the concepts of space and place concludes by emphasizing a third construct, that of "landscape," as more useful for archaeologists. For him,

> a landscape is a series of named locales, a set of relational places linked by paths, movements and narratives. It is a 'natural' topography perspectivally linked to the existential Being of the body in societal space. It is a cultural code for living, an anonymous 'text' to be read and interpreted, a writing pad for inscription, a scape of and for human praxis, a mode of dwelling and a mode of experience.
>
> (Tilley 1994: 34)

Tilley views landscape as an ordering and signifying system that produces social relations. He maintains that the concept of place emphasizes difference and singularity, while landscape is more holistic, encompassing a wider range of social processes and relationships.

Barbara Bender (1993) contends that "landscapes are created by people – through their experience and engagement with the world around them" (1993: 1) regardless of the scale, distance or degree of imagination. Pamela Stewart and Andrew Strathern add that it is landscape, and the perceptions of and values attached to landscapes that "encode values and fix memories to places that become sites of historical identity" (Stewart and Strathern 2003: 1). Victor Buchli (2013), in *The Anthropology of Architecture*, makes a similar point in his investigation of the materiality of place through an interrogation of how an assemblage of building materials, architectural objects or complex built environments enable human relations. Buchli along with Bender, Tilley, Stewart and Strathern prioritize the materiality of place and use material culture and the landscape as entry points for understanding the human experience of being-in-the-world.

Bernard Knapp and Wendy Ashmore (1999) agree with these material culture analyses, suggesting that archaeologists, while interested in space and spatial relations, should study the human past through landscapes. They trace the shift in archaeological theory from viewing landscape as a backdrop for arraying archaeological remains to contemporary notions that emphasize social and symbolic dimensions. In this transition, the passive landscape is replaced by one that is actively perceived, experienced and acted upon much like the transition in theories of space from absolute and relational to space as a capacity and constituted by social relationships.

Many of the changes in archaeological theories of space and place focus on the role of human agency. Processual theorists such as Kent Flannery (1999) view agents as biological individuals possessing psychological characteristics and varying abilities to bring about change (Patterson 2005). Post-processual theorists, such as Lynn Meskell (1999), instead see human agents as individuals with social identities that are produced and expressed within specific historical and political contexts. Cynthia Robin (2002) adds the notion of lived space to reflect how people organize their living spaces and live out the spatial rhythms of their lives. Thomas Patterson's (2005) review of these theories concludes that subjectivity, intersubjectivity and identity are now critical to understanding the complexities of human spatial lives in the archaeological record.

Space and place

These genealogical traditions reflect part of an ongoing dialogue on space and place that links philosophy, social theory and the social sciences (Blake 2004). The contrasting modalities and contradictions that characterize them often lead to new approaches and theoretical imperatives. Nevertheless, some of the distinctions and their related claims carefully laid out in theory seem less critical when the researcher is grappling with the methodological realities of undertaking an empirical spatial analysis.

From my vantage point, it is useful to imagine space and place as a continuum of global to intimate interrelations (Massey 2005) or as a range of geographical scales from the surface of the earth to an architectural structure (Smith 1984). Lefebvre's (1991) tripartite model of the social production of space also works well as an analytic framework.

Returning to the discussion of the conceptual relationship of space and place, I consider space to be the more general and abstract construct retaining its social production and materialist origins. Space, in my rendering, is preeminently social, produced by bodies and groups of people, as well as historical and political forces. Place is used in the sense of a space that is inhabited and appropriated through the attribution of personal and group meanings, feelings, sensory perceptions and understandings (Cresswell 2015, Sen and Silverman 2014). It is the spatial location of subjectivities, intersubjectivities and identities that transform space into places – that is, the lived spaces of human and nonhuman importance. While place may be studied phenomenologically through individual or collective experiences, it also derives its meaning from the social, political and economic forces and class relationships that produce its spatial, material and social form.

In the following chapters on the social production of space and the social construction of space, my understanding and definition of these concepts is further illuminated through a number of ethnographic examples. The concepts of space and place are clarified and transformed a number of times as they are put into practice by researchers in diverse ethnographic contexts and with different theoretical leanings. The remainder of the book elucidates the six conceptual frames discussed in the introduction – social production, social construction, language and discourse, emotion and affect, embodied space and translocality.

Note

1 The study of the causal relations between geographical phenomena occurring within a particular region. The study of the spatial distribution of organisms.

Chapter 3

The social production of space

Introduction

Understanding the social production of space is a useful starting point for an ethnography of space and place project. It is not the only way to begin, but the historical and political economic approach to space and the built environment offers an in-depth temporal and broad spatial perspective. The social production lens illuminates how a space or place comes into existence and opens up questions about the political, economic and historical motives of its planning and development. It emphasizes the material aspects of space and place-making, but also uncovers the manifest and latent ideologies that underlie this materiality.

For example, a social production of space lens reveals how the Latin American colonial plaza evolved from both indigenous and Spanish influences, producing a new spatial form (Low 2000). The planning and design are syncretic in the sense that it is not Spanish or indigenous but through a series of historical and sociopolitical processes became emblematic of Latin American public culture. This conceptual frame uncovers the ways in which the plaza retains spatial, architectural and physical elements from both cultural traditions such that the tensions of conquest and resistance remain encoded in the built environment. Even today, the Zócalo in Mexico City continues to be a contested terrain of architectural and political representation with the Aztec Templo Mayor and the Spanish colonial Cathedral as its symbols (Photo 3.1 Cathedral and Templo Mayor, Mexico City). The archaeological restoration of the Templo Mayor and the resulting destabilization of the surrounding colonial structures is a model of how social and political struggles of the past become part of the contemporary landscape. Ideologically and materially, the plaza portrays indigenous peoples' cultural resistance in the face of Spanish hegemony, resulting in an indigenously and colonially produced urban space.

The conceptual frame of the social production of space thus focuses on the social, political and economic forces that produce space and, conversely, the impact of socially produced space on social action. It is an interdisciplinary endeavor with seminal work by Marxist and cultural geographers (Smith 1990, Harvey 2003, Mitchell 2008), urban sociologists (Zukin 1991, Logan

Photo 3.1 Cathedral and Templo Mayor, Mexico City (Joel Lefkowitz)

and Molotch 1987, Brenner and Theodore 2002), architectural and urban historians (King 1980, Blackmar 1979; Rosenweig 1979; Hayden 2002, 2003) and anthropologists (Peattie 1970; Kuper 1972; Rabinow 1989, Holston 1989, Rotenberg 1995, Pellow 2002; Low 2000).

Contemporary ethnographers employ a number of theoretical and methodological understandings of social production to analyze the built environment. These can be considered loosely defined "schools of thought," although this organization may over emphasize their coherence and relationship to one another. They include 1) social history and development of the built environment; 2) political economy of space; 3) social production, reproduction and resistance; and 4) social control and spatial governmentality. Each emphasizes distinct ways of framing problems with methodological implications, yet they all include an analysis of how historical, political and economic forces shape the material environment. Each critically examines how and why a space or place appears or disappears and then uses this inquiry to question the assumed neutrality and naturalness of specific built environments, spatial forms and the social inequalities created.

This chapter reviews these schools of thought and identifies the theoretical and methodological focus of each. A few ethnographies are discussed briefly to illustrate their use and additional works are included as references that will be helpful to the reader. At the conclusion of the review section, the four approaches are integrated in their application to two longer ethnographic examples.

Approaches to the social production of space

Social history and development of the built environment

The social development of the built environment offers a historical and architectural approach to the ethnographic study of space and place. An early proponent, Anthony King based his inquiries on buildings, but his insight that "buildings, indeed, the entire built environment, are essentially social and cultural products" (1980: 1) also provides a framework for understanding space and place as well. He argues against the environmental and cultural determinism that dominates the architectural history field and instead suggests that the built environment is socially produced in complex political and historically specific ways:

> Buildings result from social needs and accommodate a variety of functions – economic, social, political, religious and cultural. Their size, appearance, location and form are governed not simply by physical factors (climate, materials or topography) but by a society's ideas, its forms of economic and social organization, its distribution of resources and authority, its activities and beliefs and values which prevail at any one period of time.
>
> (King 1980: 1)

As society changes new buildings emerge and others become obsolete, thus society produces buildings that maintain and/or reinforce its social forms.

The study of the architecture of colonialism also addresses the relationship of built form to the modern world system and global economy (King 1976, 1984; Buchli 2013). Global urban systems were integrated through architecture and spatial relations introduced as part of Spanish, Portuguese, British, French, Dutch and American physical plans and governance strategies for their colonies. Colonial space and architecture functioned as both producer and product, defining new spaces and instigating new economic, social, political and cultural practices.

Urban historians who employ feminist and Marxist theories critique the capitalist and gender-biased intentions of particular spatial and built forms. For example, a special issue of the *Radical History Review* traces the sociohistorical development of U.S. housing (Blackmar 1979) and parks (Rosenweig 1979) to uncover the ideological purpose of their social development. Dolores Hayden's (1981, 2002, 1995) gender-based analysis of domestic space and housing design, feminist history of work and family life and studies of the erasure of working peoples' landscapes reflect her commitment to reclaiming these spaces by documenting their social histories and reinserting material evidence of their existence through public history projects.

The social history and architectural development of a society or culture also has been studied through the ethnohistory of the house and home (Behar 1986, Low and Chambers 1989, Birdwell-Pheasant and Lawrence Zuñiga 1999, Rodman 2001, Pellow 2002). For example, the "archaeology of the house" (Behar 1986: 55) reveals how rural social relations are reproduced by spatial proximity and inheritance patterns in the evolution of Spanish village houses. A comparative ethnography of "sites and services" housing built by the government or auto-constructed by squatters after the 1976 Guatemala earthquake uncovers how the different social histories of residents produced distinct house types (Low 1988). An ethnohistory of the house compound based on family genealogies and house plans illustrates how marginalized Hausa migrants in Accra, Ghana, build social and spatial institutions to promote "legitimate behaviors and gradually gain the credibility of tradition" (Pellow 2002: 7). In the New Hebrides, the relationship of British colonial space to feelings of home are captured through historical descriptions of house design and furnishings (Rodman 2001) while tracing the historic preservation practices of Latino migrants offers a way to understand the transformation of the facades of their Los Angeles homes (Lawrence-Zuñiga 2016). These ethnographies are just a few of the many that emphasize the social development of housing and domestic spatial relations as a basis for understanding community continuity, conflict and cooperation, as well as offering a basis for political action.

Studying the social history and development of the built environment provides a basic understanding of the evolution of architectural and spatial form and reveals its ideological, political and economic underpinnings. The following three sections discuss other formulations of social production that include this basic historical and social development perspective, but also highlight other theoretical formulations.

Political economy of space

While social history studies document how buildings are socially produced and the consequences of their emplacement and form, other schools of thought underscore the underlying political and economic relations that initiate and drive spatial production. Regardless of whether it is an analysis of the production of space due to the bourgeois desire for money and commodities (Harvey 2006), the real estate market (Smith 1996, Logan and Molotch 1987), the financial markets (Sassen 2002), cultural consumption (Zukin 1991, 1996) or urban development (Fainstein 1994), it is the control of the means of production defended and augmented by the authoritative power of government that plays the dominant role. Even though society creates a physical landscape appropriate to its production and reproduction, "this process of creating space is full of contradictions and tensions and . . . the class relations in capitalist society inevitably spawn strong cross-currents of conflict" (Harvey 1976: 265). By examining the structural inequality of capital and labor in the process of the production of space, it is possible to articulate how and why struggles over the built environment and its use are inevitable.

Studies of city-forming processes often focus on urban form as an expression of the unequal distribution of capital accumulation, especially in terms of the reproduction of class relations through space allocations determined by urban planning (Harvey 1973, 1985, 2003). By way of an example, David Harvey (2003) reanalyzes George-Eugène Haussmann's attempt to destabilize the political activism of the 1848 French revolution by building three boulevards that ripped through the working classes' and working poor's homes and neighborhoods in Paris. The new spatial relations produced by the implementation of Haussmann's transportation and housing plans highlight the critical role of political economic power when combined with state hegemony and, if necessary, physical violence in urban space formation.

Capitalists' recurrent innovation and restructuring often result in cycles of economic growth and contraction. The resulting creative destruction produces dramatically different landscapes depending on whether the landscape is part of the production and service economy or part of the thriving real estate development, finance and entertainment sectors. Sharon Zukin (1991) identifies this tension between "market" and "place" as resulting in distinct and disparate landscapes, such as the deindustrialized city, the suburban city, the gentrified center city and the Disney World facade.

The increasing globalization of labor flows and manufacturing, erosion of the state and the intensification of competition, however, mark a shift in strategies to promote capital growth. This change in capital and labor practices and economic controls is accompanied by decreased state responsibility for worker welfare and social reproduction (Brenner and Theodore 2002, Peck and Tickell 2002, Smith 2008 and Harvey 2005). These processes have been subsumed under the rubric of neoliberalism.[1] The spatial consequences of neoliberalism have been devastating to working-class communities (Susser 1982) and isolated the urban poor in deteriorating hyperghettos (Wacquant 2008) while at the same time protecting the middle and upper classes in citadels such as gated communities (Low 2003). Much of the recent political economy of space literature focuses on the production of these neoliberal spaces, such as business improvement districts, redevelopment zones, shopping malls and private town centers, accompanied by the surveillance and containment of public space, including streets, parks and plazas, as well as other forms of uneven global development within this new regime (Smith 1984, Low and Smith 2006).

These underlying political economic processes of spatial production are exposed by paying closer attention to "what struggle in and over the landscape is about" (Mitchell 2008: 33). Don Mitchell (2008) emphasizes how landscape is actively produced through its political, social, geographical and relational functions within ongoing power dynamics that must be queried. His axioms for research include that landscape must be understood in its regional and global context, as a site of investment, shaped by the current state of technology and considered a concretization of social relations as well as the foundation for the formation of those relations.

A number of ethnographies utilize a political economic point of entry for the study of spatial inequality resulting from the uneven development of land and resources. Lisa Redfield Peattie's (1970) study of a low-income workers' neighborhood in Ciudad Guyana, an industrial city built in the 1960s to improve access to oil and gas resources in the interior of Venezuela, is an early example. She documents how the city came into existence, how it was planned, where the money for development was spent and, ultimately, how the material conditions privileged the engineers and corporate employees and neglected workers and their families. Her portrayal of the residents' struggle against environmental injustice and social inequality provides a methodologically useful account of how the economic and imperialist motives of U.S. and Venezuelan governments and U.S. Steel and Bethlehem Steel coalesced in the creation of this planned city.

U.S-based ethnographies often focus on class conflicts over the deterioration and destruction of housing, shopping, community centers and other services of poorer neighborhoods that suffer due to deindustrialization and fiscal crises (Susser 1982, Pappas 1989). Another aspect of this unequal power equation is a study of Columbia University's acquisition of poor residents' homes and small businesses in nearby Morningside Heights through state-mandated eminent domain (Gregory 2013). Julian Brash's (2011) ethnography of Mayor Michael Bloomberg's New York City similarly analyzes the spatialization of elite class interests through the creation of a luxury city and the abandonment of housing and public spaces for the working poor and homeless. His ethnography of the Hudson Yards, a development that was to transform Manhattan's far west side into a "high-end district," however, demonstrates how this development was ultimately thwarted by activists and entrenched local interests.

Much of this ethnographic work draws, directly or indirectly, upon Marxist and neo-Marxist theoretical frameworks as developed by Harvey (1976, 1998), Smith (1984), Zukin (1991), Mitchell (1995, 2008) and others, but is further developed and explicated through its cultural and political expression in ethnographic field sites. By viewing these political economic processes through the realities of everyday life, political economic theories of space and place are transformed into more nuanced interpretations and contextualized methodologies.

Social production, reproduction and resistance

While almost all theories of social production employ a political economic approach based on Marxism or historical materialism, some formulations are distinguished by their attention to social reproduction and resistance as fundamental concerns. Social reproduction refers to the conditions necessary to reproduce social class and in this context is defined as how everyday activities, beliefs and practices, as well as social and spatial structures transmit social inequality to the next generation. Resistance to these spatial arrangements, structures and activities through passive interventions, social movements and political mobilization also characterizes the social production process. These concerns have been taken up by a large number of neo-Marxists who incorporate feminist, psychoanalytic and other cultural frameworks into their explications of political economic processes. In this discussion, however, only a few who focus explicitly on the role of space and whose work has been heavily drawn upon by ethnographers are included.

Lefebvre (1991 [1974]) is concerned with how the capitalist system continues to grow in the face of contestation and spontaneous resistance. He argues that the capitalist mode of production has become so successful not just by owning the means of production but also by occupying and producing space, and he examines how surplus capital is transformed by real estate investment and the construction of infrastructure (Merrifield 2002, Brenner and Elden 2009). His insight is that social space is consumed and yet also politically instrumental in the control of society and the reproduction of property relations.

A number of ethnographers have drawn inspiration from Lefebvre and use his theoretical framework ethnographically. In Stuart Rockefeller's study of a village in highland Bolivia, he draws upon Lefebvre's adaptation of Marx, "production is an inherently human activity and implies action oriented to an end" (Rockefeller 2009: 23), to focus on how people's intentional activities give rise to spaces they did not anticipate. Adriana Premat is interested in how space and social action are worked out and finds Lefebvre's ideas useful because he does not assume an antagonistic relationship between those who regulate space and those who inhabit it (Premat 2009). Li Zhang (2010) draws upon Lefebvre's insights on the constitutive relationship of spatial production and new social formations in her ethnography of the spatialization of class in Kunming, China.

Architecture and planning serve unacknowledged ideological and economic ends in the reproduction of urban space and structures of class inequality. But instead of focusing on the production of space through state apparatus and professional plans, Manuel Castells (1983, 1996) studies social movements of renters, housing advocates as well as neighborhood preservation and political consolidation processes to document the role local residents play in the allocation and control of neighborhood space. For Castells,

> space is not, contrary to what others may say, a reflection of society but one of society's fundamental material dimensions . . . Therefore spatial forms . . . will be produced by human action, as are all other objects, and will express and perform the interests of the dominant class according to a given mode of production and to a specific mode of development . . . At the same time, spatial forms will also be marked by resistance from exploited classes, oppressed subjects, and abused women . . . Finally from time to time social movements will arise, challenging the meaning of spatial structure and therefore attempting new functions and forms.
>
> (Castells 1983: 312)

Ethnographic studies of urban design and planning as modes of social production, reproduction and resistance include a number of important anthropological works (Abram and Weszkalnys 2013). Gary McDonogh's (1999) history of planning politics in Barcelona and Emanuela Guano's (2003) study of the narrative reworking of neighborhood histories and urban planning in Buenos Aires affirm Castells's contention that social movements resist and reinterpret the spatial tyrannies of colonial and contemporary planning schemes. James Holston's (2008) work on insurgent citizenship of *favela* dwellers in Rio de Janeiro focuses on the impact of workers' movements to establish the right to housing and urban space.

These ethnographies offer methodological strategies for studying spatial reproduction and resistance based on neighborhood-based participant observation, interviews with community leaders and elders and active participation in resident organizing. Similar to the work of Castells (1983) and Hayden (1995), they also retrace and uncover the often erased material evidence of local history that was important in the social production of their own communities, which is discussed further in Chapter 4. From Lefebvre

(1991) and Castells (1983), ethnographers have explored the complex and mutually constitutive relationship of space and society through studies of how space is produced and reproduced not only by hegemonic elites and planning departments, but through resistance to these schemes by activists, residents and local commentators.

Social control and spatial governmentality

The study of social control through the structuring and manipulation of space and other forms of spatial governmentality offers another approach that can be employed in an ethnographic exploration of space and place. This approach is derived from Foucault's (2007) concept of governmentality that he defines as the ensemble of institutions, indicators and techniques of power that has a population as its target. Governmentality is also a type of power, sovereignty or discipline base that is called "government" and the process by which the administrative state is "governmentalized" (Foucault 2007). Spatial governmentality as a subset of these strategies "is typically portrayed as a recent technology of governance, but the use of spatial separation as a form of governance is ancient" (Merry 2001: 17, also see Foucault 2007: 108). Medieval towns, ancient Islamic cities and Chinese lineage villages were enclosed to protect inhabitants, to keep others out and to act as an indicator of economic status, religious and familial solidarity and social exclusivity. The expansion of the technique of spatial governmentality to produce social order is considered one of the characteristics of modern state governance (Merry 2001).

Foucault's well-known illustration of how spatial governmentality works is Jeremy Bentham's 1787 plan for the Panopticon, a model prison representing disciplinary control in its ideal form (1975). The Panopticon was designed as an arrangement of cell-like spaces, each of which could be seen only by the supervisor and without the knowledge of the individual being observed. Through this spatial organization of surveillance, inmates are encouraged to behave as if under surveillance at all times, ultimately becoming their own guardians.

In his post-structural writings, Foucault (1984, 1986) also describes spaces of possibility or "heterotopias" where the technologies and discipline of social order are broken down, or at least temporarily suspended, and reordered to produce new spaces where microcosms of society are transformed and protected. Their characteristics suggest alternative means of producing space that depend on the breaking down or building up of the boundaries separating these spaces from everyday life (Dehaene and DeCauter 2008). This spatial imaginary is explored in a study of Viennese gardens as a kind of heterotopia that expresses utopian ideals, resolves conflicting values, transforms time and is bounded by the ordinary and yet mystifies everyday experience (Rotenberg 1995).

Space is also a technology of social control employed as a disciplinary mechanism of colonialism initially introduced in modern Egypt (Mitchell 1988). French colonists thought that through the reconstruction of government villages and towns they could produce a new social order and colonial citizen. Mitchell defines this new ordering process as one of "enframing," "a method of dividing up and containing, as in the construction of barracks or the rebuilding of villages, which operates by conjuring up a neutral space or volume called 'space' " (Mitchell 1988: 44).

Colonial planners in Morocco under the leadership of Hubert Lyautey also built *villes nouvelles*, modern French settlements, next to, but separate from, Morocco's existing cities (Rabinow 1989). In this way, urban planning and design would produce an environment that maintained the French-imposed social hierarchy. A study of Moroccan colonial planning in Casablanca reiterates the importance of spatial and ethnic segregation for the "civilizing" of Moroccan subjects and identifies the connection between urbanism and hygiene as part of the rationalizing discourse (Maghraoui 2008).

Many ethnographers who study contemporary urban space employ Foucault's (2007) theories of territory, security and space to accomplish state goals, but they complicate the story with examples of local resistance, contested memories, legal strategies and even sabotage (Little 2014). Private corporations and governmental interests were successful in the redesign of Times Square, New York City, when the developers, planners, managers and architects agreed to create a public space that would protect consumers, businesses and tourists from crime and fear and exclude "undesirables' "(Chesluk 2008: 49). The addition of spatial partitioning with controlled sight lines, policing from a dedicated NYPD station and private security patrols with guard dogs, as well as employees who clean the sidewalks are used to remove homeless people, panhandlers, vendors and any suspicious "others" to keep tourists and shoppers feeling safe and secure.

Other ethnographic studies focus on spatial governmentality and the management of space to control people by the use of special spatial zones and rules of inclusion and exclusion (Merry 2001, Robins 2002). Patty Kelly's (2008) ethnography of the Zona Galáctica in the city of Tuxtla Gutiérrez, Mexico, documents the building and management of a government-created brothel where sex workers are regulated and supervised as part of a regional neoliberal modernization project. Teresa Caldeira (2000) explores the impact of the retreat of the state and the ensuing increase in crime and fear talk on the building of gated communities in São Paulo, Brazil. The comparative study of gated communities in the United States, Latin America and China, however, suggests that while fear of others and crime is a component of all gating, the mode of social production varies by region and cultural context, creating very different spatial patterns, degrees of public and private involvement and cultural meanings (Low 2007).

Foucault's theories of spatial control and governmentality have had a significant impact on the ethnography of space and place, especially from a social production of space point of view. The writings of Lefebvre (1991), Harvey (1998), Castells (1983) and many others have been equally generative as ethnographers have looked for theories that would help to explain the spatial configurations and power dynamics found in the field. Ethnographers have utilized these theories of social production for their own ends and generated new insights into the internal workings and external realities of the relationship of space and power. This review is brief and does not include the work of recent feminist theorists and Black race theorists who are challenging this established canon. Their contributions are discussed in Chapters 4 and 5. Two ethnographic examples illustrate the application of a social production of space and place approach. The first describes the history and development of Parque Central in San José, Costa Rica (Low 2000) and the second the evolution of the Shilin Night Market in the center of Taipei, Taiwan (Chiu 2013).

Ethnographic examples

The social production of the Parque Central in San José, Costa Rica

Introduction and methodology

The ethnographic example of Parque Central in downtown San José (Figure 3.1 Map of Costa Rica, San José and Parque Central) shows how competing and conflicting class interests, global capital investments and political ideologies socially produced this emblematic urban space. It traces how San José's colonial and republican history, agricultural to industrial economic transition, liberal to neoliberal political transformation, national to global capital investment and ideological and cultural shift in urban planning and design technology produced many of its spatial characteristics, patterns of habitation and built environment. Through ethnographic research supported by historical, archival and photographic documentation, it was possible to document the city's evolution and the increasing social inequality of residents and uneven development of this central and socially significant public space. The methods and techniques employed to undertake this analysis can be applied to any spatial or built form with similar results.

The methodology utilized for the fifteen years of plaza fieldwork was multisited and multidisciplinary with four overlapping phases. The first was ethnographic and consisted of recording daily life on two urban plazas through behavioral observation by sectors; participant observation; behavioral mapping; and interviews with users, local residents and owners of the surrounding buildings and institutions. It included photo-documentation of

Parque Central

Figure 3.1 Map of Costa Rica, San José and Parque Central (Erin Lilli)

Figure 3.1 (Continued)

the architectural context of the two plazas and detailed mapping of the businesses, vacant land and activities that surrounded the location and provided the architectural and social context. Participant observation developed into deeper relationships with some of the daily users and more nuanced understandings of their routines, intentions and everyday practices. Some plaza users and "characters" were harder to form a relationship with, so formal interviews and photography sessions were scheduled to capture their stories. In-depth interviews were also completed with local anthropologists and historians, as well as with members of the architecture faculty at the Universidad de Costa Rica and the architects and planners who had worked on the plaza designs.

Another part of this first phase was to count plaza users and to sketch their locations and spatial practices. A series of movement maps (Figure 3.2 Movement map of Parque Central) recorded the dance-like movements and trajectories of plaza users and passersby. Movement maps were

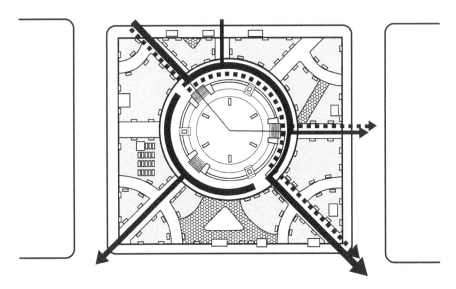

Figure 3.2 Movement map of Parque Central (Stephane Tonnelat, redrawn by Erin Lilli)

able to capture elements of the nonverbal and out-of-awareness aspects of social and physical life.[2] The quantitative procedures included counting the number of people in the plaza by day, hour and week or weekend. Gender, number of people in the group and age of the people were recorded. These counts substantiated many of the ethnographic findings such as the gendered and temporal nature of activities throughout the day and during the week versus the weekend.

The second phase of the project focused on the history of the Spanish American plaza and included architectural and ethnohistorical strategies of archival and documentary research. At the John Carter Brown Library, post-conquest texts and 1492–1501 maps and original letters were located to document the planning and design of early post-conquest plazas. Mesoamerican archaeology colleagues identified pre- and post-colonial archaeological sites that were investigated to provide alternative understandings of the processes of city planning, building and plaza design during the New World conquest and early colonial period.

The third phase involved returning to San José multiple times and adding new users, changes in the urban context and new spatial patterns that emerged. Expert interviews with the Minister of Culture, directors of the Teatro Nacional and the Banco Central and the President of Costa Rica, Oscar Arias, were completed in an effort to understand the politics of decisions that were made about public space funding and design style.

At one point in this process, the city decided to close down the Parque Central to redesign it and to move most of the then current users to other public space sites. This redesign enabled a third round of fieldwork that included interviewing those involved in the decision-making process, recording the protests of the ongoing design project and undertaking a "post-occupancy evaluation" (POE). A POE is often used in environmental psychology as a strategy for evaluating the impact of the new design on the remaining users, including those who have been relocated to other public spaces, and the new users who now find the site more appealing. The POE also created the opportunity to begin a fourth public anthropology phase of the project, where my findings became of interest to city officials and the news media in 2013.

Thus researching the social production of the plaza required a layered set of methodologies that crosscut time and space. Ethnohistorical documents and archaeological site reports, as well as architectural drawings and designs, were as important as long-term fieldwork in determining how these spaces were co-produced by the state, its citizens and the plaza users.[3] The following ethnographic example is a summary of this fieldwork and archival research from 1985 through 2013.

History and urban setting

Parque Central was first mentioned in 1761 in relation to the original town hall on the northeast corner of the plaza. It began as a grassy, tree-covered public space used as a weekend market place and was oriented as a square city block, with north-south and east-west roads as its boundaries. The civic and religious institutions of the Spanish settlers quickly surrounded it. Iglesia Parroquial (the first church) was built on the eastern side of the plaza in 1776 and became the national Cathedral in 1851 (DeMora 1973). The military barracks on the northern side were built next, and the new Casa del Cabildo (town hall) was completed on the northeast corner in 1799. At the same time, private buildings were being constructed; Capitán Don Miguel Jiménez built a house on the plaza as early as 1761, and the remaining building sites were eventually filled with private residences of newly rich tobacco growers and small businesses, including the Botica Francesa (a pharmacy) and a small hotel on the southern edge (González Viquez 1973, Vega Carballo 1981).

Parque Central retained its colonial form until Costa Rica's independence from Spain and the accession of San José as Costa Rica's republican capital in 1821. The emerging coffee elite and elected government officials began a series of improvements to represent Costa Rica as a modern republic and made use of Parque Central and its surrounding municipal architecture in this endeavor. In 1825, San José consisted of six blocks surrounding Parque Central, but by 1849, lower income families were located on the outskirts of the city beyond Calle de la Ronda where they worked odd jobs or as artisans, while the upper-middle-class professionals, business people and coffee farmers remained located along the principal streets. The most important individuals lived north of Second Avenue and Parque Central and northeast of the city center (Vega Carballo 1981). By the 1850s, the coffee elite had developed European tastes materially expressed in the growth of urban infrastructure and services, including street lamps, paved roads and flourishing stores and pharmacies (Molina and Palmer 2007).

In 1861, Ramón Quirós, the governor, the chief of police and the president of the municipality created a public walkway shaded with forty-four large white fig trees, twenty-four fig saplings and four mountain orange trees in front of the Cathedral. During the mid-nineteenth-century period, President Castro Madriz completely redesigned and refurbished the plaza with all the trappings of European bourgeois elegance. Francisco Maria Yglesias donated a fountain imported from England to supply water to the city in 1869, and an elaborate French iron fence was added in 1870. The wooden Victorian Japanese-style kiosk in which the military band would play for the Sunday *retreta* was constructed in 1890.

With this redesign, Parque Central became the center of the coffee elite's social life. In order to protect wealthy strollers from workers and poorer residents who also used the space, guards were added and watchmen patrolled in the evenings, calling out the hour and lighting gas lamps. Electric lights were added in 1889, and by 1907, the dirt paths were paved into curvilinear walkways. In 1908, another complete renovation of the park was undertaken that replaced the deteriorated Victorian kiosk with a copy in the same place and installed mosaic tiles along the walkways. Increasingly, the coffee elite appropriated Parque Central to display their version of civic life and to discipline the lower classes (Quesada 2006).

But this elite modernization and disciplining project could not disguise the growing class inequality in San José and the social heterogeneity of the mostly male park users. For instance, photographs from 1870 show workers in open shirts and barefoot boys resting in the plaza, and a well-known 1915 portrait of middle-class men with their children sitting on the ledge of the fountain captures a barefoot boy standing on the side of the scene (Banco Nacional de Costa Rica 1972). Photographs of the walkways along the fenced edge of the plaza in 1917 include barefoot *campesinos* (peasants from the countryside) as well as well-dressed urban businessmen (Banco Nacional de Costa Rica 1972). Novels of the period describe street children and poor people, including women, living in or along the edges (Trullás y Aulet 1913). Artisans and workers, as well as a subculture of sex workers and petty criminals, known as "apaches," also took over public spaces and became perceived as problematic with the illegal use of opium and marijuana (Molina and Palmer 2007).

This elite version of Parque Central did not change until the late 1930s when the fence and gating was removed during the paving of city streets. In 1944, the fountain and the Victorian kiosk were removed to make room for a modern cement kiosk donated by Anastasio Somoza, a Nicaraguan industrialist. Below the kiosk was a nightclub that was eventually replaced by the Carmen Lyra Children's Library (Figure 3.3 1976 plan of Parque Central).

Throughout this period and into the 1950s, the edges of the Parque Central retained some of the original private residences of elite families, the Botica Francesa and the military barracks transformed into a school. Cafés lined the northwestern corner and elite and middle-class people still came on Sunday for the evening *retreta* of the military band (see Chapter 5 for a description of the *retreta*). At the same time, industrialists' interests and economic alliances with Central and North American countries were already beginning to restructure the built environment.

The dramatic economic changes of the 1950s period resulted in greater urban density, crowding, crime and fumes from automobiles and buses. Most upper- and middle-class families moved to the western sector of the city or to the suburbs, abandoning the central city to the poor and working classes. The elite residences were replaced with the architecture of a new kind of global economy, one based on debt and world banking controls and dependent on foreign capital: national and international banks, movie theaters playing English-language movies, soda shops, North American fast food chains and small businesses now surrounded Parque Central, replacing the residential context of earlier plaza life.

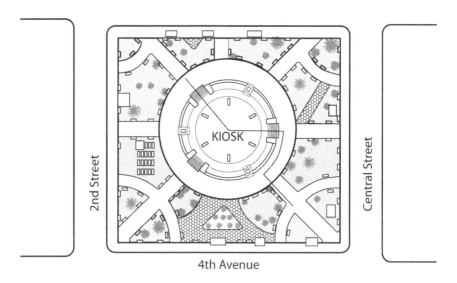

Figure 3.3 1976 plan of Parque Central (Setha Low, redrawn by Erin Lilli)

The increase in unemployment due to the declining value of agricultural exports and escalating rural migration to the city encouraged the growth of an informal economy that was visible in Parque Central. Public spaces were increasingly used as workplaces: shoeshine men controlled the northeast corner, ambulatory vendors used the sidewalks and pathways, salesmen used benches as offices, construction workers waited for pickup jobs under the arbor, sex workers stood in the kiosk or sat on benches and men moved through the crowd selling stolen goods or gambling. The influx of refugees from Nicaragua, El Salvador and Guatemala augmented the number of vendors and the competition among them, as well as contributed to the presence of homeless adults and street children.

In response, middle-class businessmen and the media generated political pressure to increase the number of police to remove "undesirables," and the state reacted in several ways. A racist discourse targeting the Nicaraguans as those responsible for the crime began to circulate more widely. Threats and xenophobia against Nicaraguans escalated with the increasing number of migrants looking for work and living in marginal squatter settlements, thus challenging the Costa Rican's myth of white exceptionalism (Sandoval-Gracía 2004, Alvarenga 2004). Downtown public spaces such as Parque Central became locations for Nicaraguans to gather, especially on weekends, appropriating these spaces and replacing the Costa Ricans who used to socialize there.

With the 1990 increase in municipal funding,[4] the police began surveillance sweeps from the top of the cement kiosk. In addition, plainclothes policemen were added to eradicate drug dealing and the selling of stolen goods. Municipal agents now required vendors to pay for the right to sell on the street or inside the park. If vendors did not have the money to pay for a license – a frequent occurrence – they forfeited their proceeds for the day.

While the changes in Parque Central were mostly due to increasing unemployment, decreasing opportunities of capital-intensive industrialization and the expansion of the service sector, there were also class-based struggles that focused on the architectural representation of civic life. For example, during the spring of 1992, there was a movement by a group of citizens to tear down the modern cement kiosk and reconstruct the original Victorian one. The conflict was so controversial that it provoked a series of well-attended town meetings. The cement kiosk and its current uses did not fit many middle-class residents' ideas of the appropriate architecture for the ceremonial and civic center of the city. The citizens who were attempting to reconstitute Parque Central in its elite turn-of-the-century image were not the daily users or the municipal designers, but professional and middle-class Josefinos yearning for an idealized past. Thus the conflict over the architectural form of the kiosk revealed an underlying cultural struggle between middle and upper-middle-class people, who wanted the park to reflect the elite turn-of-the-century cultural tastes, and the everyday working-class and low-income users who were comfortable in the park as it currently existed.

By the early 1990s, Parque Central was located in the most densely populated district of San José, with 10,669 inhabitants per square kilometer (*Ministerio de Economía, Industria y Comercio* 1992). The park encompassed 7,569 square meters surrounded by numerous banks, Burger King and the traditional Soda Palace and Soda La Perla. The overcrowding, high levels of pollution from diesel buses and increase in petty crime contributed to the perception that Parque Central was the cause of the deterioration of the central city, which resulted in its redesign.

The renovation of Parque Central (Figure 3.4 1993 plan of Parque Central) did little to alleviate the problems produced by the restructuring of the economy and neoliberal urban policies and practices. In the final version, the kiosk was remodeled and a replica fountain added; at the same time, the trees, the arbor, the working spaces and comfortable stone benches were removed to

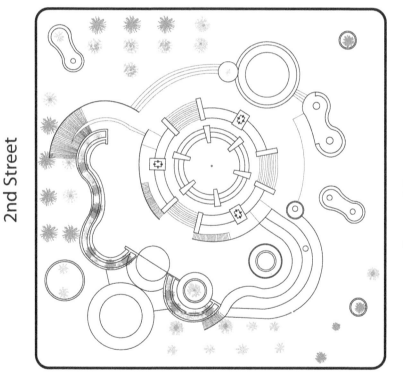

Figure 3.4 1993 plan of Parque Central (Municipalidad de San José, Costa Rica, redrawn by Erin Lilli)

correspond to an image of middle-class civility and to discourage the activities of its previous users. The new plaza included an art gallery for national artists to exhibit in the space below the kiosk where the children's library had been, twenty-four telephone booths along the eastern edge of the park and a municipal police station to protect the public from escalating juvenile crime. The shoeshine men and flower stalls were moved to another area a few blocks away. When it was reopened, new rules went into effect, including that ambulatory vendors would no longer be allowed; all edge construction would be restricted to the height of the original buildings (seven meters), and all bus stops, used mostly by the poor and working classes, were replaced by taxi stands.

The design objective was to reclaim the public space by displacing the current users. Removing the vendors and adding more police was intended to keep it clean and safe,[5] while small and curving benches and extensive paving changed its character and level of comfort. The municipality explicitly wanted to produce a new kind of public space, one that excluded many of the traditional users and restricted commercial activities. The new design appeared safer to some middle-class residents and tourists with its open vistas, and it was more modern and European with its reconstructed fountain, paved walkways and promenades.

Yet the goals of the designers were only partially realized because of the changing social environment of San José. The increasing number of Nicaraguan refugees found a place to meet family and friends, and gangs of teenagers found a hangout close to where stolen goods and credit cards were sold and near downtown stores where tourists with money were known to visit. During fieldwork in 2008–2009, the anthropologist Jeremy Rayner walked through Parque Central a couple times a week and confirmed that most users were poor and many were Nicaraguan, but there were still quite a few people using the park.

In many ways, the redesign of Parque Central was an attempt to mask the municipality's desire to clean up this central public space by removing the architectural affordances – the arbor, the trees and the benches – that invited older pensioners and the unemployed to spend the day. The cleanup restricted commercial activities to other areas of the city, removing the vendors and shoeshine men who had worked there for more than fifty years and who had kept more dangerous crime contained in the public market area many blocks away. With these restrictions, however, new forms of criminal activity invaded the public space, including narco-trafficking and other kinds of organized crime (Molina and Palmer 2007).

Underlying class bias produced a design that the municipality, the designers and the Ministry of Culture thought would reinscribe an earlier vision of elite civic life in Parque Central. But instead, the political economic realities of increasing poverty and unemployment, the de-stabilization of the welfare state by neoliberal practices and the uneven development of the city produced by global capital investments that bypassed the needs of the poor and working people located in the downtown area were more powerful. Parque Central became socially fragmented and disconnected, inhabited by marginalized and racialized Nicaraguan immigrants, dangerous because of the presence of teenage gangs and avoided by middle-class Costa Ricans and tourists because of frequent muggings.

Contemporary planning and policing

In an effort to address some of these problems, a series of policies for sustainable urban development have been legislated, and a land use plan was put in place. The goals were to reconstruct the parks, rescue the rivers, provide clean air and water and improve the overall quality of urban life. These governmental reforms and the land use plan created the basis for the renovation of many of the parks and plazas in San José. Only some of these renovations, however, were completed, and the renovation of Parque Central in 1993 (Photo 3.2 Parque Central, 2003) has been viewed as insufficient since it is still perceived as not a safe place to visit (Palmer and Molina 2006).[6]

Recent physical planning projects, however, have addressed the need for more public space in ways that facilitate shopping, cultural programming and commercial activities. A pedestrian shopping street and mini-mall have been built along Avenida Central (Central Avenue) and are protected by policing and

Photo 3.2 Parque Central, 2003 (Setha Low)

surveillance towers (Photo 3.3 Surveillance tower on pedestrian mall). This increase in urban policing and surveillance of public space from imposing police towers did not exist until 2009, but is now a prominent feature in Parque Central as well as other parks and plazas (Photo 3.4 Police talking in Parque Central). There was always a minimal amount of policing at both plazas from 1985 through 2000, but it has increased based on 2013 field observations (Photo 3.5 Parque Central, 2013).

Field notes from 2013 fieldwork reflect this downturn in the economic trajectory and social life of Parque Central:

> The faded facade of the kiosk no longer retains any of its original sculptural detail and is surrounded by dying trees and sidewalks with trash and debris. It is odd, as I can see female street sweepers talking on a bench next to the bronze statue of a male street sweeper. The plaza looks worn, shabby and smells of ripe garbage. People are dispersed compared to the clusters of users that frequented the corner benches (Photo 3.6 Dispersed people in Parque Central); now there is only one shoeshine man in each section. When asked, the remaining shoeshine men report (Photo 3.7 Isolated shoeshine man) that the police keep them separated from one another, and they are not sure why. One policeman said that it is because they don't like anyone to gather in small groups that can create the semblance of gangs.

Photo 3.3 Surveillance tower on pedestrian mall (Setha Low)

Photo 3.4 Police talking in Parque Central (Joel Lefkowitz)

Photo 3.5 Parque Central, 2013 (Joel Lefkowitz)

Photo 3.6 Dispersed people in Parque Central (Setha Low)

Photo 3.7 Isolated shoeshine man (Joel Lefkowitz)

The two photographers are still working at the base of the kiosk and the southwest corner is filled with Nicaraguans rather than with Costa Rican pensioners. The oldest pensioners are now sitting by the post office where they were relocated when the plaza was first closed.

The businesses and many of the banks that previously lined the plaza have mostly been replaced by fast food establishments from the U.S. The Soda Palace, a male bastion of civility and a supposed Mafia hangout, is gone, replaced by Papa John's and other markers of North American capitalism, including a Burger King, Carl's Jr., Popeye's, Wendy's and Applebee's. Only the Costa Rican ice cream store, Pop's, is still in its original location.

Some of the plaza "characters" remain, including a preacher in a blue robe tied with a rope belt who is carrying a paper banner with words of the gospel on it (Photo 3.8 Preacher in Parque Central). He is walking through the park and stopping to preach whenever a crowd gathers.

New surveillance towers located at the southeast and southwest corners allow police to monitor activities without having to engage directly with the park users or passers-by. The kiosk that used to be the gathering place of the police is occupied by five young men dressed in a variety

Photo 3.8 Preacher in Parque Central (Setha Low)

of costumes and female clothes smoking and flirting. There are a few vendors walking around the park trying to sell chips, toothbrushes and necklaces, but they scatter when the police approach them. There are few tourists or foreigners, I assume because of all the warning signs stating that there are pickpockets and gangs that frequent the space. But the disjointed seating and resulting lack of lively social groups also might not attract them.

(March 16, 2013 1:00–4:00 p.m.)

Since the late 1990s, economic development has increasingly relied on a system of social production of space based on the interests of transnational capital (Pearson 2012). The increasingly unequal distribution of wealth and income and break down in political openness resulted in a series of large-scale protests and community mobilizations. These experiences of community organizing set the groundwork for an upsurge in social movement activity in San José, including a series of successful protests, strikes and roadblocks in opposition to the proposal to privatize the Costa Rican Electricity Institute (ICE) in 2000 (Rayner 2008, 2014a, 2014b).

The protests, however, were only able to slow down the privatization of public institutions, including public spaces. President Miguel Angel Rodríguez (1998–2002) continued to push for privatization and by 2002–2006, under the leadership of President Abel Pacheco, neoliberals tried a new strategy by taking advantage of the Central American Free Trade Agreement (CAFTA) to open a number of public services to private corporation competition. Grassroots social movements, however, reemerged in 2005 as a decentralized network of rural and urban Patriotic Committees to fight, albeit unsuccessfully, the CAFTA-DR referendum in October 2007 (Rayner 2014a). To date, these political mobilizations have not changed Parque Central, except to increase the deterioration and lack of attention from the municipal and national government. Instead, the privatization of public spaces has accelerated with a number of pedestrian streets being created and funded by the surrounding businesses to increase the number of shoppers. In many ways, as in the United States, shopping streets and "mini-malls" are taking over the social role of urban plazas for middle- and working-class Costa Ricans with the caveat that you must pay for the price of entrance.

Shilin Market in Taipei, Taiwan

Introduction and methodology

Street markets are growing as significant social, political and economic urban spaces throughout the global South. These sites and their complicated systems of municipal policies and practices of policing offer insights into the spatial vulnerability of this growing sector of the informal economy (Hansen, Little and Milgram 2013; Milgram 2014; Gengzhi, Zue and Li 2014). The night markets of Taipei, Taiwan, are a special kind of street market characterized by their dynamic commercial life and successful social relations that share much of the same class diversity and sociality of the plazas in Costa Rica.

Shilin Night Market is one of the oldest of these food and dry goods markets located in front of the Zichen Temple in the downtown area of Taipei (Photo 3.9 Shilin Night Market). When the municipal government moved the market, the remaining vendors, local residents and officials were concerned that such a planning decision would destroy this place of social interaction for locals and remove a popular tourist attraction.

Chihsin Chiu (2013), an architect and environmental psychologist, became interested in how to preserve and redesign night markets to maintain their social and tourist functions. At a time when night markets were listed as the top tourist attraction for foreign tourists within a rapidly modernizing city, it was crucial to find a way to integrate these cultural icons into the emerging new landscape. Through his long-term ethnographic study of the Shilin Night Market, Chiu was able to recommend design solutions to local planners. At the same time, he became intrigued by the complicated system of informal management and interactive performance between the vendors and the police that produced and preserved this social space.

Photo 3.9 Shilin Night Market (Chihsin Chiu)

Chiu's methodology focused on intensive participant observation with the legal and illegal vendors and the local police tracking their movements in what he describes as a highly choreographed form of performance. Drawing on Goffman's theory of impression management, he studied the interplay of movement and social interactions, including how the vendors became "invisible" or "visible" to their customers, the police and to each other. Through mapping the spaces of the market, tracing the circulation of goods and people and recording the presence or absence of vendors, he was able to document how these everyday practices produced the vibrant space and attraction of the market. Another aspect of his fieldwork included searching the municipal archives for planning documents and historical maps of Taipei's central core. Working with the city planners and designers who were concerned with modernizing the night markets without destroying them, he was able to participate in conferences and meetings about the fate of these spaces.

Instead of a grand narrative of the production of space through changes in economic and political trends, his ethnography characterizes social production as an interactive process among the actors involved in regulating and maintaining the market's commercial and public spaces. The municipal government maintains control over the use of public streets and buildings through policy, planning and design practices that regulate the urban environment and impact the construction and repair of infrastructure, circulation of goods and functioning of the night market. Private businesses have the ability to lease and sublease the commercial spaces both inside and outside of their stores in ways that often contest the rules and regulations of the municipality. The police face the paradox of being responsible for keeping streets clear for pedestrians and vehicular passage by removing illegal vendors, but at the same time, they are encouraged to tolerate the illegal vending that promotes economic viability.

In response to these forms of regulation and control, the street vendors cooperate with one another and the store owners where they rent space to evade removal by the police, thus becoming agents of a different kind of social production process than the historical accretions, elite hegemony and discursive practices of Parque Central. Instead, in the Shilin Night Market, street vendors appropriate both public and private property and deal with the municipality and local businesses through legal, extralegal and illegal practices that produce what Chiu calls "fluid occupancy," a strategy that results in a vibrant and constantly changing configuration of urban space (Chiu 2013: 335).

History and urban setting

The market evolved through the activities of the Chinese immigrants who first lived on the south side of Taipei's Shilin District and built Zichen Temple in a central space surrounded by four main streets (Figure 3.5 Map of Taiwan, Taipei and Shilin Night Market). The area became known for wholesale fish and produce because of its location near the Kilong River, and the Japanese colonial government built two indoor markets in 1909 to accommodate the produce vendors (Chiu 2013 citing Yu 1995). In the 1950s, the space in front of the Zichen Temple became a popular day market that by the 1960s also had a number of established night market vendors who sold traditional Taiwanese dishes to students at the three nearby universities. The traditional Taiwanese food vendors located outside the wholesale markets became successful as retail markets took over much of the fish and produce demand. Shilin Night Market was well established by 1970 through the increase in food vendors and their local customers (Chiu 2013).

The regulation of the nighttime vendors eventually became a problem for the community. While vendors initially occupied the temple plaza, they intruded on the temple property, creating a nuisance for the temple

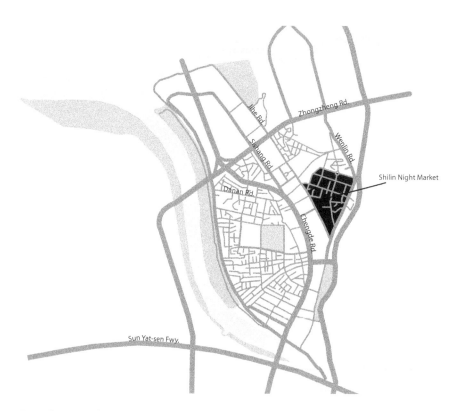

Figure 3.5 Map of Taiwan, Taipei and Shilin Night Market (Erin Lilli)

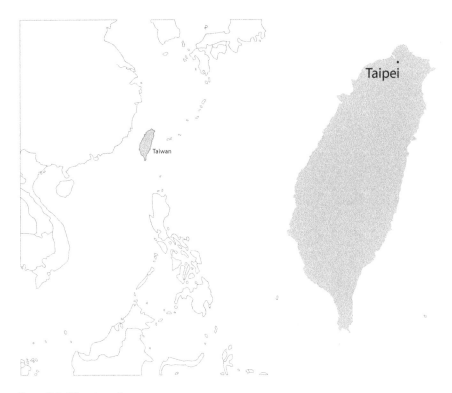

Taipei

Taiwan

Figure 3.5 (Continued)

administrator (Chiu 2013). The municipality at first designed an open lot with utilities behind the temple for which they charged rent. But many vendors persisted in selling in front of the temple and ultimately forced the municipality to put a roof over the vending area and to open two wholesale markets that could be used at night. Vendors drew lots for these covered spaces and 535 vendors received licenses for which they had to pay monthly fees and register with the market administration for the use of these fixed locations (Chiu 2013).

But there remained "various forms of extralegal – unlicensed and unregistered – groups of vendors" (Chiu 2013: 341) who did not have access to the municipality run stalls and locations, especially after 1990 when they stopped legalizing vendors. These extralegal vendors found other solutions for locating vending space. Some rented storefront arcades from the local shop owners while others created "self-regulated communities that appropriated the center of Dadong Road" (Chiu 2013:341). These different kinds of vending strategies – legalized with fixed stalls and locations, extralegal self-regulated communities and quasi-legal renting of private space from shop owners coexisted as part of the tourist economy of the late 1990s.

The social production of informality

This configuration of legal, extralegal and illegal vendors came under great scrutiny with the emergence of Taipei as a global city branded as a modern international business and tourism destination. Efforts to relocate vendors into large, multistoried buildings that initially seemed promising did not provide the vitality and liveliness of the traditional street vending locations. Further, street vending had always been an employment opportunity for the urban poor and unemployed in Taipei, and it was not in the best interests of the city to close off this part of the informal economy. At the same time, street vendors could offer considerable political support for politicians such that many elected officials were unlikely to oppose even the illegal vendors by closing the markets or forcing vendors into undesirable interior spaces (Chiu 2013). A complex ecology of street vending emerged that succeeded in producing and promoting the market, while at the same time maintaining the facade that the municipality and the police were actively clearing the roadways and removing illegal vendors, following municipal health and safety laws.

This production of informal market space relies on a number of different transactions and strategies. For example, while some unlicensed and unregistered vendors rent space in the storefront arcades from shop owners, other local power brokers also claim the right to regulate sidewalks and streets adjacent to them (Figure 3.6 Plan of Shilin Night Market). Thus the vendors have to pay both the shop owners and the additional local power brokers to use the shop front and arcade areas. Vendors who work in the street pay these individuals US$500 a month (Chiu 2013) for a tiny space, about a square foot, and they then protect the vendors by paying off the local police.

The police, though, must be in evidence and act as if they are clearing the street so the vendors have developed other ways to avoid being fined or caught. One vendor is designated as a lookout or gatekeeper and signals the others that the police are on their way. Cell phones and speakers are also used to warn the vendors that the police are arriving in an attempt to avoid being ticketed. Vendors then close up their tables and suitcases of goods and move away to a hidden corner or alleyway, sometimes with customers still buying their merchandise (Chiu 2013). Where there are no hidden corners or places to wait, vendors cover their wares and try to act as if they are not selling. In other cases, vendors take turns being the one to be "caught" and fined, while the rest retreat until the police have left. Street vendors, regardless of

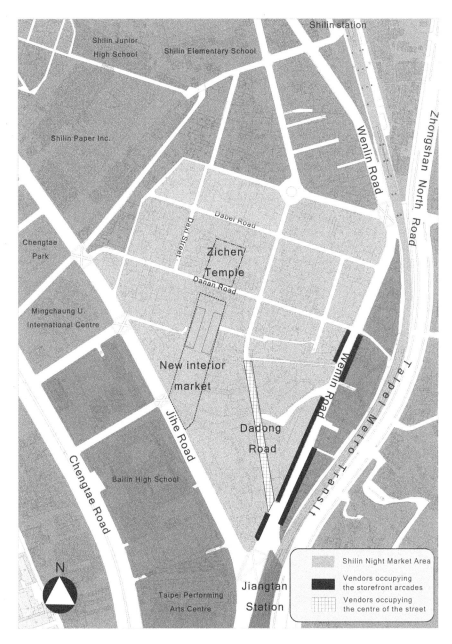

Figure 3.6 Plan of Shilin Night Market (Chihsin Chiu)

whether they are hiding in an alleyway, covering their wares or simply walk-ing off and acting as shoppers with a suitcase, return to their vending sites as soon as the danger has passed.

These moments of apparent chaos with the disappearance of the vendors when the police arrive add to the drama and interest of the market for shop-pers and tourists. The performances play an important role not only in pro-ducing the actual physical space of the night market, but also how the space is reproduced in ever-changing forms, collectivities and assemblages of people and locations through the fluid occupancy of the vendors. By employing eth-nographic and environmental psychology methods to understand the produc-tion of space at a microsociological level, Chiu demonstrates how the informal economy that thrives on the poorly regulated spaces of the night market coex-ist within a complex system of formal mechanisms that include city planning, urban management, private property ownership and law enforcement used to regulate urban public space. The interactive performance of street vendors and police in the space of the night market offers another example of the value of the ethnography of space and place when studying the social production of space at a micro- as well as macro-sociological scale.

Conclusion

The strength of a social production of space approach is its ability to connect far-reaching historical, economic, political and social forces with specific sites and physical locations and their architecture, planning and urban design. It is a powerful method for linking macro- and micro-social processes, generating empirical evidence of how the social and political goals of one group – in the Parque Central example, the local and transnational elites – are implicated in the production of a material environment that restricts resources and access to public goods for the majority of the poor and working-class residents. Social production also offers a means for understanding why a place is in a certain location, how it developed into its present form and how it maintains and accommodates unequal power and social relations found between ven-dors and the police in the Shilin Night Market. A social production of space analysis provides insights into the many processes of uneven development and the multiple ways that capitalism destroys and recreates the built envi-ronment in its never-ending quest for profit through investment of surplus value and also highlights how locals contest and confront these incursions.

There are, however, limitations to a solely social production point of view in that it does not answer questions about people's ability to give meaning to and appropriate everyday lived space. A complementary methodology and way to understand space that social scientists also frequently employ is studying the social construction of space through individual meanings, intentions, thoughts and dreams, which is the subject of the next chapter.

Notes

1 A theory of political economic practices that proposes that human well-being can best be advanced by liberating individual entrepreneurial freedoms and skills within an institutional framework characterized by strong private property rights, free markets and free trade. The role of the state is to create and preserve an institutional framework appropriate to such practices (Harvey 2005).
2 These movement maps were conceived of before mobility studies had emerged, but increasing interest in mobility and walking has reinforced the importance of what at the time seemed like an unorthodox method, as discussed in Chapter 5.
3 Bruno Latour's (2005) actor network theory (ANT) approach helps to explain why I included buildings, materials and construction processes, as well as the designers and users as equal or "symmetrical" partners in the production process. On the other hand, beginning with the idea of social production of space as a form of uneven capitalist development encouraged the uncovering of asymmetrical power relations that continue to undermine social justice in the city today.
4 Since the municipality of San José did not have the legal right to tax its citizens, all funds for urban development and planning came from the minimal 1 percent allocation of the federal budget for urban services. In 1990, however, President Oscar Arias reformed the city governance laws and instituted a 10 percent income tax on those living there.
5 See Mitchell and Staeheli (2006) for a discussion of clean and safe public space discourses and practices.
6 This phase of economic and political domination included Central American regional integration through large-scale infrastructure development projects such as the Plan Puebla Panama that from 2001 to 2008 developed highways, ports, electrical grids and railroads to attract foreign investment (Pearson 2012). Regional corridors of biodiversity conservation brought together neoliberal discourse with sustainability goals (Pearson 2012). At the same time, regional elites promoted regional free-trade agreements, such as the United States–Dominican Republic–Central American Free Trade Agreement (CAFTA-DR) to liberalize these new markets (Raventós 2013, Pearson 2012).

Chapter 4

The social construction of space

Introduction

A social construction conceptual frame assumes that space and place are abstractions – not a set of physical properties – made up of shared understandings and social structural differences such as race, class and gender. Thus they cannot be used as "place-as-matter" to explain the world (Brown 2005: 9). Yet changes in the physical environment, its interpretation and its forms of representation also influence the social construction of space and with it people's sense of inclusion and the ability to appropriate space for their needs. In this sense, then, a social constructivist methodology requires an ethnographic sensitivity to the unstable relationship between the many forms of social abstractions that make up space and place meanings and the materiality of the environments that make up the everyday world.

A working definition of the social construction of space and place includes the transformations and contestations that occur through peoples' social interactions, memories, feelings, imaginings and daily use – or lack thereof – that are made into places, scenes and actions that convey particular meanings (Low 1996). Studies of space and place that employ a social constructionist approach often examine differentially distributed meanings, experiences, local knowledge and individual, as well as collective, understandings of place, spatial relations and representations. It is one of the most useful and certainly the most ubiquitous of the conceptual lenses presented, yet in many ways it is difficult to characterize because it is made up of a variety of approaches and has many qualities that require further unpacking. Ironically, social scientists often take social constructivist conceptions of space and place for granted and fail to go far enough in interrogating underlying assumptions and social processes or clarifying how a constructivist explanation can lend a critical edge to a spatial analysis.

For example, visitors to Orchard Beach in the Bronx, New York, socially construct and communicate local meanings through symbolic forms and practices such as music, dance, food, decoration and recreational activities. The spatial appropriation, routine practices and park experience narratives of "Latinos," "seniors" and "naturalists" – three groups that are often marginalized elsewhere in the city – create unexpected forms of place-making and inscriptions of meaning. The seniors have found an abandoned concession stand where they meet each day to talk, have coffee and remember friends whose pictures are pinned to the wall. They call this place their "clubhouse" and consider it a home away from home. For the Latinos, during the summer there are *salsa* concerts and families celebrate birthdays and family reunions under tents on the beach or under shade trees in the picnic areas. Friends and family bring hammocks for *siestas*, card tables for dominos and cookout grills for making chicken and *chorizo*. The naturalists, on the other hand, do not mark their presence by playing music or altering the environment as a means of place-making. Instead, daily walks along the beach, forays into the forest and "hunting and gathering" activities are the way naturalists inscribe and appropriate park space. These different strategies of meaning-making underscore the multiplicity of ways that individuals and groups socially construct space and give it meaning.

Power relations always underlie the social construction of space and are embedded in race, class and gender inequality; disputed claims to history, heritage and collective memory; limited access to territory and resources; and other contested social processes. Space and its arrangement and allocation are assumed to be transparent, but they rarely are. Instead, when critically examined, the social construction of space and resulting spatial formations and relationships yield insights into unacknowledged biases, prejudices and inequalities in a particularly forceful way.

Michael Peter Smith's assertion, "social theories are largely constitutive of the reality we see, tell stories about, and act upon" (2001: 8), succinctly summarizes the social constructionist approach. Structures as well as the makers of these structures are also "socially constructed understandings of how the world works . . . produced by historically specific discourses and practices situated in different 'subject positions' " (2001: 8–9). Therefore, a social construction of space analysis uncovers explicit as well as implicit assumptions about the world through the careful observation of the material and discursive practices of social actors (Lussault 2007). Ethnographies of the social construction of space decode and deconstruct the struggles, contestations and power dynamics underlying existing social and spatial relations.

In the following sections, a number of theoretical approaches to the social construction of space are presented. Diverse perspectives and ethnographic methodologies are illustrated by focusing on three areas of research: contestation and conflict; memory, heritage and attachment; and the social construction of race, class and gender. The chapter concludes with two ethnographic examples. The first is an engaged anthropology project of the African American experience and sense of historical erasure at Independence National Historical Park in Philadelphia (Low, Taplin and Scheld 2005, Fanelli 2014) that illustrates the importance of symbolic representation for the continued use and meaning of space. The second is the ethnography of the Solidere redevelopment of downtown Beirut, Lebanon and local residents' attempt to resist the destruction of historically important buildings and places based on the research of Aseel Sawalha (2010), Deen Sharp (Sharp and Panetta 2016) and Kristin Monroe (2016).

Theoretical approaches to social construction

Constructivism and social construction

In reaction to the positivism and scientism of the 1950s in which reality was assumed to be objective and entirely "out there," constructivists posited that reality might be better understood as a product of human practices and intentions, and thus subjective and dependent on language and symbols for its communication. Beginning with the 1960s and expanding during the 1980s into the 1990s, this epistemological perspective became a dominant paradigm such that any cultural expression learned by socialization or acculturation was considered inherently constructionist. This system of explanation remains ubiquitous within the social sciences.

Lester Ward (1905), an American botanist, paleontologist and sociologist, was the first to use the concept in his discussion of the evolution of a social structure as "something that has been constructed, and a study of social structure is the study of a process and a product. Our task therefore, is . . . to inquire into the methods of social construction" (as cited in Best 2008: 41). This early articulation of social constructivism was remarkably prescient – not least because it recognized that social structure, as a phenomenon created by processes of social construction, required sociological analysis to uncover its underlying form and meaning (Best 2008).

James Faubion and George Marcus describe anthropological constructionism as made up of four kinds of analysis: 1) the functionalist inquiry into practical consequences, 2) the semiological constitution of meanings, 3) the rhetorical use of speech and 4) the hermeneutical process of interpretation (2008). They then apply these methodological approaches to three distinct categories of constructivist theorization. The first category begins with the work of Emile Durkheim (1982), who considered the form and content of social organization responsible for the moral and cognitive patterns of organized interaction and "particular habits of heart and mind" (2008:73). In the work by Durkheim (1982), as well as in Victor Turner's (1968) and Mary Douglas's (1970) writings, meaning is constructed through ritual symbols and events. The second category of constructionism centers on Bourdieu's (1977, 1984) studies of power and sociocultural reproduction and the construction of meaning through everyday practices. Faubion and Marcus (2008) then attempt to untangle the many strands of structural semiology, their third category that includes the microanalysis of communicative interaction, symbolic anthropology and the anthropology of performance. Two well-known, but opposing, theories of constructionism in anthropology are highlighted in their discussion of semiology: the binary opposition of Lévi-Strauss's structuralism in which the biological mind imposes social categories on experience and the cultural relativism of Geertz in which "man [sic] is an animal suspended in webs of significance he himself has spun" (1973: 5).

There are, of course, other ways of understanding the pervasiveness of social construction theory. In Peter Berger and Thomas Luckmann's (1967) model of the social construction of reality, face-to-face interaction is the basis by which the subjectivity of the other person is easily perceived through expressive acts. In this intimate situation, people share and apprehend the reality of everyday life as a continuum of "typifications," which are standard social constructions that become general knowledge and a way to know something other than through direct experience. Typifications become more abstract the farther one moves from one's communication group or community. They are subject to "objectivation" – that is, the externalization of the social construction process in which ideas, objects and other forms of "reality" are assumed to be stable and objective – rather than based on the subjective processes of their producers (Berger and Luckmann 1967).

Social structure is the sum total of these typifications and shared objectivations that serve as enduring indices of subjective meanings. The most important case of objectivation is found in language, as it is able to be detached from face-to-face interaction and convey signification at a distance. Language can typify experience and build up "semantic fields and zones of meaning that are linguistically circumscribed" (Berger and Luckmann 1967: 41), such as "gender" or "class" that shape everyday life and play a critical role in the social construction of space. John Searle (1995) calls these objectivations "institutional facts" that are matters of culture and society as distinct from the "brute facts" of physics and biology and distinguishes facts that can exist independently from language from those that "require special human institutions for their very existence" (Searle 1995: 27, also see Mounin 1980).

The work of Bruno Latour (2005), however, challenges this assumed distinction between biological and physical facts from socially constructed or institutional ones. For Latour (2005), there is no *a priori* divide between the human and nonhuman, organic and inorganic; instead, he treats all entities equally and in the same terms. Differences and categories are generated through networks of relations and are not presumed, while previous divisions and distinctions that constitute the "social" should be ignored (Latour 2005: 76). The term "construction" or "social construction" in this scheme requires visiting the site – such as a building construction site – where the process of construction is occurring and then tracking how the assembling of disparate elements creates something (a place, a building, a kind of sociability) (Latour 2005: 88–89). Latour is interested in tracing how the "construction" is made regardless of whether it is an architectural or sociological project. From this point of view, social construction processes emerge from a collection or grouping – an assemblage – of interrelated facts and phenomena.

Social construction of space

These conceptualizations of social constructivism have been utilized by social scientists and particularly anthropologists and sociologists interested in explaining how space and sites communicate and encode social meaning. Ethnographic studies have been especially helpful in this regard in that long-term fieldwork and in-depth accounts of the creation of spaces, their uses and their subsequent social and symbolic meanings can provide important insights into the social construction process.

Early examples of ethnographic work exploring space as a socially con-structed phenomenon include the work of Hilda Kuper (1972) and Miles Richardson (1982). For Hilda Kuper (1972), the power of space lies in its capacity to communicate meanings articulated through a complex system of social and ideational associations. She develops a spatial analysis of the interaction of territorial units and ideational elements and employs the term "social construction of space" to define sites as "a particular piece of social space, a place socially and ideologically demarcated and separated from other places" (1972: 420). Some sites have more power and significance than others, but these qualities have no fixed relationship to the physical environment and are only activated during political events such as chal-lenges to the political hierarchy. Her ethnography, in which sites make up a flexible spatial and symbolic language activated by human intervention, takes the ideas of structural semiology and applies them to a spatial analysis in which the ideational and classificatory aspects take on more importance than the physical setting.

Miles Richardson (1982) employs a different theoretical framework to reveal the social construction of space by drawing upon a more individual-istic and phenomenological perspective to consider how people transform experience into symbols, including artifacts, gestures and words. These sym-bolic transformations, he argues, give space its meaning, and the spatial realities created communicate the basic dynamics of culture. Richardson proposes that the construction of social reality occurs through the symbolic processes by which human experience and feelings become anchored to ele-ments of the material environment. This anchoring process is more experi-ential than linguistic and highlights how human perception and the senses play a role in constructing space as culturally meaningful, which is a model of social construction based on a person-centered world (Richardson 1984a and b). I will return to similar phenomenological and sensory approaches to space and place in Chapter 5.

During the late 1980s and into the beginning of the 1990s, the social construction of space perspective became ubiquitous. Social scientists and design professionals began to refer to socially constructed spaces as "places" and the social construction process as "place-making" (Rodman 1992, Feld and Basso 1996, Sen and Silverman 2014). A major proponent, Margaret Rodman (1992), argues that places are socially constructed by the people who live there and include "politicized, culturally relative, historically specific, and local and multiple constructions" (Rodman 1992: 15). For Rodman, place is a unique reality for each person so that any place is made up of all the social constructions of spatial meanings enacted and embedded at the site.

The concept of place-making is expanded by processes of land-marking, place-naming, soundscaping and imagining, ways that a sense of place can be restored when "emptied" of place attachment by violence, terror and fear (Riaño-Alcalá 2002). It is also expressed through the ritual inscription and the design of space. John Gray (2006) employs the semiological systems of Douglas (1970) and Turner (1968) in his exploration of place-making through the ritual inscription of the Nepalese house. He argues that domestic architecture is inhabited space intentionally constructed with designs and layouts that symbolically represent the ideal life, the social order and the cosmos through habitation.

Some researchers have moved beyond place-making to integrate both the social construction and production of the built environment in their analyses. Examples of such integration can be found in the work of Pellow (2002), Limbert (2008) and Fennell (2011) who link the sociospatial meanings of Hausa compounds (Pellow 2002), Oman ruins (Limbert 2008) and Chicago public housing (Fennell 2011) with the histories and ideologies of their social production. Recent anthropological work on infrastructure has been particularly illustrative in this regard.

Infrastructure refers to the basic material and ideological structures that underlie the operation of the physical, social and sensory environment. Brian Larkin maintains that

> Infrastructures are built networks that facilitate the flow of goods, people, or ideas and allow for their exchange over space. As physical forms they shape the nature of a network, the speed and direction of its movement, its temporalities, and its vulnerability to breakdown. They comprise the architecture for circulation, literally providing the undergirding of modern societies and they generate the ambient environment of everyday life.

(2013: 328)

In his study of media technologies in urban Nigeria, Larkin (2008) looks at how the radio, audio cassette and mobile cinema have facilitated changes in both the physical shape of the city and the circulation and meaning of cultural goods. He is particularly concerned with the representational qualities of these infrastructures and their early ideological roles in educating and developing Nigerians into "modern colonial citizens" (Larkin 2008: 3). But he also points out that these technologies are vulnerable to failure or subversion, frequently spinning off in unexpected directions with intended and/or unintended outcomes. As he explains, this vulnerability is a function of the fundamental instability of the relationship between the technologies, their social uses and their attributed meanings (Larkin 2008).

In her analysis of architecture and the Soviet imagination, Caroline Humphrey (2005) draws a similar conclusion about the fraught relationship between ideology and infrastructure. She argues that while the Marxist materialist perspective suggested that the task of Soviet construction was to build the material foundations that would create a socialist society, in practice, the relationship was far less straightforward. In fact, rather than acting as a template, Soviet architecture acted as a "prism," deflecting ideas embedded in its design (Humphrey 2005: 39). Humphrey's contention that the architecture "gathered meanings and scattered them" (Humphrey 2005: 55) resonates with Larkin's claim that infrastructural forms are highly unstable and vulnerable to all kinds of practical and ideological intervention that subvert their intended uses and meanings.

In her ethnography of East German built infrastructure in post-war Vinh, Vietnam, Christina Schwenkel (2013) also looks at the representational qualities of infrastructural forms – albeit from a different perspective. She shows how bricks have figured prominently both in building construction and in the ideological and social meaning of urban reconstruction for local residents. Her explanation for this congruence is that during the colonial era, bricks were an elite construction technology, usually reserved for elite buildings and housing, as well as a form of material production. Through their political meaning and elite materiality transferred to post-revolution public housing, bricks "harnessed political passions and utopian sentiments, [that] over time came to signify [the] unfulfilled promises of the social state and dystopic ruins [that] today stand in the way of capitalist redevelopment" (Schwenkel 2013: 252). Similarly, the urban water systems and water-related facilities that are decaying and inadequate for a housing complex in Vinh City signify both the promise of the socialist state and its systemic neglect (Schwenkel 2015). In tracing the evolving relationship of Vinh's residents to the bricks and urban water systems, Schwenkel also underscores the instability of infrastructural forms. In so doing, she, along with Larkin and Humphrey, highlight how the analysis of infrastructure is a particularly good way of examining how the social production and social construction of space come together.

Thus the social construction of space is made up of a wide range of perspectives that explain how meaning is inscribed in the landscape and built environment, as well as the role that politics, unstable meanings and culture play in place-making. These different approaches coexist as alternative strategies, and in a few cases, as competing points of view. Some researchers privilege a language-based methodology to reveal underlying social construction processes, and these ethnographies are discussed in greater detail in Chapter 6. Others employ phenomenological, affective and infrastructural approaches that are explored further in Chapters 5 and 7.

Social construction of space methodologies

Contestation and conflict

One of the most effective ways to investigate the social construction of space is through an analysis of "contested spaces," those "sites where conflicts in the form of opposition, confrontation, subversion, and resistance engage actors" – often with differential access to power and resources (Low and Lawrence-Zuñiga 2003: 18). These conflicts frequently center on the control of the construction of local meanings, but they also reveal broader social struggles over deeply held beliefs and practices as well as political and economic realities that shape everyday life. Many of the ethnographic examples and research vignettes found in this book are about contestation because they expose the social, political, economic and cultural schisms embedded in spatial relations at multiple geographical scales

Urban public space provides frequent opportunities for spatial contestation because the complex structures and differentiated social institutions often collide and compete for control over material and symbolic resources. For example, conflicts over the cultural meanings of the Parque Central for users, the media and middle-class citizens in San José, Costa Rica, ultimately resulted in the closing and redesign of this iconic urban space as discussed in Chapter 3. Spaces of political struggle, from Cathedral Square in São Paulo (Arantes 1996), Zuccotti Park in New York City (Maharawal 2012, Shiffman et.al. 2012), Syntagma Square in Athens (Dalakoglou 2013) to Tahrir Square in Cairo (Ghannam 2012, Winegar 2012) are examples of how urban space takes on conflicting ideological meanings that provide a forum for dissent and protest, including violence and fighting.

Conflict between the exchange and use value of land is one of the main points of contention in struggles over urban space (Cooper and Rodman 1990). Redevelopment and renovation practices bring into stark contrast the needs and attachments of local residents with the profit goals of land developers and the political goals of city officials as discussed in Chapters 3 and 6. These conflicts often take on a moral dimension, as in the case of bars in Barcelona's Barrio Chino where conflictive systems of categorization of space, class and gender affirm hegemonic ideas of a place as "good" or "bad" (McDonogh 1992). British and Australian politicians and policy makers mobilize similar urban moral geographies to secure social norms through legal graffiti walls that become contested sites of respect and inclusion for street artists (McAuliffe n.d.). Even the simple act of cleaning up the sidewalk in post-Katrina New Orleans, takes on moral and conflicting meanings when redefined in terms of the maintenance of the commons and shared space (Ehrenfeucht 2012).

Another kind of moral geography is produced by conflicting colonial constructions of space that marginalize indigenous "sited identity," defined as a collective concept of self located within a specific landscape (Thomas 2002: 372). Place-making, Philip Thomas (2002) argues, should be understood in terms of sited identity, but also in relation to the difference and marginality of the system of signs bequeathed by the colonial encounter. In southeast Madagascar, colonial symbols construct a moral geography of "native" marginality within the post-colonial present that helps to explain local peoples' ambivalence toward modernity. Moral geographies are also created through religious practices and post-colonial narratives of diaspora, where religious processions and performances transform the streets of Manchester, U.K., into sacred and moral ground (Werbner 2002).

The post-apartheid cities of South Africa offer some of the most jarring examples of how multiple and overlapping layers of socially constructed meanings carve conflict onto a racialized urban landscape. Leslie Bank's (2011) ethnography of East London reveals how these disarticulated spaces create a new type of urbanization, one he calls "fractured urbanism." But he uses this term in a positive way by demonstrating how women struggle to reintegrate these segregated spaces and reinscribe them with their own meanings through ritual and everyday practices.

Ethnographies of spatial contestation and conflict provide one methodological framework for uncovering how space and place are constructed, often for hegemonic purposes. These same processes of social construction, however, are equally available to those who are resisting spatial control and change. In this way, contested spaces give material expression to and act as loci for creating and promulgating, countering and negotiating dominant cultural themes and political practices. Space is contested precisely because it concretizes the fundamental and recurring, but otherwise unexamined, ideological and social frameworks that structure social life (Low and Lawrence-Zuñiga 2003).

Memory, heritage and place attachment

Studies of place-making and the social construction of space frequently draw upon memory and memory-making as a dominant mode of inscribing meaning at various scales from the most intimate to the national and transnational. Edward Said (2000) asserts that the overlapping areas of memory and geography and "specifically, the study of human space" (2000: 175), has actually created a new field of inquiry that touches upon significant questions of identity, nationalism, power and authority. Memories and their representations, he argues, are never neutral recitations of facts, but to some considerable extent always underlie what he defines as a nationalist or elite effort. Thus memories construct and substantiate, as well as repudiate received notions of territoriality and sense of place.

The ethnography of collective memory and place offers a way to study what Gastón Gordillo describes as the "experiential dimensions of place-making with the political economy that makes it possible by examining the materiality of memory, its embodiment in practice, and its constitution as a social force in the production of places" (2004: 4). He argues that "every memory is a memory of a place" (2004: 4) such that the spatiality of memory is part of the dynamic process of space production. The underlying tensions between memory and the places it constructs reflect the structural constraints of place-making for the people and territory in question. For example, Gordillo (2004) attempts to unravel the historical experiences, tensions and places of the Toba people in the Argentina Chaco by examining Toba memories and historical practices that created the "bush" physically, politically and culturally through the opposition of wage labor to Toba foraging.

Hegemonic constructions of histories that justify the political and economic control of wealthy elites and transnational corporations are infamous for excluding the memory and local history of residents facing neighborhood gentrification and urban redevelopment. Struggles over the right to live in a historic neighborhood such as the center of Rome, Beirut or Cairo are fraught with conflicting narratives and memories that poor and marginalized residents recruit to support their land claims (Herzfeld 2009, Sawalha 2010, Ghannam 2002). But powerful government officials and capitalist interests elide these claims by asserting their own histories in the name of the nation and discrediting local evidence so that residents are eventually evicted and the land expropriated (Herzfeld 2009, 2003, Ghannam 2011, Harms 2012). Christa Salamandra (2004) makes the point that debates about representation, preservation and the restoration of the Old City of Damascus, Syria, are always about status competition and identity construction by the ruling elites. Even heritage projects with the imprint of UNESCO and ICOMOS (the International Council on Monuments and Sites of UNESCO) often face highly conflictive discussions of whether or not a place or object should be designated as part of a society's or group's "heritage" depending on the ruling elites (Schmitt 2005).

Memory and place-making also figure prominently in diaspora studies where associations of people, culture and place are historically and socially constructed (Brun 2001). Researchers working with refugees, forced relocation victims and diasporic populations often write about places as "symbolic anchors" of community and how constructions of homeland – as territories and imagined places – are part of a politics of memory (Gupta and Ferguson 1997). For example, Alyssa Howe (2001) discusses the social construction of San Francisco as a queer homeland that has become a pilgrimage site, offering a symbolic refuge for the elaboration of queer identity. Andrea Smith (2003) and William Bissell (2005) study the colonial nostalgia of people who remember and idealize the past in ways that coexist, combine or conflict to restructure urban space in the case of Zanzibar (Bissell 2005) or to explain Maltese pilgrimage (Smith 2003).

Archival and ethnographic work on Liberty Island (where the Statue of Liberty stands) draws upon similar constructions of history, memory, nostalgia and forms of place-making to explain peoples' deep attachment to the site (Low, Bendiner-Viani and Hung 2005). Place attachment, briefly discussed in Chapter 2, refers to the emotional and affective relationship of people to a space or piece of land and the associated symbolic meanings and modes of attachment (Low and Altman 1992). In this case, place attachment is expressed through competing social constructions of what the statue and island represent – from an image of a freed Black slave to a Native American princess – based on the different experiences, conflicting memories and multiple constructions of history elicited from interviewees. Pilgrimage to Liberty Island, replicas of the Statue of Liberty and stories, recordings and songs of the people who have resided, visited or worked there illustrate the intensity of the connection and the sense of belonging and national myth-making that characterizes this kind of nationalist constructed space.

Nationalist social constructions are also embedded in personal life trajectories that draw upon multiple inscribed meanings. Based on the life stories of Israeli veterans of the 1973 Yom Kippur War, Edna Lomsky-Feder contends that memory is "embedded within, designed by, and derives its meaning from, a memory field that offers different interpretations" (2004: 82). She finds that this memory field is not an open space in that the "remembering subject is not free to choose any interpretation that he wishes" (2004: 82). Instead, access to collective memories is differentially distributed according to cultural criteria that dictate who is entitled to remember and what should be remembered. This provocative finding also applies to memories of place when social and cultural entitlements such as access to knowledge and control of space shape people's memories, as portrayed in the ethnographic examples of Independence National History Park in Philadelphia and the destruction and rebuilding of downtown Beirut. Erased landscapes and memories of exclusion create what has been called "dissonant heritage" (Meskell 1999), the negative relationship of people to a place or a place forcibly stripped of meaning and attachment. These ethnographies provide examples of how space and memory are based on multiple intersecting, conflicting and inherently unstable social constructions that are continuously shaped and reshaped by the power dynamics of historical, political, economic and social forces.

The social construction of race, class and gender

Contemporary research on the social construction of space often focuses on the inscription, contestation and politics of race, class, gender, sexual orientation, age, ability and other social categories. These national, neighborhood/community and local constructions reinforce structural constraints, inequality and exclusion as well as offer opportunities for group and place attachment (Bank 2011, Carter 2014, Hoffman 2002).

Ethnographic studies of gendered spaces illuminate how patterns of everyday behaviors, symbolic representations and spatial allocations distinguish gendered places, as well as how particular locales are invested with gendered meanings or are sites where gender-differentiated practices occur. Ethnographies of spatially differentiated gendered practices as diverse as Patty Kelly's (2008) ethnography of the Zona Glactica, a state-run brothel in Chiapas, Mexico; Henrietta Moore's (1986) interpretation of Marakwet space in Kenya; and Deborah Pellow's (2002) analysis of the historical construction of gender and space through "socio-spatial practices within the Hausa *zongo* in Accra, Ghana, discussed previously, illustrate the centrality of gender in all forms of place-making."

The investigation of the racialization of space has its roots in early groundbreaking studies of race, place and exclusion (Drake and Cayton 1970 [1945]) challenging the social and spatial construction of the "Black ghetto." Steven Gregory's (1998) social history of Corona, Queens, New York provides an in-depth critique of the micropolitics of Black activists and city officials involved in "the racialization of place" and the negative impact of racial and class power dynamics on the neighborhood. In a Southern U.S. context, Mieka Polanco (2014) explores the consequences of the federal recognition of Union, Virginia, as a historically Black district that racializes and homogenizes residents by erasing old-timer White and newcomer Black residents' sense of homeplace, identity and community. And Jacqueline Brown's ethnography of the racialization of Black Liverpool in the United Kingdom concludes with the assertion that "place is an axis of power in its own right" (2005: 8) in her historical analysis of the association of Liverpool with its Black residents and the consequences of this racialized urban identity.

The social construction of "whiteness" in gated communities provides another example of how intersecting constructions of race and class permeate the suburbs to constitute a purified and privileged social space (Low 2009, 2003). Whiteness is not only about race, but it is also a historical and cultural construct actively produced and reproduced to further and/or improve an individual or social group's position. It refers to the systematic advantage of one group over others where whiteness becomes the location of advantage in societies structured by racial dominance (Frankenberg 1996, 2001).

The power dynamics of whiteness for suburban residents in the United States are hidden and rarely challenged because White socialization occurs in largely racially segregated housing. The mechanisms associated with race privilege vary with socioeconomic status and gender, but are salient across most individuals. They include distancing, denial, superiority, belonging and solidarity. These mechanisms for defending whiteness can be observed in gated communities as justifications for living in a White, secured enclave. Thus the physical space of the neighborhood and its racial composition become synonymous. This racialized spatial ordering and the identification of a space with a group of people is a fundamental aspect of how suburban landscapes reinforce racial prejudice and discrimination. In these communities, "whiteness has the social power to define itself as the normal, as the point where normality can be produced and elided with the orderliness of the social order" (Fiske 1998: 86). Thus whiteness becomes both the foundation for and the practice of normalization. Gated communities enhance residents' visual surveillance of boundaries and therefore spatially promote its maintenance.

An analysis of U.S. middle-class insecurity is similarly explored in Rachel Heiman's (2015) ethnography of how suburban residents living in New Jersey struggle to maintain their class affiliation by gating their communities and driving large SUVs. She documents how families that escape to the suburbs to buy more affordable houses and a middle-class White lifestyle are increasingly finding it difficult to keep up with the pressures of class-related consumerism and local deficits due to economic restructuring. Residents' fragile claims to middle-class status and financial security are increasingly exposed by their inability to support better schools, open space and other amenities, as well as their escalating sense of insecurity and anxiety. Driving SUVs and a sense of "rugged entitlement" are reflections of the economic constraints faced by residents and their failure to achieve the trappings of the American Dream.

These ethnographies of how the social constructions of race, class and gender are inscribed in space and given material form offer another template for understanding the way that space and place can obscure underlying exclusionary practices and racial prejudices. Place can be used as the basis for the construction of many kinds of difference, hierarchy and identity and effectively rationalizes economic and political inequality, but its effects are not limited to the spatial domain. Spatial inequalities also have an impact on individual and group health, well-being and life chances of those whose neighborhoods and communities are bypassed by social services and access to financial, education and legal resources.

The following ethnographic examples provide a more detailed examination of how a social construction of space and place frame was employed in two cultural contexts. Both ethnographies highlight some of the ways that memory, erased landscapes, racialization of space and struggles over access and use occurred over a twenty-year period at Independence National Historical Park in Philadelphia, Pennsylvania, in the United States and during the post-war renovation of downtown Beirut in Lebanon.

Ethnographic examples

Representation and exclusion of African Americans at Independence National Historical Park (INDE), Philadelphia

Introduction and methodology

This first ethnographic example addresses the racialization of space through the gentrification of downtown Philadelphia, Pennsylvania, that accompanied the designation of Independence National Historical Park (INDE) and explores the park's subsequent social construction as a White space for tourists and visitors. It also documents how an ethnography of space and place, in this case, a rapid ethnographic assessment procedure (REAP), can become the impetus and blueprint for attempts by the National Park Service and local Black communities to redress this history by reinstating African American spaces and representations at the park to increase inclusion and sense of belonging. The ethnographic description is based on a REAP[1] completed 1994–1995 (Low, Taplin and Scheld 2005) and an assessment of the impact of these findings for African Americans and other local residents twenty years later (Fanelli 2014). It included a litany of qualitative methods, including participant observation, interviewing, focus groups and archival research, as well as the more specialized collection of cultural resource use maps for the groups studied (see Low, Taplin and Scheld 2005 for a full discussion of the methodology). It is an example of how ethnographies of space and place can be a kind of engaged anthropology because they are based on community collaboration with the potential of revealing exclusionary and racist processes encoded in spatial relations and the built environment.

History and urban setting

The idea of a national historical park in Philadelphia originated with the Federal Historic Sites Act of 1935. Planning and site acquisition began in the late 1940s and demolition, site preparation and building took place throughout the 1950s. The major controversy during this period was how much of the existing city fabric was to be removed to create a setting for the eighteenth-century structures associated with American Independence. The blocks both east and north of Independence Square were dense with commercial structures of granite, marble and brownstone that were anywhere from forty to one hundred years old, with the bulk having been built between 1860 and 1890. In the 1950s climate of slum clearance and urban renewal, such blocks of buildings were regarded as symbols of decline and threats to the continued prosperity of the central city. Others, particularly architects and historians, were advocating an architecturally sensitive approach to renewal, one that would leave some of the more distinguished structures intact.

The INDE project became part of a larger effort to renew Society Hill, an area east of Eighth Street and south of Walnut, adjacent to the new national park (Figure 4.1 Map of downtown Philadelphia and Independence National Historical Park). The neighborhood, close to the Philadelphia immigration center on the Delaware at Washington Avenue, originally housed a multiethnic population, which included African Americans, Eastern European Jews, Italians, Polish, Irish and Ukrainians. By the 1940s, the neighborhood had become increasingly poor, as well as African American, although pockets of immigrant populations remained.

Because of the proximity of this neighborhood to the projected park area and the high quality of much of its building stock, the city saw the INDE process as an opportunity to restore the neighborhood. Whole sections of Society Hill were designated as redevelopment areas and homeowners were given the choice to restore their properties according to strict historic preservation guidelines or to sell them to the redevelopment authority. Since few could afford the costly restoration, most sold. The city then offered the properties for a nominal price to buyers who could prove that they had the financial resources to obtain a mortgage and complete the restoration. The banks, the real estate industry and the news media cooperated with the city to project a favorable image of the redevelopment area, thereby creating a market of affluent, mostly White buyers. Thus, over a period of roughly fifteen years, a new community of predominantly White professionals dispersed and replaced the predominantly poor, heterogeneous and African American community of long standing.

The social and physical upheaval involved in the creation of Independence National Historical Park was exacerbated by an absence of communication with local communities and the extensive demolition that removed the settings of life, play and work that had any special meaning. The national park became a new, artificially produced built environment from which most signs of the city's nineteenth- and early twentieth-century history were carefully scrubbed away.

African American experience and perception of INDE

Interviews and focus groups with African Americans living in Southwark, a housing project a few blocks south of the park reflect this legacy of social and physical uprooting. One man reported, "I don't visit [the park] because it has nothing to do for or with me . . . it doesn't show Black history or culture. It doesn't represent us and we helped build this country."

Independence National
Historical Park

Market St.
Chestnut St.
Walnut St.

Race St.
Arch St.

S. Broad St.

I-95

S. 4th St.
S. 5th St.

S. 6th St.
S. 10th St.

I-676

I-76

Schuylkill Exp.

Figure 4.1 Map of downtown Philadelphia and Independence National Historical Park (Erin Lilli)

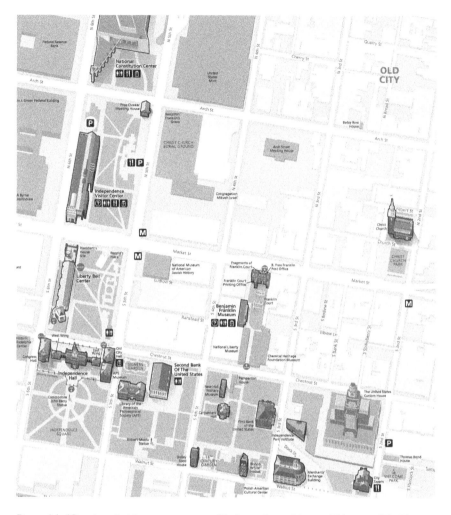

Figure 4.1 (Continued, this map courtesy of Independence National Historical Park)

A woman added, "Yes, it's history . . . a part of teaching about history and some people have lived here all of their lives and haven't visited. There's lots of history here that people don't know about . . . Black history." Charles Blockson, a local historian, felt that African Americans could have a strong cultural identification with the park if there were some physical marking or interpretation of Black history and participation:

> African Americans were involved from the inception of the park . . . although we were considered three-fifths of a person, most of them,

slave labor, and free African Americans – carpenters and laborers – helped to build, create Independence Hall. We must tell their history.

He went on to explain that Washington Square, on the southeastern corner of the park was the original burying ground for African Americans and later was used as a gathering place, referred to as "Congo Square." This grassy square, part of William Penn's plan for Philadelphia, holds great significance for African American residents, but at the time of the 1995 interviews, the city had not commemorated or officially included it in the park.

Most African Americans, however, said that the park had no particular meaning for them. One elderly woman commented, "No special feeling . . . I'm not gonna tell no lies . . . when the kids were small [it was more important]." A middle-aged woman said, "no special feeling . . . the Bell is cracked . . . What's to see, it's cracked . . . We all know that." A younger woman asserts,

> The Liberty Bell, I don't care. We won't benefit at all . . . It's not beneficial to the people, we don't have any money. When something up there needs fixing up they come down here to ask about it. What about fixing up something down here [in Southwark]? The park ain't done nothing for the people here. This part of town is in isolation. This is not a location on the map. I took my kin to Penn's Landing, and we were looking at the map. We're not on the map. This place is no place.

A man commented that the area had no meaning for him because it was not designed for local Black visitors:

> The area is for tourists. It is a White area. The intention is for White people to see the Bell. It is not important for African Americans visiting. It's not for African Americans. The only thing Black at the park is the ink used.

Another interviewee added, "it's [the park] not important for African Americans, that's why there are no African Americans visiting." A third interviewee stated that, "most people who go there go to look at their own people. It's a showcase for White people."

The feeling that African Americans are not welcome appears to have a long history. One woman in a focus group recounted that, in the past,

> not everyone was welcome, not everyone was allowed in the park. Now it's different [but back then] some of our children were not allowed to go into the park . . . they knew they lived on the wrong side of the

neighborhood and that they could not go in. They couldn't have picnics there [so] we didn't go.

The focus group leader then asked, "Was there something in particular that made you feel you couldn't go there?" The woman responded, "No, not really. You just knew you weren't allowed. If you were there you weren't there for the right reason."

Pastor Leath of Mother Bethel Church adjacent to the park added that

there is not a clear message presented in the park . . . diversity is not displayed . . . one could walk through the park and not know that there were African Americans in colonial Philadelphia.

Members of the Nazareth Baptist Church remarked on the need for different cultures to be able to identify with the park: "Different cultures need something to grab, the children need something to grasp at." The speaker, a churchgoing man, felt that there is not a solid identity expressed by the park for African Americans to relate to. Cultural history starts here, he added, "with the church and the committee . . . the church is the root for us as African Americans." But many others in the focus group felt that the park should be relevant as well and agreed with another interviewee who opined that, "every child should learn about how we got our freedom."

The ethnographic research at INDE revealed how important cultural representation is for a sense of identification and a meaningful relationship with a place. The erasure of historical buildings and resulting amnesia about historically significant places as well as the everyday racist practices of some park employees, uncovered how people, especially African Americans, read and responded to exclusionary cues in the built environment. These cues and erasures are part of the social construction of the park as a colonial White space that marginalized other racial, gender, ethnic and class claims to this iconic American heritage site.

Reprise

But the story does not end in 1995. Dr. Doris Fanelli (2014), who directed the National Park Service side of the project in 1995, commissioned Dr. Tony Whitehead (2002) to undertake an in-depth study that confirmed the findings that African Americans did not see a connection with the park. Since that time, the National Park Service has emphasized inclusion in its recruitment and promotion practices and in its interpretive and cultural resource programs. In 2000, INDE wrote an amendment to its National Register nomination to include sites related to the Underground Railroad and anti-slavery movement and an exhibit was added to the visitor's center in 2007.

An important opportunity for African American interpretation of and presence at INDE occurred in 2002. An independent scholar, Edward Lawler, published an article in the *Pennsylvania Magazine of History and Biography* about the house that Washington occupied while he was president. The article was about the architecture of the property, but Lawler mentioned that the Washingtons had nine of their slaves living at the house. This reawakened public memory and rallied local community groups in the African American community to demand that the story of the first president as a slave owner be told at the site.

Today the President's House, located at Sixth and Market Streets immediately before entering the Liberty Bell Center, incorporates text and videos of the life of the Washington slaves. All of these buildings are on the new Independence Mall, which is the outgrowth of the planning for the General Management Plan that included the original ethnographic study. The President's House has increased the audience in the African American community and spawned a cottage industry of publications, artistic expressions and opinions.

In addition to the President's House project, when Independence Mall was developed for the new National Constitution Center, documentary research revealed that the founding meetings of the African Episcopal Church of St. Thomas were held in the home of James Dexter, a former slave, located within the boundaries of the new Constitution Center. The church still exists and is, with Mother Bethel, one of the two oldest Black churches in the country. Both churches asked the National Park Service to conduct an archaeological dig to see if anything survived from Dexter's occupancy. Four plaques at the National Constitution Center currently mark the site and St. Thomas Church is now a "traditionally associated group" to the park and consulted regarding relevant projects.

INDE also assumed stewardship of Washington Square, including an area known for its use by the congregation of free and enslaved Blacks during the eighteenth century and served as a burying ground. Today, African American groups hold special libation ceremonies there.

As part of the original research findings concerning the community's desire for more representation and recognition, INDE also rewrote the exhibit script for the new Liberty Bell Center that opened in 2003. The script now explains the history of the Bell and its growth as a symbol for human rights beginning with its adoption by the Anti-Slavery Society in the early nineteenth century. The Martin Luther King Center for the Study of Nonviolence holds a ceremony at the Liberty Bell every Martin Luther King Day. The National Freedom Day Association also holds an annual ceremony to commemorate the date (February 1) that Lincoln signed the resolution proposing the thirteenth amendment. Interpretive tours incorporate the history of freedom for enslaved Africans and discussions of race and slavery as much as possible into the story of the creation of the U.S. government.

In many ways, INDE has expanded its audience and developed tours that draw other marginalized groups not covered in our initial research. For example, a ranger developed a tour about gay rights that has been well received. The park also actively consults with federally recognized tribes who consider land within the park's boundaries as part of their ancestral homeland and are now involved in any deep excavation in the park because that is where indigenous artifacts are likely to be found. In addition, there continue to be discussions about undertaking Spanish translations of interpretive writings and to initiate tours about Spanish American relations in the past.

Returning to INDE today to interview African American residents would yield different perceptions and problems than those elicited twenty years ago. The original rapid ethnography played a part in increasing the representation of African American history and sacred sites, and the local African American churches and history centers are integrated into the interpretive fabric of the park. These changes have created a series of sites that are socially constructed now as Black by the park and its visitors and resident users.

Reconstructing Beirut: Memory and space in a post-war Arab city

Introduction and methodology

The second example is drawn from Aseel Sawalha's (2010) ethnography of the reconstruction of Beirut after the sixteen-year civil war that formally ended in 1991 (Figure 4.2 Map of downtown Beirut, Solidere and Ayn el-Mreisse neighborhood). Her fieldwork began in 1995 and was made up of field visits to Beirut through 2005. During that time, she examined the work of Solidere (the Lebanese Company for the Development and Reconstruction of the Beirut Central District), which was founded by then prime minister Rafik Hariri to implement a massive inner city and waterfront renewal project. Working in various neighborhoods to explore the project's impact on the city's residents and its urban fabric, she met with intellectual leaders, religious leaders, politicians, property owners and residents who had squatted in abandoned buildings during the war. She used multisited ethnography and other methodological techniques, including discourse analysis of newspapers, expert and local interviews, participant observation through living in one of the neighborhoods and becoming a part of it, as well as working with locals to try to save the historic environment. By analyzing their debates, struggles, and narratives pertaining to the urban renewal project, she found that memories of old Beirut played a dominant role in residents' anxieties about the future of their neighborhoods and communities. Moreover, she discovered that these memories played a central role in the various efforts of local groups to resist Solidere's spatial incursions.

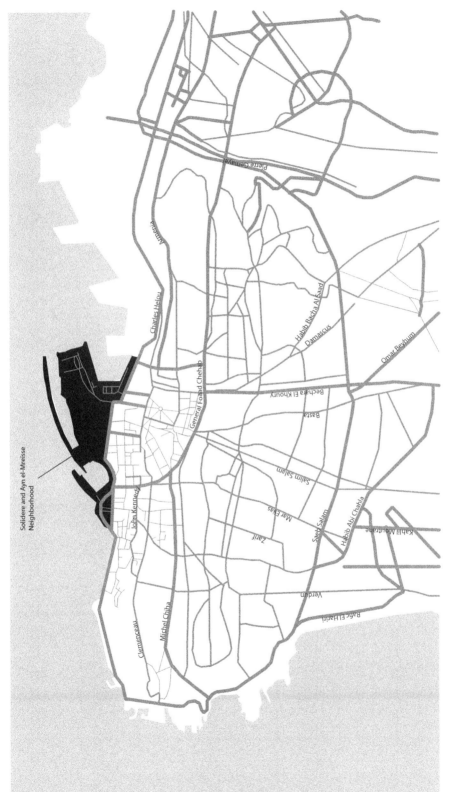

Figure 4.2 Map of downtown Beirut, Solidere and Ayn el-Mreisse neighborhood (Erin Lilli)

History and urban setting

A government-sponsored joint stock offering that excluded the participation of all but the wealthiest citizens and international development companies lead to the creation of Solidere. At the time of its inauguration in 1994, Solidere was one of the largest urban renewal projects in the world, turning 1.8 million square meters and an additional 608,000 square meters of reclaimed land into a corporate-directed redevelopment project. The ostensible goal of the project was to refashion the landscape to create "Beirut an Ancient City of the Future" (Sawalha 2010: 23). To that end, Solidere's promotional material claimed it was interested in preserving Beirut's heritage; however, in practice, the reconstruction company began by destroying what remained of the war-ravaged city center and obliterating many of the most sacred and historic places in the downtown area. What quickly became clear is that the power to determine "in whose image and to whose benefit" (Sawalha 2010:23) the new downtown would be rebuilt was in the hands of Solidere and Rafik Hariri and his government.

Beirut residents were shocked and saddened by the disappearance of many of the city's landmarks and religious structures. For residents and community groups living in the destroyed and decaying neighborhoods, it seemed that all vestiges of the past, in particular a culturally and religiously diverse past and the historic buildings that represented that past, were torn down to make room for Hariri's version of a modern future. Moreover, the destruction of large swaths of the urban fabric – and particularly traditional places for socializing – had a major impact on their daily life. The removal of spaces such as the hairdresser, the tailor, relatives' homes, local shops and, especially, Western cafés changed forms of sociality for Beirutis – especially among middle-class women. In response, residents filled the daily newspapers with personal narratives of their memories of the city. While they could not stop the destruction, city residents wrote about these erased landscapes, while historic preservation professionals urged Solidere to protect historically valuable buildings (Sawalha 2010). In addition, religious parties issued *fatwas*, religious decrees, against the company, its employees and shareholders, and they harbored the suspicion that the project intended to exploit the poor for the benefit of the rich. However, despite their various calls to stop the destruction, valuable historical sites continued to be demolished without proper documentation or archaeological assessment.

Resistance, redevelopment and cultural identity

At the same time, internationally based commercial establishments were being built on the newly cleared sites. Protests from local neighborhood groups such as the Mosque Committee of Ayn el-Mreisse, a neighborhood adjacent to downtown where Sawalha spent much of her time, fought to stop the building of a Hard Rock Cafe a few feet away from the old Otto-man mosque. But despite their struggle, the café was opened in 1997 and loud Western music competed with the mosque's call to prayer (Sawalha 2010). Residents felt alienated from these international incursions and simi-larly to the previous example of African American residents who lived near Independence Historical National Park, Ayn el-Mreisse residents explained, "These foreign businesses are not built for us [the local residents]; they are for the rich and the tourists" (Sawalha 2010: 74). Very few residents ever visited the Hard Rock Cafe, but when a visit was attempted, the neighbors felt insulted by the short skirt and rudeness of the waitress (Sawalha 2010).

The Association for the Revival of the Heritage of Ayn el-Mreisse orga-nized another act of resistance to the destruction of their spatial and mate-rial history. This local organization headed by Najem, a middle-aged retired fireman, was composed of members of three ethnoreligious groups – Druze, Sunni and Christian – who banded together to record their memories in a local museum. Najem transformed his house into what he called the Museum of Ayn el-Mreisse and preserved anything "old, authentic, and used by the people of Ayn el-Mreisse" (Sawalha 2010: 78). This flexible definition of heritage was successful in filling three rooms of Najem's house with memo-rabilia and was seen by the community as a way to protect the threatened past and guarantee its existence in the future.

In Sawalha's analysis of Beirut, urban space was socially constructed in multiple ways to accommodate and represent conflicting political, social, class and religious beliefs and practices. These social constructions, in many cases, were quite specific as to the cultural assumptions embedded in the built environment and were disturbed and manipulated as part of the rebuilding process. Sawalha emphasizes how residents' images of what the city should look like were often in conflict with the government, real estate and financial objectives of Solidere that were represented by an image of a modern city produced by creative destruction. Many local residents, women, religious and political groups contested this modernist image in an attempt to protect their sense of cultural identity previously encoded in historic buildings and intimate public/private spaces.

At the same time, Sawalha is careful not to reduce the spatial conflicts to a simple contrast of the state/Solidere versus the local residents. On the contrary, she is attentive to the nuances of shifting power hierarchies in the city, recognizing that Soldiere was not the only culprit in creating dramatic changes in the historic urban landscape. In Ayn el-Mreisse, for example, decision-making power was also shared by the political parties that had evolved out of wartime sects and militia and revived governmental institu-tions such as the Municipality of Beirut and the newly formed Ministry of the Displaced, as well as international and national financial investors (Saw-alha 2010). Thus to understand the urban transformation of Beirut required an analysis of the role of each of these institutions in reforming the city.

Unfortunately, in contrast to the Independence National Historical Site case, the poor and middle-class residents of Beirut were not successful. Their social constructions of urban space were erased through the recon-struction process. Solidere itself, which had been at the center of Beirut's fragile post-war experience in the 1990s and early 2000s, has been only partly successful and marred by assassination of its principal sponsor, Rafik Hariri, in 2005 and a "sit-in" by opponents of the government in 2006. Following these events was a war with Israel and Hezbollah, further fighting between Lebanese factions in 2009 and greater instability with Syria following the protests in 2011. However, by 2014, celebrating its twentieth anniversary, Solidere had radically changed the arrangement of both space and political power in Lebanon (Sharp and Panetta 2016). Yet many of the contemporary urban problems facing neighborhoods in Beirut, from a lack of effective planning and management of public space to an unpredictable transportation system of roadblocks, holdups and rundown roads, stem from the priority of rebuilding high-profile and high-end areas like downtown to attract international capital rather than attending to the basic infrastructure of housing, schools and services in local neighborhoods (Monroe 2016).

Conclusion

The national and city decision makers, urban designers and planners involved in the redevelopment of both downtown Philadelphia and the cen-tral city of Beirut intended to produce internationally acclaimed cities and tourist sites with limited consideration for the people who historically lived there. It is certainly no surprise that in Philadelphia contemporary African American residents saw INDE as not holding any meaning or significance for them since they were designed out in the beginning. The dialogic rela-tionship of social production and social construction helps to explain how the political and economic intentions of the National Park Service and the city of Philadelphia were retained in the landscape and understood through its spatial vocabulary and also points to ways that sites can be physically changed, spatially reconfigured and reinterpreted to create new social and racial meanings.

Even though the Beirut example is not a tale of local community success in the face of dominant state constructions of the city as "modern and interna-tional," Sawalha's ethnography captures the intricacies and complex inter-actions of how the social construction space and place plays a decisive role in determining the shape of the future urban landscape. The various groups she studied mobilized different urban discourses of the past in an attempt to fight the transformation of the urban landscape – and, in particular, what were perceived as immoral commercial enterprises within their community space. It offers a useful ethnographic model for similar studies. The next chapter on embodied space integrates elements of the social construction and social production approaches to the ethnographic study of space and place by focusing on how bodies make space through movement, trajectories and intentions.

Note

1 The REAP methodology for the study of space and place is presented as part of the Moore Street ethnographic example presented in Chapter 8.

Chapter 5

Embodied space

Introduction

The conceptual frame of "embodied space" integrates body/space/culture and connects microanalyses of individual bodies and place-making to macroanalyses of social, economic and political forces.[1] Embodied space addresses both the experiential and material aspects of the body in space as well as the merging of body/space as a location that can communicate, transform and contest existing social structures. The addition of the idea that embodied spaces have "trajectories" as well as time- and space-specific goals and intentions that are personally, culturally and politically directed brings greater agency and an appreciation of power dynamics to the theorization of individual and collective bodies and their movements.

While spatial analyses often neglect the body because of difficulties in resolving the dualism of the subjective and objective body and distinctions between the material and representational aspects of the body (Harris and Robb 2012), embodied space draws these disparate notions together. It underscores the importance of the body as a physical and biological entity, as lived experience and as a center of agency – a location for speaking and acting on the world. The conceptual lens that views space as always embodied offers a different approach to the ethnography of space and place by considering human and nonhuman "bodies" as simultaneous spaces as well as producers and products of space.

For example, imagine a woman walking in a white pine and oak forest listening to the wind rustling the dried leaves that remain on the late autumn trees and looking for the few remaining birds and deer. She walks with heavy boots making her own path by compacting loose dirt underfoot and removing branches and undergrowth in her way. Through her bodily movements and physical efforts, she is making a path that allows her to cross through the woods to another trail. The older trail, now marked with red and white paint, is a product of off-road bikers who have used this town reserve many times before, inscribing their own trajectories on the landscape. These paths have also opened this part of the woods to hunters searching for deer and small game. Hunters – men carrying rifles – shoot the deer who also wander on these paths, disturbing the birds, leaves and tranquility of the space with the sudden sound of gunfire. The hunters and the fleeing birds and deer are also transforming this space through their bodily actions, movements and intentions. The conflicts and tensions between these users have erupted into a political battle about town land rights and resident safety, adjudicated in the local and state courts. Thus an embodied spatial analysis includes individual place-making, new modes of circulation and conflicts that are political as well as personal inscribed in the materiality of the site.

In this chapter, the term "body" refers to its biological, emotional, cognitive and social characteristics, and "embodiment" is defined as an "indeterminate methodological field defined by perceptual experience and mode of presence and engagement in the world" (Csordas 1999: 12). The term "sensorium" is used to characterize bodily sensibilities and dispositions (Hirschkind 2011) and the multiple senses and sensory modes of apprehending the world. "Embodied space" encompasses these concepts – human and nonhuman body and bodies, forms of embodiment and sensorium – as the location where human experience, consciousness and political subjectivity take on material and spatial form.

After identifying the inherent difficulties in defining the body, body space and cultural explanations of body experience, approaches to embodied space focusing on proxemics (Hall 1966), phenomenology (Richardson 1982, Rodman 1992), sensorium (Stoller 1989, Desjarlais 1992, Weiss 2011, Hirschkind 2006, 2011; Brahinsky 2012; Mazzarella 2013), spatial field and orientation (Munn 1996, Rockefeller 2009), movement (Ingold 2004, 2007; 2010, Ingold and Vergunst 2008) and mobility and circulation (Pred 1984; Katz 1999; Amin and Thrift 2002; Hannam, Sheller and Urry 2006; Spinney 2011; Sopranzetti 2014) are explored. The chapter concludes with three ethnographic examples of how embodied spaces are socially, ritually and politically created and lived through the *corso* in Serbia, the *retreta* and *paseo* in Costa Rica and the Critical Mass bicycle movement in Budapest. Based on this discussion, embodied space is posited as a heuristic model for understanding the creation of space and place through trajectories, movements and actions.

The body

What constitutes the space of the body is strikingly illustrated by Harold Searles's (1960) schizophrenic patient trying to convey something of the world he inhabits by saying, "Doctor, you don't know what it's like, looking out on the world through square eyes." Searles interprets this statement to mean the patient could not differentiate his body from the volume of the room – the square eyes being the windows of the room looking out at the world (as cited in Hall 1973). Thus the patient's body incorporates the room and his experience and social interactions are mediated by this unorthodox spatial sense of the self.

The space occupied by the body, and the perception and experience of one's body and space, contracts and expands in relationship to a person's emotions, state of mind, sense of self, social relations and cultural predispositions. In Western culture, the self is perceived as naturally placed in the body, as a kind of precultural given (Scheper-Hughes and Lock 1987). People imagine themselves as experiencing the world through a social skin, the surface of the body representing "a kind of common frontier of society which becomes the symbolic stage upon which the drama of socialization is enacted" (Turner 1980: 112). The schizophrenic's distortion challenges this accepted notion of isomorphism of the body/self/social skin by separating the relationship of the physical and biological body, the self and the perceived boundary between the body/self and the rest of the world.

Bryan Turner (1984) points out that it is an obvious fact that human beings "have bodies" and "are bodies." Human beings are embodied and everyday life dominated by the details of corporeal existence. But he cautions that biological reductionism deters scholars from focusing on the ways in which the body is also inherently social and cultural. Terence Turner (1995) comments that even though the body is an individual organism, it biologically depends for its reproduction, nurturance and existence on other individuals and the environment, so even this biological individuality is relative and dependent on other social beings.

The body is often conceived as a multiplicity: the "two bodies" of the social and physical (Douglas 1970), the "three bodies" of the individual body, social body and body politic (Scheper-Hughes and Lock 1987) or the "five bodies" with the addition of the consumer body and the medical body to the three (O'Neil 1985). A fundamental question within anthropology is how to understand apparently incommensurate perspectives on the body such as whether human bodies can transform into animals or objects (Harris and Robb 2012). Anthropological concerns also include questioning the "secular body" as a means of studying subject formation (Asad 2011, Hirschkind 2011, Farman 2013) or employing the racialized body to interrogate racial identity and class (McCallum 2005). These discussions suggest that the "body is ontologically multimodal" (Harris and Robb 2012: 676), experienced and understood differently depending on local knowledge, circumstances, social relations and cultural principles and practices.

From a Marxist perspective, David Harvey conceptualizes the body as an accumulation strategy: "the 'measure of all things' is itself a site of contestation for the very forces that create it" (1998: 420). He argues that the body is open and porous to the world such that culture, discourses and representations are not separate from it, but part of its materialization. Marx was aware of the role of bodily materializations in the circulation of capital under capitalist social relations, but Harvey (1998) adds it is also the locus

of political resistance made evident in his Baltimore study of workers' struggle for a living wage. Harvey's (1998) contribution integrates the physical/
biological body as both a material sociopolitical formation and an active
agent of change.

Body space

The importance of the body for an understanding of space and place was
recognized quite early in psychoanalytic theory with Harold Searles (1960)
writings on human attachment and the external environment and Erik Erikson's (1950) attribution of gender and genital modes with spatial modalities.
In Erikson's research on child development, young boys build tall block structures to heights that topple over, while young girls create places with static
interiors and enclosed spaces. He concludes that in young children, representational space is structured by an interpenetration of the biological, cultural
and psychological aspects of gender expressed externally in architectural form.

Anthropologists who offer other psychoanalytic interpretations of bodily
spaces have criticized Erikson's spatial analyses (Pandolfo 1989). For instance,
Robert Paul (1976) agrees with Erikson's contention that there is a relationship between the psyche and built spaces by revealing how the Sherpa temple
can be seen as an objectification of subjective, internal experience. He modi-
fies this understanding, however, by reading temple architecture as a guide
to Sherpa secret psychic life. Mariella Pandolfi (1990), on the other hand,
suggests while there is some minimal identity derived from the experience
of the body as a way of describing and expressing the self, identity is better
defined by historical social structures that inscribe the body and naturalize
a person's existence in the world. It is not biology/psychology that produces
gendered body spaces and their representations, but the inscription of sociopolitical and cultural relations on the body.

Feminist scholars take this critique even further by exploring the epistemological implications of knowledge as embodied, engendered and embedded
in place (Duncan 1996). By disrupting the binary mind/body by positionality
(Boys 1998) and focusing on the situated and colonized body (Scott 1996),
states of mind become loosened from the location of social and spatial relationships (Munt 1998). Donna Haraway (1991) argues that personal and
social bodies cannot be seen as natural, but only as part of a self-creating
process of human labor. Her emphasis on *location*, a position in a web of
social connections, eliminates passivity of the female body and replaces it
with a site of action and of agency (Haraway 1991). Judith Butler (2004),
nonetheless, adds that to persist in one's own being still depends on norms
of recognition of what constitutes an "I" and a gendered body.

The majority of sociologists and anthropologists emphasize the intrin-
sically social and cultural character of the human body. Marcel Mauss
(1950) argues that acquired habits and somatic tactics, what he calls the

"techniques of the body," incorporate all the "cultural arts" of using and being in the body and the world. The body is at the same time the original tool with which humans shape their world and the substance out of which the world is shaped (Mauss 1950, also see Csordas 1999). As discussed in Chapter 2, Bourdieu (1984) employs habitus to characterize the way the body, mind and emotions are simultaneously trained and uses this concept to understand how social status and class position become embodied in everyday life.

The body is also a medium of communication with a direct relationship to spatial arrangements and social structures that begins with the symbolism of the body and body boundaries (Douglas 1971). In later work, Mauss (1979) analyzes the importance of the human body as a metaphor, noting that architecture draws its imagery from human experience, while both Douglas (1978) and Bourdieu (1984) explore how body symbolism is transformed into spaces within the home and neighborhood.

Cultural groups often draw upon the human body as a template for spatial and social relations. The Dogon describe village spatial structure in anthropomorphic terms spiraling down in scale to the plan of the house representing a man lying on his side, procreating (Griaule 1954), and the Batammalibans endow their social structure and architecture with body symbolism (Blier 1987). Many anthropologists use metaphor analysis to interpret the ways the human body is linked to myths and cosmology and describe how spatial and temporal processes are encoded with body symbolism (Hugh-Jones 1979, Johnson 1988). Other studies explore the body as isomorphic with the landscape, where the landscape provides a metaphor that is an expressive device transmitting memory, morality and emotion (Bastien 1985, Fernandez 1986).

These "bodyscapes," the various representations of bodies at multiple scales from bodies as landscapes, bodies moving through space or individual body differences tend to idealize societal norms (Geller 2009). The biomedical bodyscape, for example, is hegemonic in Western societies, influencing scientific and social practices and reinforcing heteronormative assumptions about sexual differences, gender and sexuality. Pamela Geller (2009) suggests that queer theory is useful in producing alternative body representations such as Michael Brown's (2000) study of "closet space" that illustrates how performativity of space equally constrains and defines the body and personal identity.

These studies of body spaces do not theorize the body, per se, but utilize it as a spatial metaphor and representational space. Even though the body is implicated as a tool in the production of cultural forms, it is treated as an empty container without consciousness or intention. Douglas, Mauss, Bourdieu and others are more concerned with the body as a metaphor for social and cultural conceptualization than with the space of the organism itself and the impact of cultural influences on it and its operations. Other studies of body space based on language models and phenomenology offer alternative perspectives.

Proxemics

The study of proxemics was one of the first attempts to explain how space and spatial relations are configured by cultural norms and practices. It provides a theoretical grounding for space and language studies, discussed in Chapter 6, and offers a methodology that has been used by businesses for training international employees to interact in a culturally appropriate manner. Edward T. Hall (1966, 1973) is the best-known proponent of proxemics and spent his career studying the influence of culture on spatial perception, behavior and use of space. He postulates that humans have an innate distancing mechanism modified by culture that helps to regulate contact in social situations. Conceptualized as a bubble surrounding each individual, personal space varies in size according to the type of social relationship and situation. Hall proposes four general kinds of personal space ranging from intimate (which permits very close contact) to public (which requires greater distance between individuals). Because these spatial aspects of behavior are tacit, actors usually become aware of the boundaries only when they are violated, often in culture contact situations. Appropriate spatial variations in social relations are learned as a feature of culture.

Hall's research casts doubt on the assumption of shared phenomenological experience: people not only structure spaces differently, but they experience them in different ways and inhabit distinct sensory worlds. There is a selective screening out of perceptual and sensory data accomplished by individuals "tuning out" one or more of the senses or by architectural interventions. Thus the body becomes a site of personal space with multiple screens for interacting with others and the environment.

Phenomenology

From a phenomenological perspective, the body is the ground of perceptual processes that end in objectification, a process discussed in Chapter 4. Merleau-Ponty recognizes that *le corps propre* (one's own body) is both physical and experiential, combining consciousness and intentionality. Through an examination of embodied activity, such as seeing, hearing, touching and feeling, he emphasizes how actions and perceptions are habitual responses to the environment. He comments that "far from my body's being for me no more than a fragment of space, there would be no space at all for me if I had no body" (Merleau-Ponty 1962: 102).

Asha Persson (2007), on the other hand, argues that embodied being-in-the-world is not solely dependent on an experiential sense of place. In her ethnographic study of Satyananda Yoga practice in Australia, she employs the notions of embodiedness and space to counter the narrowness of a phenomenological approach that exclusively focuses on emplacement. Instead she emphasizes "the cultural diversity of spatial experiences and the multimodality of embodied being-in-the-world, inviting a different understanding of the ways in which embodied practices produce and configure meaningful space" (Persson 2007: 45).

Bridging phenomenological approaches and considerations of political economy is another problem faced by ethnographers interested in experiential and agentive narratives of everyday life. Robert Desjarlais (1997) struggles with the limitations of a phenomenological approach that privileges the "internal" experience of mentally ill homeless individuals to find a way to understand not just what people feel but with how they come to feel in this way. He suggests that the ethnographer link the "modalities of sensation, perception and subjectivity to pervasive political arrangements and forms of economic production and consumption" (Desjarlais 1997: 25). Using the architecture of the building of a homeless shelter and tracing the movements and orientations of the residents, he is able to understand the multifaceted modalities of "sensing, knowing, remembering and listening" common to everyday life in the shelter (Desjarlais 1997: 27). The spatiality of Desjarlais's (1997) and Persson's (2007) ethnographies offer an important step in the development of an embodied space analysis.

Sensorium

Paul Stoller (1989, 2002), Mary Hufford (1992) and Josh Brahinsky (2012) also use a phenomenological approach, but one that emphasizes the sensory context – smell, texture, sound, sight and taste of a place – that must be accounted for as aspects of the sentient body that anchor human experience in the world. A focus on the senses or sensuous scholarship (Stoller 1989) rejects mind/body duality and redefines bodily experience holistically, with an emphasis on knowing the world through the senses. This ethnographic approach focuses on body logics, the messy process of oscillating between sensory modes of experience and understanding (Brahinsky 2012).

The study of sensorium has been most notable in studies of healing, illness and religion, where religious conversion, spirit possession and shamanistic healing take on mystical and dramatic form (Desjarlais 1992, Brahinsky 2012, I. M. Lewis 1971). Often the ethnographer's bodily experience is implicated through an intensive form of participant observation used to document the healing or religious transformation through fasting, sleep deprivation, ingestion of hallucinatory drugs and chanting. Ethnographers attempt to understand the experience of their informants through their own feelings of elation, sadness, belief, calm or out of body awareness based on the cultivation of the distinct sensorium deemed appropriate to the cultural context. Not unlike the bodily discipline of yoga described by Persson (2007), religion and body training require the cultivation of ways of sensing as well as being-in-the-world. This approach has become increasingly recognized for its ability to answer old questions in new ways. For example, Charles Hirschkind (2011) and Talal Asad (2011) use the configuration of the human sensorium that includes embodied dispositions, sensibilities and feelings as a methodology for challenging assumed notions of what it means to be secular or religious in the Middle East today.

The relationship of a sensory approach to space and place is most developed in *The Senses of Place* (Feld and Basso 1996), which provides rich ethnographic examples of sensory cuing of local meanings in the landscape. Research on the culinary concept of *terroir*, the local environmental conditions of the land where a food is produced or grown, also draws upon a sensory approach to understand the complex relationship of taste and place. For example, Brad Weiss (2011) examines how food is spatialized through its experiential qualities and its role in constituting expressive places. By asking "how is place made," he traces the ways that local foods operate by drawing upon Lefebvre (1991) for his analysis of the social production of space. Like Desjarlais (1997), he is interested in integrating political economy – in this case, environmental justice and sustainability aspects of local pork production – with his sensory analysis that links taste to a discerning public and market thus creating and constructing notions of "place" and "locality" (Weiss 2011).

Another sensory approach to embodied space is Stefan Helmreich's (2007) discussion of the immersive soundscapes of an anthropologist underwater. He argues that the term "transductive" is more appropriate when attending to the "embodied capacitances of the ethnographer" in the field. These various sensory approaches to embodied space offer the ethnographer new methodologies and techniques for understanding space and place. They expand earlier phenomenological approaches by integrating macropolitical economic concerns into an intimate, intense and sensory-rich form of auto-ethnography of space and place.

Mobile spatial fields

Nancy Munn combines aspects of this phenomenological work with a social practice perspective by considering space-time "as a symbolic nexus of relations produced out of interactions between bodily actors and terrestrial spaces" (Munn 1996: 449). Drawing upon Lefebvre's concepts of "field of action" and "basis of action," as well as his insistence that embodied practices and experiences actively produce and consume space, she constructs the notion of a "mobile spatial field." Her spatiotemporal construct can be understood as a culturally defined, corporeal-sensual field stretching out from the body at a given locale or moving through locales.

Munn's (1996) ethnographic illustration is the spatial interdiction that occurs when Aborigines treat the land according to ancestral Aboriginal law. She is interested in the specific kind of spatial form being produced, "a space of deletions or of delimitations constraining one's presence at particular locales" (Munn 1996: 448) that creates a variable range of excluded or restricted regions for each person throughout his or her life. For instance, in following their moral-religious law, Aborigines make detours that must be far enough away to avoid seeing an ancient place or hearing the ritual singing currently going on there. By detouring, actors carve out a "negative space" that extends beyond their spatial field of vision: "This act projects a signifier of limitation upon the land or place by forming *transient but repeatable boundaries out of the moving body*" (Munn 1996: 452). Munn applies this idea to contemporary Aborigines' encounters with powerful topographic centers and "dangerous" ancestral places.

The importance of this analysis for the ethnography of space and place is the way Munn demonstrates how the ancestral law's power of spatial limitation becomes "embodied" in an actor-centered, mobile body, separate from any fixed center or place. "Excluded spaces" become spatiotemporal formations produced out of the interaction of actors' moving spatial fields and the terrestrial spaces of body action. Further, these detours, what she calls the production of "negative space," are a new kind of spatialization of respect and a model for understanding the relationship of distance, detour, social regard and status in other cultural groups, including one's own. Her theory goes well beyond Hall's concept of proxemics with culturally constituted spatial orientations and interpersonal distances and phenomenological understandings of being-in-the-world. Instead, she suggests constructing the person (actor) as an embodied space in which the body, conceived of as a moving spatial field, makes its own place in the world.

Stuart Rockefeller (2009) develops this notion of mobile spatial fields into a theory of public places formed by individual movements, trips and digressions of migrants crossing national boundaries. Starting with Munn's idea that the person makes space by moving through it, he traces how movement patterns collectively make up and reproduce locality. Places, he argues, are not in the landscape, but simultaneously in the land, people's minds, customs and bodily practices. By tracing the crossings of labor migrants between Bolivia and Argentina, Rockefeller uses this formulation to theorize how actors' embodied spaces occupy and create transnational spaces in the same way that the vendors and shoppers at the Moore Street Market create translocal space through their exchange of food stuffs and merchandise from Latin America discussed in Chapter 8.

Walking, movement and rhythm

The importance of walking and movement in the creation of space redefines place as movement and intersecting pathways rather than a container (Pandya 1990). For example, the geographer Allan Pred (1984) traces the history of the microgeographies of daily life in southern Sweden to determine the ways that everyday movement and behavior generate spatial transformations in land tenure and local social structure. De Certeau's (1984) analysis of the spatial tactics of orientation and movement discussed in Chapter 2 similarly focuses on how the mundane acts of walking and meandering resist state order and regimes of city planning. Tom Hall and Rob Smith (2013) add "rhythmanalysis," Lefebvre's (1996, 2005) method for analyzing the rhythms of urban spaces and the effects of those rhythms on inhabitants, to better understand outreach workers on pedestrian patrols. They trace how the walking and navigation of outreach workers on the streets of Cardiff in the U.K. must coincide with their rough sleeper clients whose urban rhythms "are (sometimes) so very out of step" (Hall 2010: 59).

Lefebvre's premise is that when there is interaction between a place, a time, and an expenditure of energy, there is *rhythm* (2005). Conceptually, rhythmanalysis interweaves both cyclical (reoccurring with intervals of repetition, including biological or environmental rhythms such as the rising and setting sun) and linear (unidirectional, point-to-point movements) aspects of everyday life (Kofman and Lebas 2005). These rhythms characterize the human body as well as integrate it into the spatiotemporal rhythms of space. Through rhythmanalysis it is possible to identify places as having distinct characteristics or set of rhythms that make up a "polyrhythmic ensemble" at a particular site (Crang and Thrift 2000).

Walking as a methodology for understanding how rhythms make up space is most clearly depicted in John Gray's (1999) ethnographic research on sheep herding in the Scottish borderlands. He argues that the *hirsel*, a unified place that includes both a shepherd's sheep and their grazing area, is constituted by the shepherds walking or cycling the hills to care for their animals (Gray 1999). The act of shepherding, or "going around the hill," is a form of place-making requiring a shepherd's detailed knowledge of the terrain and also of how the sheep bond to parts of the terrain, as well as how paths link these parts together to form the *hirsel*. The emphasis on walking the hills demonstrates the ways places that may be separately named and recalled, but are still connected to one another in a unified whole. The relationship of place-naming and space is discussed in greater detail in Chapter 6.

Dance improvisations of Black and Brown youth similarly reflect a form of embodied knowledge production produced through rhythm and tempo with political potential. Aimee Cox (2014) emphasizes dance as a form of self-expression and political power that enables Black girls to create their own spaces of freedom and safety in a deteriorating neighborhood. Rosemarie Roberts (2013) describes the "accumulated excess" of hip-hop with its gestures and dynamic movements that reach beyond a single body to inform other knowing Black and Brown bodies. Dancing bodies produce a relational and dialogic experience that reveals "the oppressive nature of structural inequalities . . . codified in hip-hop dance" (Roberts 2013: 12).

Tim Ingold (2004, 2007) integrates elements of these perceptual, rhythmic, sensory and embodied approaches by incorporating the ecological psychology theory of James Gibson. Gibson (1979) argues that perception is a psychosomatic act that can only be experienced through the body. Ingold (2007) argues that linear movement connects body movement and visual perception through lines of vision and the lines and paths of walking. He contrasts lines as free-flowing movement in an open landscape with lines that connect predetermined points of arrival and departure. Multiple forms of linear movement integrate the person, memory, experience and the environment.

Ethnographic research carried out in 2004–2005 in northeast Scotland by Ingold and Vergunst (2008) takes the notions of lines and body movement and applies them to walking. They argue that the relationship between walking, embodiment and sociability is crucial:

> That is, we do not assume *a priori* that walking affords an experience of embodiment, or that social life hovers above the road we tread in our material life. Rather, walking affords an experience of embodiment to the extent that it is grounded in an inherently sociable engagement between self and environment.
>
> (Ingold and Vergunst 2008: 2)

Based on a study of Aberdeen walkers, they conceptualize the relationship between bodies and the environment in three ways: 1) the walker may look or sense the environment; 2) the walker may turn inward to thoughts, memories or stories while experiencing the sensory perception; and 3) walkers may become aware of or even cross the boundary of the body and environment through their embodied and emotional interactions (Ingold and Vergunst 2008). The details of each step are integral to how the walk proceeds, while emotions are engendered not only by grand vistas but also by the care taken in maintaining balance or wayfinding.

In another ethnographic project on Union Street in Aberdeen, Scotland Jo Vergunst (2010) uses sound, movement, rhythm and shape of the walker's body as a means for understanding the city's historical development. By interviewing walkers while walking, he is able to trace their wayfinding decisions and adjustments in speed, tempo and diversion. His discussion of "walking the mat," that is, walking down Union Street in small, single-gender groups and during the walk meeting up with another group of the opposite gender is reminiscent of the *retreta* and *paseo* in Spanish American culture, as well as the *corso* in the Balkan culture described in the following ethnographic examples. By tracing the legal underpinnings of this practice, Vergunst (2010) is able to link the loss of the embodied practice with the loss of the ritual space.

Walking, dancing and other forms of movement are more than the inscription of footprints or footfalls on the ground; they create tracks and paths as well as networks and nodes of human and nonhuman places. These movements include gestures, postures, rhythms, sequences and timings that create variegated and unique emplacements in the world. Movements such as walking or dancing, however, are not just about making space and place but also generate knowledge through the interconnection and communication of bodies and the walking, breathing and knowing of everyday movement (Ingold 2010).

Mobility, circulation and trajectory

Embodied practices, physical activities, daily rhythms and bodily movements can be combined with an individual's goals and intentions through time-geography, another methodological approach useful for ethnographers. Similar to Vergunst's description of Union Street walking, Munn's analysis of excluded spaces and Ingold's lines and paths, Pred (1984) argues that place-making is based on the temporal and spatial attributes of users' walking and intentional activity that when viewed over time form paths and projects:

> Since each of the actions and events consecutively making up the existence of an individual has both temporal and spatial attributes, time-geography allows that the biography of a person may be conceptualized and diagramed at daily or lengthier scales of observation as an unbroken continuous *path* through time-space subject to times of constraint. In time-geographic terms a *project* consists of the entire sequence of simple or complex tasks necessary to the completion of any intention-inspired or goal-oriented behavior.
>
> (Pred 1984: 256)

These time-geography behavior sequences and their emotional effects are tracked in a study of drivers' road rage in Los Angeles, California. Jack Katz (1999) argues that the metaphysical merging of the driver and his car explains a driver's sudden anger when another "automobilized person" interrupts the drivers' intended path by cutting off a preferred route, disrupting the timing of a turn or obstructing the preferred driving speed. The tacit embodiment of car, action and personal identity explains how becoming angry "is a practical project in which the driver attempts to regain a taken-for-granted intertwining with the environment" (Katz 1999: 32).

Paths, projects and human-machine embodiment are part of a new way of thinking about cities, space and place-making. Ash Amin and Nigel Thrift (2002) reimagine the city as spatially open and made up of a multiplicity of mobilities and flows of people, culture, commodities and information, with much of this interaction occurring at a distance. Their discussion of circulation as a "central characteristic of the city" (2002: 81) contributes to an understanding of the role that movement plays in urban encounters, nodes and entanglements that take on spatial expression. As they define it,

> cities exist as means of movement, as means to engineer *encounters* through collection, transport and collation. They produce, thereby, a complex pattern of traces, a threadwork of intensities which is antecedent to the sustained work of revealing the city minute on minute, hour on hour, day on day, and so on. These forces are distinguished in four ways: by what they carry, by how they carry, by their stretch in space and by their cyclicity.
>
> (Amin and Thrift 2002: 81–82)

The city has long been identified as the point of articulation of the flow of goods, cash, labor and services between the metropole and the countryside (Leeds 1973), although there generally has been less focus on internal spatial systems of transportation and encounter. There are, however, a few important exceptions. André Czeglédy's (2004) ethnography of transportation in post-apartheid Johannesburg documents how the circulation of people restricts movement and reinscribes social relationships along racial and class lines. He examines the primacy of private automobiles in contemporary suburban development, urban planning and physical design, as well as how public versus private modes of transportation differentiate the mobility of rich and poor resegregating urban and suburban space. Automobile transportation in Beirut, Lebanon, is also a way to understand everyday security practices and how citizenship is asserted through one's ability (or inability) to move through the city (Monroe 2016).

Urban youth circulation in Douala, Cameroon, however, can also forge new possibilities and collaborations rather than limitations through young peoples' mobility (Simone 2005). For Simone, circulation refers

> to a practice of lateral, transversal movement, whereby individuals attempt to get out of their neighborhoods and familiar social relationships, to demonstrate a capacity to navigate a wide range of different

quarters and an availability to engage in different activities, as well as an availability to become parts of different stories, games, transactions being elaborated by others elsewhere in the city.

(2005: 518)

These ethnographic studies are part of the "new mobilities paradigm," a theoretical framework that traces contemporary and historical mobility through the movement of people, objects, capital and information, globally as well as locally (Hannam, Sheller and Urry 2006). The "mobilities turn" encompasses a wide array of concerns from studies of walking, circulation and transportation, such as those identified in this discussion, to research on migration, tourism and travel; virtual and informational mobility; mobility nodes and spatial mobility; and materiality and mobility (Hannam, Sheller and Urry 2006). Much of the literature concentrates on how space and place are made through the intersection and entanglement of these circuits of movement, whether of people, materials or capital, and therefore contributes a rich theoretical background for a movement-based concept of embodied space. Further, research on how information modalities and web-based social networking create new spaces of possibility and transform existing spaces into centers for action are helpful in thinking through the political implications of an embodied spatial analysis.

Mobilities theory expands the concept of embodied space as a mobile spatial field to include the capacity for social relations and through the patterning of everyday movements to produce place and landscape. These embodied spatial patterns of movement and circulation are the substrate of Pred's (1984) paths and projects, and they encompass emotion and affect as well as surrounding objects and environments as illustrated in Katz's (1999) automobile drivers or Vergunst's (2010) Aberdeen walkers. Further, as Pred (1984) points out, these paths and projects are intentional and goal oriented, although one could imagine an unintentional fall or forced march in which an individual's intentionality is compromised. The intentionality and goal orientation of Pred's and Katz's contributions allow for greater agency to be accorded to the actor(s).

This agency when combined with the idea of patterned movement, however, I think is better captured by the term "trajectory," as in a path that is being actively projected or an object/person moving because of some given internal or external force. When added to the concept of embodied space, the term trajectory transforms the spatiotemporal unit into a construct with agency, power and direction. Through personal and cultural trajectories, the embodied space(s) of individuals and collectivities take on social, ritual, cultural and political dimensions. The material and social impact of embodied space is illustrated in the ritual walking, strolling and bicycle riding described in the following ethnographic examples drawn from ethnographic fieldwork in Costa Rica, Serbia and Hungary.

Ethnographic examples

Ritual walking and strolling

Introduction

People who have spent time walking, dancing or physically training in a particular location have probably experienced "knowing" or "creating" a space through their bodies, a sense that reoccurs each time, even if it is many years later. There are a number of ethnographic examples of this kind of bodily knowing and space-making. Deborah Kapchan (2006) writes about the body intimacy created in a salsa dance club in Austin, Texas, where regulars claim space through dance competence and bodily contact with other dancers. Over time and through numerous repetitions of music and dance steps, participants create a space where dancers feel at home in what is otherwise perceived as a nomadic world. Arafaat Valiani (2010) explores the darker aspect of body routines by suggesting that Hindu Nationalist Movement volunteers who take part in physical training are encouraged not only to identify with the Hindu nation and its territory but also to participate in improvised ethnic cleansing through this ideologically prescribed ritual activity. Other everyday examples include the practice of yoga at a specific place or time, or walking to the bus, the store or on a favorite path as part of a daily routine. On familiar walks, the routinized body takes over even when thoughts and dreams are distracting, and walkers usually find themselves arriving at their destination often without knowing how they got there. This body/knowledge/space exists in relationship to different cultural and bodily contexts.

There are important rituals of walking, such as religious and secular processions (Rodríguez 1996, Davis 1986), cruising (Chappell 2010) or going around the hill (Gray 1999), that capture salient elements of cultural tradition and meaning in an embodied form. In Latin America and Europe, there are a number of kinds of strolling that traditionally enabled young people to meet, talk, flirt and court in public spaces. These distinctive walking circuits around a square or park or along the main street in a town or village were made up of single-gender strolling groups. Ritual walking has many names depending on the country and language, including the *corso* in Serbia (Vesna Vučinić-Nešković and Jelena Miloradović 2006) and the *retreta* in Costa Rica (Richardson 1982, Low 2000).

Employing an embodied spatial analysis demonstrates how this ritual walking creates gendered and class-based space through movement and through trajectories inscribes the landscape with social, cultural and political meanings. Both the *retreta* and the *corso* are semiformal institutions in which all age groups take part, but in a narrower sense, are informal cultural practices of young people. Historically, the generations participated at the same time, but contemporary practices include a significant temporal transition with adults and children strolling before dinner and youth gathering after dinner or the movies. In some cases, ritual strolling includes leisurely forms of shopping and other consumption practices.

The gendered inscription of the retreta

The *retreta* is a traditional form of heterosexual socializing and courting that still occurs in small villages and towns throughout Latin America. The term refers to the *verbatim* translation of *la retreta* as the retreat played by a military band or an open-air military band concert that became associated with people strolling around the plaza or square after the concert was over. Colloquially and ethnographically, the *retreta* refers to the groups of young men who walk arm in arm in one direction, while groups of young women walk arm in arm in the opposite direction, enabling the two groups to face one another as they pass by. The idea is to catch the eye of an admirer and then, in some cases, meet the person at the end of the turn, alone or accompanied by friends. The exact form and location varies based on the unique practices of the village, town and country.

Research on the *retreta* started through my initial participation in the Christmas festivities in downtown San José, Costa Rica (Figure 5.1 Map of San José city center). The *retreta* had already moved from Parque Central and become a holiday custom along the stretch of Avenida Central (Central Avenue), that fronted the main department stores and local gift shops in December 1985. Young people were throwing confetti as they walked arm in arm facing one another on the street that was temporarily closed for pedestrians and shoppers. The walking and confetti throwing were stopped for many years because of the massive cleanup and health hazards, but the custom has been revived in the past few years (Maria Eugenia Bozzoli de Wille 2013, personal communication).

To learn more about ritual strolling, I turned to the municipal archives, popular histories of San José and novels and memoirs of social customs (Low 2000). I also interviewed older residents about their experiences in Parque Central as well as anthropologists who had worked in San José. Based on these interviews, observations and archival documents a description of the *retreta* in San José emerged.

Historically, the *retreta* created a space where middle- and upper-middle-class young men and women could flirt and talk to one another in what was then a relatively gender-segregated society. Yet it appears that this early form of spatial and cultural inscription has been retained in other strolling contexts. Window-shopping rather than walking around the plaza to meet a *novio* or *novia* (boyfriend or girlfriend) continues to be a culturally valued activity and the accepted social and spatial context for meeting friends (Photo 5.1 Pedestrians shopping at new *retreta* in San José). The gender-based embodied space and circulating trajectories are still part of the urban environment, inscribing and creating spaces of sociability.

Figure 5.1 Map of San José city center (Erin Lilli)

Photo 5.1 Pedestrians shopping at new *retreta* in San José (Setha Low)

Until the 1960s, the *retreta* was a clockwise and counterclockwise walk around the Parque Central bandstand, with boys moving in one direction and girls in the other. In informants' earliest recollections and stories, it convened after Sunday services in the Cathedral let out, and the military band played. Later when Parque Central became surrounded by movie houses, the *retreta* occurred after the movies ended. Memories of this ritualized walking and its accompanying sociability are part of what many older Josefinos remember fondly.

Alvaro Wille spent time in Parque Central as a young man in the 1930s and 1940s. He is one of the few people interviewed during my 1993 and 1997 field trips who actually participated in the *retreta* as it has been historically described. Alvaro talked about his experiences while laughing when asked about living in downtown San José when he was growing up.

ALVARO (A): On Sunday afternoon, young people would get together and walk around the park with the girls on the inside and the boys where they could see them. It was a way to meet someone. I did it; yes, I went sometimes.

SETHA (S): What year was this?

A: I do not remember exactly, but in the 1940s. I would have been at least fourteen years old in 1940.

s: And how was the experience? How did you feel about it?
a: Well, it interested me the first time – everyone told me that I had to do it because it was the custom. So I went after the three o'clock movie at Las Palmas. I went with my friends and we would walk around. But this experience did not convert me into a regular. I did not have a single girlfriend to look at and would not have one; there was plenty of reason to attend only if you had a girlfriend. Thus it was a park of teenage romance. And afterwards, I am sure there were evening romances as we became more adult.
s: So this was in the afternoon?
a: In the afternoon about 5:00. And we would stay until it got dark or a bit later. I went two, three or four times, not much more than that.

Alvaro's wife is the well-known Costa Rican anthropologist Maria Eugenia Bozzoli de Wille. Although much younger than Alvaro, she also remembers walking in Parque Central in the 1950s and early 1960s, but her circuit included more of the downtown area, including a stop for snacks. She remembers this walking as a *paseo*,[2] a circular stroll or linear promenade, taken with her friends as a two-part event associated with going to the movies. In Maria Eugenia's *paseo*, groups of same-gender friends still walked together:

> For young people the idea was to stroll down the avenue past the movie theater, make a circle of the park, and then continue on to Chelles. We would stop at the corner of Chelles because it was the bar with the best little pastries and *los arreglados* [flaky pastry shells filled with meat, vegetables or cheese]. The people who went to Chelles, however, were more adult because it was a bar and people would go to drink. This trip to Chelles was part of the entire *paseo* in the early hours of the evening. Everyone would leave the movie theater about 5:00 p.m. and make a circle before going down to Chelles. Some people would enter the movies at 7:00 p.m. and leave about 9:00 p.m., but even those that left at 9:00 p.m. spent a little time walking around. At other times, the parade was down the avenue, and the boys and men would stop at the corner as the girls and women walked by – boys watching the girls and men watching the women. Some girls would come alone, but normally a girl would not come with a boy. She would meet him at the corner.

In Maria Eugenia's story, the *paseo* she describes also takes on an embodied form and becomes her personal space in the city. By walking the streets and stopping at special places, her spatial practices are like de Certeau's "tactics" in which individuals make the city their own through everyday bodily practices. In the *paseo*, nodes of social interaction interrupt the linear and circular movements creating new social spaces and places inhabited by the strollers. Further, the walkers' trajectories intersect at corners creating spatial entanglements of attraction and desire. The goal is the sociability of the walking, yet through the rhythms of the *paseo*, the city becomes one's own, legible through bodily movement.[3]

The social inscription of the corso

Vesna Vučinić-Nešković and Jelena Miloradović (2006) have undertaken extensive ethnographic and historical research on the youth *corso (korzo)* in Serbia from 1930 to 2001, as well as in the old town of Dubrovnik in the 1990s (Vučinić-Nešković 1999). They argue that the *corso* is a "total social phenomena" drawing on Marcel Mauss's (1979) concept, and their methodological approach and findings suggest a broader interpretation of this ritual promenade.

Their study of the *corso* traced a complex social institution over from 1930 to 2001, combining anthropological, historical and geographical techniques. Participant observation utilized for the study of the contemporary *corso* in the 1990s was augmented with in-depth interviews based on a standardized questionnaire for the entire research period, with ten respondents for each decade. City plans, photographs and other relevant documents were gathered from the archive of the Smederevska Palanka Municipality on the major changes in urban planning and use of buildings on the *corso* route. The analysis of the data included mapping spatial behavior on the *corso* for every decade, recording the walking paths and standing places and a content analysis of the interviews and field notes.

The term *corso* originated from the Latin *cursus* and the Italian *corso* translated as "running, race, running track, flow, circulation or street promenade" (Vučinić-Nešković and Miloradović 2006: 231). In medieval Italy, the *corso* was a space for sports competitions illustrated in Sydel Silverman's (1978) ethnography of an Italian hill town where the *corso* was a circuit of horse racing based on interneighborhood competition. *Corso* as a promenade has been practiced in areas along the Adriatic coast and throughout the Balkan Peninsula.

In Smederevska Palanka, Serbia, the *corso* stands for both the space where the promenade takes place and the accompanying walking, standing and social interactions. Similar to the *retreta*, historically the *corso* took place along a specified route in the downtown area and was an everyday activity – although it was more popular on Saturday and Sunday – and mostly attended by high school students who walked in gender-specific groups (Photo 5.2 Gender-specific groups of youths strolling in *corso*). Until the 1960s, adults also had their own *corso*, but increasingly only the youth continued the custom since it became a socially acceptable way to have a romantic relationship in this relatively small Orthodox Christian community. Also, similar to the *retreta*, the ritual promenade was associated with going to the movies or for moving between favorite cafés and leisure youth activities.

Photo 5.2 Gender-specific groups of youths strolling in *corso* (Petar Dekić)

Vučinić-Nešković and Miloradović (2006) describe the physical context of the *corso* in great detail and examine the locations of where people stood and watched as well as walked (Photo 5.3 Stopping and watching the *corso*). The paths of the *corso* were along socially significant streets with two sides for walking. One side of the street was used for the ritual promenade and the other for those hurrying to complete their errands characterized as being "where the peasants went," creating status-based spaces (2006: 239). After the 1990s, the weekday *corso* receded and was replaced by repetitive circulation between middle-class cafés (Photo 5.4 Upper part of the *corso* with shopping stalls).

One of the most important findings is the relationship of the people who use the *corso* standing places and where these standing places occur along the *corso* path. Until the 1980s, only male *corso* participants had "standing places," and while females after the 1980s could stand with male companions, even today they do not have standing places similar to the men (2006: 241). This spatially inscribed gender hierarchy intersects with the class-based territories and the age segregation that has evolved over time.

Vučinić-Nešković and Miloradović (2006) conclude that the embodied spaces and changing trajectories of the *corso* are about the spatial and place-specific differentiation of gender, status, age and other forms of social phenomena rather than the more personal and gendered embodied space found in Costa Rica. Their historical ethnography of space and place uncovers both how the *corso* was produced by walking and how the structural

Photo 5.3 Stopping and watching the *corso* (Petar Dekić)

Photo 5.4 Upper part of the *corso* with shopping stalls (Petar Dekić)

constraints of gender, status and age are embodied and a hierarchical form of spatialized culture created.

Critical Mass and the politics of bicycling

A final example of an embodied space analysis is of Critical Mass, a grassroots bicycle movement that is reclaiming cyclists' right to the city. Éva Teszsza Udvarhelyi (2009) compared the Critical Mass movements in New York City and Budapest and found that bicycle riding and advocacy in Budapest was tolerated by the state. The police actually assisted with the organization of the Critical Mass rides, as they were considered protests requiring acknowledgment by the local police. Critical Mass rallies and bicycle rides in New York City, on the other hand, were heavily policed, restricted and controlled. Although the Critical Mass rides in Budapest no longer occur, they live on under the new name of I Bike Budapest.

Based on her ethnographic research and through experiences as a cyclist on regular Critical Mass rides, she suggests that in post-socialist Hungary,

> the Budapest Critical Mass can be read as the spatialized enactment of a direct and embodied form of democratic participation that goes beyond and at the same time transforms representative democracy.
>
> (Udvarhelyi 2009: 121)

Since bicycle riding in both cities was her main form of transportation, Udvarhelyi became aware of the discrimination and violence of a car-dominated city. She developed a visceral understanding of the embodied politics of cyclists riding together as an assertion of political rights. Cycling profoundly changes a rider's relationship with the urban environment through the combination of direct personal experience, a strong identity created by cycling with others and the bodily motion of cycling. Critical Mass riders develop a connection to the city, one that politically empowers them to make claims and have a stake in its future.

Udvarhelyi's research was based on participant observation as well as formal and informal interviews. She took part in all the rides organized by the two groups, engaged in informal conversations with participants and monitored the conversations that took place on the mailing lists of core organizers. She also observed the communications and social interactions on the Hungarian movement's interactive website where cyclists and activists shared experiences and exchanged opinions on Critical Mass and other issues related to urban cycling. She completed interviews with the organizers and participants of both Critical Masses as well as representatives of the Budapest and New York City Police Departments and the Budapest City Hall. Most interviews took place in person, while some were conducted over e-mail.

Udvarhelyi posits that it is because of Critical Mass's understanding of the importance of the embodied nature of cycling that the movement uses organized "rides" as a way to protest and reclaim public space. She documents that Earth Day and Car-Free Day in Budapest draw up to eighty thousand participants, evidence of how mass biking in traffic upsets the assumption that the road is only for cars and instead begins a spatial dialogue about transportation and public space in a political sense (Udvarhelyi 2009).

The example of bicycling as an embodied practice with citywide trajectories of individual riders reclaiming the streets is provocative in its political potential as well as narrative importance (Freudendal-Pedersen 2015). The Critical Mass movement offers a concrete example of how embodiment can be linked to political action, in this case, through the body trajectory of the cyclist. In this ethnographic example, embodied trajectories are not creating space and place, but they are reclaiming space that has been restricted by other embodied practices.

Conclusion

What is significant in terms of this conceptual review and the ethnographic examples is that these scholars have brought diverse perspectives to the ethnography space and place, where the body has been so often overlooked. They offer an understanding of body/space/culture in new and creative ways that theorize and imagine the body as a moving, speaking, cultural space.

The trajectories of young people strolling around Parque Central or along the main streets of Smederevska Palanka create distinct embodied spaces that are important to cultural continuity and community. These body/culture/spaces constitute and are constituted by the social production and social construction of each site yet also exceed existing structural and semiological limitations. The trajectories of Critical Mass bicycle riders, for example, actually transform the city through their various modes of circulation, creating new spaces through movement, bodily actions and political practices.

Embodied space and the intentionality of individual and group trajectories do more than create space and place; they also open up space to innovative political and social possibilities and imaginings. Embodied space offers one strategy for integrating the social production and social construction conceptual frames by locating space in bodies, individual, collective, human and nonhuman, in such a way that the materiality of the body and body knowledge and cognition are recognized as equally important to understanding space and place from an ethnographic point of view.

Notes

1 The idea of embodied space was first discussed in Low and Lawrence-Zúñiga 2003.
2 Another Spanish term for "taking a walk" is *paseo*. Costa Ricans often talk about their *paseo*, which can mean anything from a Sunday stroll in the neighborhood to a picnic in the countryside or visit to the United States. A *paseo* is more of a leisurely family walk than a gendered and ritualized walking sequence or promenade.
3 These Costa Rican descriptions, especially the *paseo* of Maria Eugenia Bozzoli de Wille, are similar to my experiences growing up in Westwood Village located in West Los Angeles. Every Saturday, I would meet my girlfriends, stroll to the bowling alley to meet other friends, stop at Baskin-Robbins for ice cream and finally end up at the Bruin Theater to see the 2:00 p.m. matinee. The boys from our high school class and a few who were in college usually hung out at the bowling alley, smoking illicit cigarettes and playing pool. Sometimes, the boys would join us in going to the Saturday matinee, but always walked together as an all-male group separate from our gaggle of girls. When a couple was "going steady," it was signaled by walking side by side and not joining either walking group. These ritualized strolls and the pattern of going to the movie (and sitting in separate rows in front of each other) created familiar and well-loved places inscribed through bodily movements and repetition. Each time I return to Westwood and retrace my steps, I momentarily become a teenager again, reliving the sociability of those times through the rhythm and tempo of my walking. More surprisingly, when I interviewed high school classmates at our last reunion, I learned that most of them had had similar experiences. Both men and women remember walking specific routes through Westwood, and even those who stayed in Los Angeles experience those places today as embodied spaces of an earlier time.

Chapter 6

Language, discourse and space

Introduction

This conceptual frame examines the ways in which language and discourse shape space and place and locates spatial analysis more firmly in social interactions, communication strategies and linguistic practices. The emphasis on language and discourse also provides a methodologically explicit way to understand how everyday communications produce, manipulate and control spatial meaning. Language and discourse analyses draw upon many of the theories and methodologies presented in Chapter 4 on the social construction of space as well as some of the embodied spatial practices and meaning-based frameworks reviewed in Chapter 5. The unstable semiological[1] relationship of language to ideas, thoughts and objects that underlies a social constructivist approach to spatial analysis informs this discussion. Further, an in-depth consideration of the material effects of language, its performative and discursive aspects and its ability to mark identity also plays a significant role in producing space and making sense of people and place interactions.

As has been the case in the previous chapters, this examination covers a number of discrete and sometimes overlapping conceptualizations and methodologies that make up a language, discourse and space approach to the ethnography of space and place. Each represents some of the many ways language and discourse function in constructing, producing and transforming space through everyday communications and national and global media and information circuits. I focus on sociolinguistic definitions, theories and ethnographic examples because of their utility in understanding the interface of language, social interaction and space. For the purposes of this chapter, language is defined as the vocabulary (words) that make up discourse, while discourse refers to the systematic organization of language as real-world text, the codified language of a field of inquiry or the relationship of language and structure and agency. The following sections review the specific relationships of language, cognition and space; place-naming; words and space; discourse and space; and textual approaches to the built environment. It concludes with a comparative ethnographic example of how talk reframes the social and spatial context of living in cooperative housing in Washington, DC and New York City.

Language and space approaches

Language, cognition and space

The relationship of language and space is most frequently assumed to be mediated by cognition, specifically the "*cognitive style* with which individuals of different cultures deal with space" (Levinson 1996: 356; emphasis in the original). Yet, as Stephan Levinson (1996) argues, social science has neglected the empirical study of everyday spatial notions due to an ethnocentric perspective that Western notions of space are universal. Neo-Whorfian findings, however, suggest that language plays an important role in molding thought, perception and action, as well as space and that there is considerable cultural variation in spatial notions and spatial orientation that correlate with culturally distinctive cognitive tendencies (Levinson 1996). Spatial descriptions of all types – from relative "left" to absolute "north," designations of front and back, and modes of wayfinding and spatial orientation – correlate with other cultural realms, including symbolic values, aesthetics, material cultural and kinesics (Levinson 1996).

The relationship of language to thought is one of the major controversies in the study of the mind. Cognitive science research has made considerable gains in demonstrating the causal link between how speakers of different languages think differently and provides evidence of how people talk can shape the way they think (Boroditsky 2010). For instance, speakers of languages that use gendered nouns, such as the feminine *la mer* (sea) in French and the masculine *el mar* (sea) in Spanish impart feminine and masculine properties to each, respectively.

The language, cognition and space linkage expressed through spatial descriptions, gendered terms and spatial orientation is a fundamental way of thinking about the relationship of language and space. But the emphasis on language as a form of cognition suggests that spatial relations are formulated solely in the mind and through thought. Some sociolinguists find this cognitive model too limited, and they have searched instead for a more practice-oriented, referential strategy where the speaker is an active agent employing language performance in a social world. Much of contemporary space and place research draws upon these language-as-practice and speech-as-action models.

Place-naming

Another kind of linguistic practice that has been used to study the relationship of language and space is through place-naming, variously referred to as toponymy or ethnogeography. Place names have been found to be of cultural significance at a variety of scales and locales, from Native American naming systems that focus on local flora and fauna, geographical features and spiritual importance to the renaming of urban streets, neighborhoods, cities, regions and nations in response to political transition or social trauma. Naming systems vary considerably, with small-scale locales often being descriptive, while large-scale place-naming, such as the renaming of Burma to Myanmar, depends on the historical, political and social meaning of the name as well as the choice of language in many post-colonial and post-Soviet contexts.

Cognitive anthropologists such as Eugene Hunn (1996) developed ethnosemantic analyses of place names in an effort to understand their cognitive foundations. He found a correspondence between toponymic density and the intensity of cultural focus in a region (Hunn 1996). For example, in the rural context of the Sahaptin Native Americans, he found that they characterize a site by the presence of plants or animals – their abundance, value, rarity (deer crossing), or mythological importance rather than empirical association (Hunn 1996). Other Native American place names are topographically based and describe terrestrial or hydrological features, such as a shoreline, with names that refer to sensory properties (roaring falls) or motion (rapid running stream). Hunn argues that for the Sahaptin of northwestern North America, the places that get named are "*places where things happen* . . . Rather than name each mountain, they named places in the mountains where they would go to dig roots, pick berries, hunt mountain goats, or encounter spirits" (Hunn 1996: 18). William Meadows (2008) adds that for another rural Native American group, the Kiowa, place names reference geographic forms and reflect sites of important historical and cultural events. Basso (1996) writing about the Apache and Karen Blu (1996) on the Lumbee, on the other hand, emphasize the moral and community identity dimensions of Native American place-naming (also discussed in Chapters 2 and 4.) These place-naming references to geography, subsistence activities, morals and history are brought together in Rupert Stasch's (2013) contention that the spatial form of the village has "poetic density" that includes cultural and landscape meanings, as well as social principles, politics and the structure of feeling for the Korowai of Papua, Indonesia.

Place-naming is a key cultural practice that situates people's minds in space and time, connecting them with local knowledge and stories and can be used critically as well as descriptively (Hedquist et.al. 2014). In a study of violence and memory in Medellín, Colombia, Pilar Riaño-Alcalá (2002) found that place names became a collective symbolic text for social commentaries and moral determination. She traces how *barrio* (neighborhood) names change due to periods of social stigma and exclusion and shows how place-naming can be used to resist negative place designations as well as to reinforce them. Toponymy was also used to track transformations in political ideology in Poland from 1949 to 1957 when the intentional renaming of cities and places was used to legitimize the ideological control of the Communist Party (Lebow 1999) or to contest the renaming in post-socialist Rumania (Light and Young 2014).

Words, movement and space

Words can also be understood through the movements that accompany them. For example, Alessandro Duranti examines the transnational Samoan expression *nofo i lalo* (sit down) and compares its use in a Western Samoan village and a suburban neighborhood in Southern California. In the Californian setting, the expression is used to establish a place for children to sit down, but also references the experience of sitting down in a Western Samoan house, one without furniture and walls. Specific commands such as *nofo i lalo* are a particular kind of interactional practice in which language, gestures and gaze are communicated through the channels of the voice, body and sight to produce a cultural space. The space created becomes part of a meaning system employed by parents to reconnect their children to an ancestral place or by cultural group member to establish a socially ordered physical space in this Samoan case.

Another way that words identify who you are and where you come from can be the contrast between slang and standard language practices. For example, the register of slang in Rio de Janeiro, Brazil, historically demarcates the physical space of the *favela* (shantytown) and the exclusion of its residents, while middle-class people claimed their class allegiance through standard language and secured communities (Roth-Gordon 2009, Caldeira 2000). Jennifer Roth-Gordon (2009) points out that in the Brazilian climate of fear and insecurity, marginalized *favela* dwellers draw on speech repertoires to claim their right to the city. Dark-skinned *favela* youth call themselves a *communidade* (community, a term not used by middle-class residents) and emphasize their shared status and suffering to highlight their social exclusion. Words such as *bum* (boom) punctuate their speech as they "manipulate linguistic registers to properly 'perform' the vulnerable citizen-subject and to inhabit or attribute the position of marginality" (Roth-Gordon 2009). The register of slang also recreates the shared safe space of the *favela* in otherwise dangerous contexts.

Other examples of the way that language is used to define identity and spatial location include the use of Mexicano to signify a rural and indigenous identity, and Spanish to signify greater urbanity in the work of Jane Hill (1995). Similarly, in Ecuador, standard Kichwa becomes associated with the city and elites, while vernacular Kichwa is associated with rural identity and authenticity (Wroblewski 2012). Thus words and their performance index space in multiple ways – linking transnational spaces, creating safe spaces and community for marginalized citizens, distinguishing rural versus urban residence and spatializing class and race.

Discourse and space

Discourse analysis and space and place

The term "discourse" refers 1) to linguistic approaches for understanding a group of utterances or texts and 2) to social theory approaches in which language or other semiotic systems construct reality and positions of knowledge and power (Hastings 2000, Foucault 1977, Modan 2007). Discourse analysis is therefore useful for exploring face-to-face social interactions as well as political economic questions in which the circulation of language and associated ideas reinforce hegemonic control. Both kinds of discourse and discourse analysis are crucial for understanding the relationship of language and space.

Many linguistic anthropologists trace their interest in practice-based approaches to the philosophers John Austin (1962) and John Searle (1969) who developed "speech act theory" that views language events as actions in the world with real consequences (Modan 2007, Hastings 2000, Schiffrin 1996). Austin (1962), in *How to do Things with Words*, notes that all utterances do not only report or describe but bring a state of affairs into being such as "I do" in a wedding ceremony. He calls these utterances "performatives" (Schiffrin 1996), speech that can make something happen, which gives agency to the speaker and redefines speaking as a material practice.

Modan (2007) and other linguists, including James Gee (1990) and Frederick Erickson (2004), use an informal way of describing the different uses and scales of discourse analysis. They employ "big D" Discourse to indicate the use of language or written text to represent and construct the world and certain ideologies (i.e., the social theory approach) and "small d" discourse to refer to the structure and organization of language (i.e., the linguistic approach). One crucial benefit of small d discourse is that it attends to linguistic structure, not just context; for example, what's said in the active voice and what's said in the passive voice reveals the way that subjective viewpoints are naturalized. Modan points out that:

> big D Discourses are also related to the little d discourses in that a social group's general ways of speaking, and the world views encoded in and promoted by those ways of speaking, are built up through an accrual of actual little d discourses over time.
>
> (2007: 277)

Modan suggests in her study of Mt. Pleasant residents living in a co-op apartment building in Washington, DC, that the residents are "a community of practice" (Lave and Wenger 1991) and participate in specific "discourses of place" (Modan 2007: 282).[2] These discourses construct the neighborhood as an urban and socially diverse space and locate it within a moral geography. Discourses of places are used to make claims to both space and rights to community membership (Modan 2007).

While multiple theories of discourse analysis have played an important role in the connection of actual talk (small d) to broader sociocultural, political, economic and historical forces (big D) within anthropology, the discursive turn in geography is derived mainly from two social theory strands of discourse analysis. The first is drawn from a Marxist critique of political economy and ideology, especially Gramsci's analysis of discourse as a tool of hegemony and recent work on discourse coalitions. The second is based on Michal Foucault's (1977) contention that language, knowledge and power are connected through discourse. The second strand is most commonly employed by critical geographers, but in practice, these approaches are often combined as is found in critical discourse analysis outlined by Fairclough (1995) and employed in my work on gated communities (Low 2003).

A fundamental tenet of sociolinguistics is that language is a form of social practice historically situated and dialectical to the social context, thus both socially shaped and socially shaping. Since language is widely perceived as transparent, it is often difficult to see how language produces, reproduces and transforms social structures and social relations. Yet it is through talk and discourse that social control and social domination are exercised – through the everyday social action of language. Critical discourse analysis offers a stronger focus on power relations to the well-established practice of ethnographically based discourse analysis that includes 1) the analysis of context, 2) the analysis of processes of text production and interpretation and 3) the analysis of the text.

One example is the way the word "nice" is used by New York and Texan gated community residents to talk about their desire for a socially controlled, middle-class White environment. "Nice" is an implicature, a linguistic term that refers to what is suggested in an utterance, even though it is not expressed or directly implied. Implicature functions by giving inexplicit information so the audience must generate its own meanings. For instance, gated communities residents talk about their insecurity and fear, but they are just as interested in finding a "nice" house in a "nice" community. In some cases, "nice" reflects the micropolitics of distinguishing oneself from the family who used to live next door. Status anxiety about downward mobility due to declining male wages and family incomes, shrinking job markets and periodic economic recessions increases concerns that their own children will not be able to sustain a middle-class lifestyle. Assurances that gated housing developments will maintain their value and attract "nice" neighbors are employed by real estate agents and developers to encourage prospective buyers to live in a gated community as a partial solution to upholding their middle- or upper-middle-class position. While nice does not specify any neighbor characteristics, gated community homebuyers hear "nice" as referring to middle-class and White residents.

Similar to the previous ethnographic example of the slang of *favela* residents in Rio de Janeiro, socially positioning oneself in contrast to others through the use of different registers and speech genres enables people to locate themselves both geographically and in terms of class or other group identities. This form of sociolinguistic variation has a historical link to regional variations in dialect and other studies of speech and pronunciation patterns. The connection of place identity and pronunciation, such as Barbara Johnstone's (2002) study of the use of the "ah" sounds in "downtown" (dahntahn) in Pittsburgh, is only one case from a large body of literature where the study of language variations reveal spatial location, human migration patterns and orientations to locally salient identity categories/positions.

Another way to link discourse and space is through a communications approach that Charles Briggs (2007) employs to understand how the state communicates its governing power to the local community through linguistic and spatial practices. He suggests that the production, circulation and reception of knowledge, values and ideas can be thought of as "communicable cartographies." In the same way that maps code subjects, produce identities and create hierarchies, acts of discourse construct their own unique communicable cartographies that can be traced as they emerge from particular places and travel through various sites and activities (Briggs 2007).

An ethnography of hip-hop and community radio in São Paulo, Brazil, also draws upon the spatial circulation of discourses such as rap songs and the places they reach to produce the idea that discourse creates a "conquering of space" with political implications (Pardue 2011). Derek Pardue argues that listening to the radio is a spatial as well as a social act for impoverished suburban residents, thus producing both a material place and a contested ideology. The marginality of hip-hop as a discursive practice "needs the presence of space to have any traction" (Pardue 2011: 107) and the materiality of such spaces combine with hip-hop discourse to produce indicators of class. Hip-hop linguistic practices and spatial referencing offer an important tool for reading social class through the study of how movements, sound and space come together at certain places and times, as well as how these nodes of space/time are interpreted and contested by their location and social context.

Discourse analysis in planning and development

Discourse analysis is frequently used in studies of urban restructuring and redevelopment that focus on how discourses of planning are manipulated by the municipal or other state authorities to change spatial representations and meanings. For example, Eugene McCann (2008) demonstrates how spatial imaginaries such as Richard Florida's creative city become geographically grounded stories, maps and texts that link policies and urban spaces in ways that obscure underlying social inequalities in Austin, Texas. Matthew Cooper (1993, 1994) examines how the Canadian royal commission's adoption of the discourse of bioregionalism, and its application to planning, helped the authorities to redraw the boundaries and reimagine the Toronto waterfront in Canada. Keith Jacobs (2004) in a study of the Chatham Maritime project in the U.K. uses discourse analysis to discuss the tensions that emerged in the context of government relations, partnership arrangements, project implementation and marketing and how the limited discursive space discouraged community involvement.

Gary McDonogh (1999) in his history of the changing "discourses of the city" in Barcelona traces the direct relationship between planning discourses such as "urban sustainability" and their material consequences in housing, social services, green spaces and the maintenance of neighborhoods, usually in ways that circumvent residents' participation. Recounting a more successful endeavor, Daniel Fisher (2012) examines efforts to remove Aboriginal people from public parks and town camps in Darwin, Australia, using a number of discourse analysis strategies to depict the complexity of the conflict. For instance, the media accounts report this land-based struggle is between the Aboriginal "mob" and the "campers," while Fisher frames it as a politics of recognition using local narratives of land ownership and memories to frame the different claims to the "bush spaces" (Fisher 2012).

The consequences of discursive practices even changed the restructuring of the early twentieth-century ghetto. Through historical documentation, Christopher Mele (2000) illustrates how state agencies and community members engaged distinct discourses to select and implement certain restructuring practices. He argues that employing discourse for urban restructuring has three explicit purposes, including 1) defining restructuring as normal and beneficial, 2) legitimizing restructuring and its social costs and 3) facilitating or rejecting the invention of a new place. The Moore Street Market, discussed in Chapter 8, is a case in which real estate agents renamed the neighborhood East Williamsburg to capitalize on the cachet of artistic Williamsburg, Brooklyn, instead of using its local name to justify the proposed closing of a Latino public market.

Of course, architectural and planning codes and standards play a role in restricting what can be built and in what form. Rather than focusing only on the discourses of planning, Ben-Joseph (2005) enumerates the rules and regulations that produce the contemporary landscape and argues that these codes and standards are the hidden language of space. The justification and naturalization of building and design codes is based on multiple discourses, including those of modernism, efficiency, health standards and governability, to convince citizens and governments that a particular redevelopment project provides a new future or greater vitality for a city or region.

Texts, landscapes and the built environment

The role of text in the environment and its semantic positioning in the landscape is a rapidly growing field within language and space studies. Studies of billboards and graffiti as means of social communication and of claiming a right to the city have been the mainstay of this research area (Masco 2005, Caldeira 2012, Iveson 2010, Borden et. al. 2001). The focus on billboards and graffiti is partly about how language in the form of written text marks and delimits space and more about the politics of the textual practices (Daveluy and Ferguson 2009).

Reading the landscape as a text has developed into the examination of written texts and the role they play in the built environment (Duncan and Ley 1993, Leeman and Modan 2010). For example, linguistic landscape studies discern the "ethnolinguistic vitality" of certain groups. The goal is to learn how minority languages, and by extension minority peoples, are faring from mapping language use and knowledge. These studies focus on the location and relationship of text in the environment and mapping of ethnolinguistic groups in multilingual and superdiversity settings (Blommaert, Collins and Slembrouck 2005).

A more recent avenue of investigation considers linguistic landscapes as social constructions that contribute to spatial meaning (Leeman and Modan 2010). These studies sample landscape texts over time or comparatively to produce insights about sociopolitical and cultural meaning. Jennifer Leeman and Gabriella Modan (2009), for example, link a microlevel analysis of Chinese language signs in Washington, DC's, Chinatown to specific sociogeographical processes of spatial commodification and gentrification.

Another approach explored by Scollon (2005) is to track the text on a can of tomatoes through its commodity cycle as an indicator of its relationship to the rapid restructuring of food production in the world system. He calls this textual project "nexus analysis" because it brings together a complex network of texts and discourses and their circulation by examining spatialized practices of daily food consumption, the worldwide industrialization of food production and the consequences for public and personal health.

Writing, reading and seeing text are also central to person-environment interactions and relations, especially in cities where they mediate people's relationships to the urban environment (Diaz Cardona 2012, 2016). Rebio Diaz Cardona (2012) argues that it is partly through texts, including technologically transmitted texts on cell phones and digital tablets as well as the plethora of signs, handbills, billboards, advertisements and storefronts, that the network society imagined by Manuel Castells (1996) becomes visible in daily life. He considers historical accounts of the increasing number of texts and readers in nineteenth century New York and their role in shaping the modern state to argue that wireless information and communication technologies furthers people's access to text and their ability to generate and circulate it.

Text, then, becomes a type of "stuff" that surrounds people and leads to an ongoing processing of written information that he conceptualizes as "ambient text," a theoretical approach that has advantages over the concept of linguistic landscape (Diaz Cardona 2016).

Ambient text is defined as text that people encounter in their multiple trajectories of daily life, and

> includes any portion of readable written text (alphabetic or otherwise) visible to a person in the immediate environment, including, for example, commercial signage and traffic signs, but also words written on mobile objects like a t-shirt or a shopping bag, the front page of a newspaper or a flyer blowing in the wind, a box of cereal or a bottle of beer, the text on a cell phone screen or a computer monitor, on all the books, smart phones and advertisements inside a subway car, on the carton held by a person asking you for a donation in the street and so on.
>
> (Diaz Cardona 2012: 3)

Text is recognizable even when reading is not possible, and it remains socially and psychologically relevant. Depending on the degree of language competence and proximity, text supports meaning-making – albeit imperfect or partial – for readers (Diaz Cardona 2012). In this sense, texts can be understood as nonhuman actors or "actants" that shape actions and outcomes in urban settings (Latour 2005, Diaz Cardona 2012). An ambient text framework calls into question the idea of the "built environment" as a static or completed product and posits instead "environmental-building," a dynamic material process that includes those texts on the street that people experience and share. This text-based analysis is useful for the ethnographic study of space and place because it offers a way to account for the agency of written texts, including signs, billboards and text messaging, and gives ambient text an active role in place-making and other forms of spatial relations.

The conceptual frame of language, discourse and space includes multiple methodological approaches from the study of place names and the relationship of words to specific locations to more complex research strategies of critical discourse analysis and ambient text. The wide range of ethnographic methods include taxonomic interviews, linguistic mapping, video and audio recording of speech acts, news media analyses and in-depth ethnographic studies of everyday conversations in the familiar and unfamiliar locations of people's lives. Language and discourse offer many entry points into an ethnography of space and place because of its ubiquity as a medium of social meaning and interaction. Yet a language and discourse approach to space can reveal unacknowledged ways that people include and exclude others and how even subtle discursive strategies produce very different kinds of space and place.

Ethnographic example

"Home and family" or "people like us"

To illustrate how these approaches to language, discourse and space are employed methodologically, two empirical studies are compared: my current fieldwork on co-ops in New York City and Modan's (2007) ethnography of a residential co-op in Mt. Pleasant, Washington, DC. In both cases, place discourses and narratives of inclusion and exclusion are used by residents to legitimate social and spatial relations and create a contested sense of community. The ethnographic cases are located in socioeconomically dissimilar cities and neighborhoods with different degrees of residential, cultural and racial diversity. However, the discursive structures of affiliation used in each reinforced, and in some cases exaggerated, these differences. (Figure 6.1 Map of Washington, DC, with Mt. Pleasant neighborhood and Figure 6.2 Map of New York City boroughs of Queens, Brooklyn and Manhattan)

The study of gated condominium communities in New York City, San Antonio, Texas; and Long Island, discussed in Chapter 7, found that the greatest impact on residents' social relations was the structure of private governance and not solely the walls and gates (Low 2003). To further investigate this counterintuitive finding, a study of market-rate housing cooperative apartment complexes – that is, co-ops, another form of private governance – was completed in 2015. The objective was to determine whether the same discourse that rationalized and legitimated social exclusionary and racist behavior in gated communities was observed in co-ops. We found that co-op residents do not talk about their fear of others and crime like gated community residents. Instead they employ a discourse of wanting to live with "people like us." They talk about the importance of the co-op board application process in creating social homogeneity by excluding those who do not pass the financial vetting or who look like they don't belong.

Gabriella Modan (2007) was also interested in the discursive practices she found in the co-op residence where she lived in Mt. Pleasant, Washington, DC. In her co-op apartment building, residents talked about their "home and family" and the importance of diversity in building a community. Phrases like "the families," referring to those who do the work in the co-op, or "the families want to purchase," referring to the people interested in buying apartments, were used (Modan 2007: 218). Unlike the New York City apartment complexes that are made up of market-rate co-op units, Modan's residence was a combination of low-equity co-op units and market-rate condominium apartments. The condominiums, however, attracted residents with different values, and the discourse in the building changed to "the family isn't what it used to be" to refer to the time when the co-op members worked closely together in a time of hardship before the influx of new residents (Modan 2007: 224).

Mount Pleasant
Neighborhood

Figure 6.1 Map of Washington, DC, with Mt. Pleasant neighborhood (Erin Lilli)

Figure 6.2 Map of New York City boroughs of Queens, Brooklyn and Manhattan (Erin Lilli)

This ethnographic example compares these contrasting discourses in the context of the two cities: New York City where gentrification, housing speculation, rising real estate values, preferred social homogeneity and exclusionary practices are well documented and Mt. Pleasant, Washington, DC, where redevelopment is moving much slower. Gentrification started much earlier in Mt. Pleasant, but stalled because of a downturn in the Washington, DC, residential market (Williams 1988).

The talk of the co-op residents distinguishes the social impact of political economic forces in each context. In Mt. Pleasant, place discourses and narratives of "home and family" are mobilized in the face of the influx of outsiders with different community values and as a strategy for contesting the ongoing transition from use value (home and living space) to exchange value (upscale condo housing). In New York City, the "people like us" discourse reinforces the increasing spatial governmentality (Merry 2001) and decreasing sociality of co-op apartment living that is emerging with the rapid appreciation of apartment prices, number of building conversions, reduction of rent stabilization programs and obsession with housing investment values. To flesh out these two ethnographic cases, I briefly present the social production of co-op housing in the United States, summarize the methodology used in New York City and Mt. Pleasant and provide examples of the discursive strategies used in each context.

Housing co-ops in the United States

The first co-op in New York City established in 1876 was known as a "home club" (Sazama 1996) and provided wealthy individuals with all the benefits and security of home-ownership while mitigating the individual responsibilities involved (Siegler and Levy 2001). Although at first rare, and intended primarily for the wealthy, co-ops became more working class and common by the twentieth century, as well as "more politically and socially progressive in their motivations" (DeFilippis 2003: 89). These politically and socially progressive goals were reflected in the adoption of a governance ethic known as the Rochdale Cooperative Principles. Established in England by the Rochdale Society of Equitable Pioneers in 1844, these Rochdale Cooperative Principles are a set of standards for the governance of all cooperatives (Conover 1959, Freeman 2002, Eisenstadt 2010).

During the Great Depression of the 1930s, many member-sponsored co-ops folded and were not revitalized until 1950 when the National Housing Act provided mortgage insurance for the buildings and residents (Sazama 1996; Goodman 2000). Starting in the 1970s, low-income co-ops, known as limited-equity co-ops, became more popular as a strategy to counteract disinvestment and abandonment in certain neighborhoods (DeFilippis 2003, Starescheski 2016). An example of this housing movement, the Mt. Pleasant co-op's struggle for ownership began in 1977 when the management company handling the rentals was indicted and the tenants fought for limited-equity cooperative ownership that was granted in 1984. Luxury and middle-class co-ops did not become popular again until the 1980s when an inability to profit from price-regulated rental units motivated landlords and tenants to convert their buildings to co-ops as a way to recoup their investment. (Goodman 2000).[3]

In co-ops, residents become members of a corporation or limited partnership that collectively owns an apartment building, apartment complex or group of attached or detached houses. Residents purchase shares that entitle them to a long-term "proprietary lease." Individual shareholders do not "own" their units, but own a percentage of shares. Fees covering maintenance, taxes and improvements are paid by residents in proportion to the number of shares they own.

The developer and/or owner(s) legally organize co-ops as corporations – that is, with a governance structure that includes a board made up of elected residents and the developer and owners if they still retain property in the development. In the New York City case, the co-op board makes all decisions about the finances and repairs and is protected by corporate legal statutes against lawsuits. However, in the Mt. Pleasant example, there is both a co-op board made up of the original owners and a condominium board that governs the new units. Two members of the co-op board are appointed to the condo board for continuity of decision making.

In New York City, the seller and the real estate agent present prospective buyers of an apartment or house to the co-op board. This involves a financial review, including tax returns and pay stubs as well as multiple letters of reference, among other materials, going back up to five years. Although co-op boards are not allowed to discriminate by race, ethnicity, age, gender and sexual orientation per U.S. housing law, they are allowed to refuse entrance to those whom the board feels are a financial risk. Co-op boards do not have to disclose their reasons for acceptance or refusal, and New York City market-rate co-ops are notorious for refusing prospective buyers who may even have already qualified for a mortgage and are ready to purchase the property.

New York City and Mt. Pleasant co-op methodologies

Gabriella Modan's (2007) ethnography of Mt. Pleasant is based on participant observation fieldwork conducted from 1996 through 1998. She took part in community activities, made detailed observations of residents' daily interactions and then interviewed them about their experiences of living in the building. As a linguistic anthropologist, she paid special attention to the role of talk and media discourse as Mt. Pleasant transitioned from a diverse and inclusive neighborhood to one struggling with conflicts generated by gentrification and increasing home prices.

Even before starting fieldwork, Modan lived in this limited-equity co-op and market-rate condo building. She describes the co-op members as "by and large working class," while the condo owners moving into the neighborhood in the mid-1980s were mostly middle- to upper-middle class (2007: 205). The renters who were living in the building were a mix. The difference in the class backgrounds between the co-op and condo members was a source of continuing conflict, which was reflected in the narratives of both groups. More condo owners were White, while the co-op members were African American, Latino, White and Caribbean/Caribbean American.[4]

The New York City co-op study began in July 2006, with data collection for the first phase completed in September 2008 after interviewing 24 co-op residents in twenty-three buildings in New York City.[5] From 2009 through 2015, a second phase focused on individual buildings with multiple interviews in each and participant observation of the shared spaces was completed (Photo 6.1 New York City co-op medium-sized building and Photo 6.2 New York City co-op large-sized building).Through personal

Photo 6.1 New York City co-op medium-sized building (Joel Lefkowitz)

contacts and interested colleagues, and in some cases, through a key informant, we located residents willing to be interviewed.

The sample of twenty-four residents used in this analysis own and reside in market-rate co-ops in Manhattan, Brooklyn and Queens. They range from twenty-seven to seventy-one years of age and a third identify as men, with the remainder identifying as female. Eighteen identify as White or Caucasian and six identify as African American, Latino, Filipino or Asian. Six of the participants identify as gay or lesbian, fourteen as heterosexual and four individuals did not identify their sexual orientation. All participants completed college and most had an advanced degree. The residents were lawyers, professors, artists, graphic designers, computer programmers, corporate vice presidents and research directors.

The open-ended interview was organized around a residential history and incorporated additional questions about doormen, the building conversion and application process. Interviews were conducted in the home with the individual or the couple together and ranged from forty minutes to one hour and forty-five minutes. Audio recordings of the interviews were made for accuracy and transcribed before the coding process commenced. Field

Photo 6.2 New York City co-op large-sized building (Joel Lefkowitz)

notes were also taken on site by the interviewer to account for visual cues that could later be used to help contextualize the analysis of interviewee responses. Buildings were located by block and neighborhood, as well as by size and configuration of the apartment, placement within the building and relationship to hallways, elevators, lobbies and other amenities. These interviews and the field notes are the basis of interview excerpts discussed in the following section.

"Home and family" in Mt. Pleasant[6]

Modan was struck by the way that the narratives and stories are structured around family and kinship terms, emphasizing family relationships between members and constructing co-op members as family (2007). She identifies two ways that kinship ties are used: 1) macrokinship linguistic strategies that "use the metaphor of family and kinship to describe relations among co-op members as a corporate group" (Modan 2007: 215) and 2) "micro-kinship strategies" that "highlight co-op members as family by pointing to members' kinship ties" (Modan 2007: 215). The use of these kinship terms contrasts with co-op members' references to the newer condominium residents as "the public." Even twenty years after the initial co-op conversion, co-op members fill their stories with kinship terms that create a value system and sense of community congruent with their struggle to gain ownership and tenant control.

Microkinship strategies include how co-op members place themselves within a family network. For example, Modan describes Joel, who calls his best friends in the building brothers and also locates them in a family network by their affinal (marital) and lineal (descendant) connections:

> It was really just myself and uh the, Flying Zavala Brothers, we called ourselves the Three Banditos. It was myself and Pedro Zavala, who was Angela's husband. And Eugene, whose daughter was just . . .
>
> (Modan 2007: 216)

Another strategy is employed by Joel to bring attention to the hardships imposed on families in the struggle to gain building ownership:

> So here we were living in the nation's capital, in supposedly the civilized center of the world, and we were living like third-world people. Without any heat or hot water and there were families there with children, and, the mothers had to, you know boil hot water to draw baths for their kids.
>
> (Modan 2007: 219)

Modan also writes about Mrs. Patterson, who links family life in the co-op (the babies had no heat) with her struggle with city political institutions to gain their recognition as tenants and owners:

> Because I was here when we all went down to Abilard Center, the school down there, and we invited Mayor Barry to come. Luisa-Luisa had um babies' bottles and different things and – you know, she's a spokesperson. And she told him that how the babies had – I mean ha – no heat! No hot water! And we had a lot of babies and those things you know.
>
> (Modan 2007: 218–219)

These discursive strategies incorporate all members   for example, Joel who is single – into the co-op kinship structure. The incorporation of individuals as both co-op and family members functions as a way to integrate and tolerate ethnic, racial, gender and value differences to produce a sense of social inclusion and home. Joel narrates his return to the co-op:

> But we felt we were acting in the best interests of the co-op and eventually – you know well we were, restored to – oh, a state of acceptance, *by the elders*. [. . .] Um I mean we've all sort of bonded with one

another even though we come from different backgrounds. [. . .] so –
and, to that extent, I'm sort of a *member of the family . . .*

(Modan 2007: 221)

The family and kinship discourse that co-op members use to recruit members into their social space is not extended to the new condominium owners, but instead developed into a discourse of "insiders" and "outsiders." Co-op members refer to condo owners as "the public" to exclude them and to criticize their values. Similar to New York City market-rate co-op members faced with newcomers with more money and class aspirations, the Mt. Pleasant co-op members resort to talking about "people from outside who came in" (Modan 2007: 232) or "selling the other units to the public" (Modan 2007: 231). The newcomers are described as treating old-timers with contempt, not recognizing who belongs to the building and not being concerned about others who live in the building, thus, as not being part of the family.

The contrast between the co-op members and the condominium owners anticipates the change in social relations that occurs when limited-equity co-op units become market rate. In the New York City example that follows, there is an absence of this discourse of family and kinship that ties people together across race, ethnicity, gender and class. Instead, a sense of safety and feeling at home is accomplished through living with "people like us."

"People like us"

At the start of the co-op project, it was assumed that co-op residents would utilize an inclusive discourse to create community rather than the "fear of crime" talk that gated community residents employ to justify keeping others out. Instead, we found that interviews elicit a discourse that employs homogeneity and indicators of socioeconomic class to construct a sense of inclusion, but at the same time functions as an exclusionary and racist strategy.

The discourse of "fear of crime" expressed by gated community residents is not just about incidents of burglary but also about those who are thought to perpetrate it (Low 2003). Gated communities do not have public places where strangers intermingle, and their relative isolation and homogeneity discourages interaction with people who are identified as "other" and seems to increase their fear of those who enter from "outside."

Co-op apartment residents, on the other hand, live in New York City, a diverse and socially complex setting. Yet instead of talking about their fear of others, co-op residents feel safe and secure in their buildings, even when they do not trust the safety of the neighborhood. This sense of security is attributed to the perceived homogeneity and the discourse of "people like us" created by the co-op board application process.

For example, Ruth, a mother with two children living on the Upper West Side of Manhattan comments on her decision to live in her co-op building: "I think it was sort of like who was in the building? You know, like who – not wanting people to be in the building if they hadn't gone through the admission process or something like that." Vanessa, a young, single professional, explains why she likes her co-op:

> . . . there is a certain feeling like knowing that anyone else had to go through the same agony to get by the co-op board, it almost makes me feel a little bit better . . . that my next door neighbor isn't this axe-murderer or that they are not paying their rent by selling drugs [laughs].

Patricia, who lives in an upscale building on the Upper East Side of Manhattan, explains her reasons for buying a unit in her building:

> I think there is a lot of homogeneity in this building . . . I really trusted the homogeneity of the building, that I was not going to find someone so very different from me.

Others perceive the same application process that produces the homogeneity most residents find comforting as racist. Without attributing the selection process to active racism, there were numerous incidents where people of color felt treated differently. Yul, a self-identified Filipino, talks about what he perceived as a racist question during his application interview:

> . . . towards the end that [White] guy asked me "What's your race?" and I could tell the [other board members] were pissed off he asked, but you know, I do get weird questions as a minority sometimes, things they won't ask in a job interview that you could sue for . . . in my Manhattan apartment one [board member] guy, they asked me "Do you cook any ethnic food that smells offensive?"

Yvonne, a young Korean American, explains her concerns about how the co-op board's ability to reject applicants without explaining their reasons can lead to a perception of racial and ethnic discrimination:

> I think co-op boards can get away with discrimination without . . . out-wardly . . . doing it outwardly because they don't have to tell you what they like and what they don't like . . . someone . . . she was an elderly woman and I think she had said "Oh could you hold the door open for me?" and if I had heard that I obviously would have held the door but I didn't . . . when she came out she was just like "You Chinese women." I was like [clap] I turned around and I was like "Are you talking to me?"

[laughs] Because I was the only Asian person around here so there will be days ... I think it has to do with, and, and it might be my perception that I think that this building is ... generally like older White and it's changing, but you know, I just, I can' ... it just shocked me. I'm like, we're in New York [laughs] and I just got called "Chinese" on the street [laughs].

Even though some residents dislike the application process and the financial vetting by the co-op board and even question it, in the final analysis, residents like Kerry decide that it is probably "a good thing" and explain why it is important:

First I'm thinking, like you know, "oh, that's a drag. Who are they to say?" ... do you just want people who – sort of haven't been vetted, walking around – But – but how do you know how to vet people? ... if you're vouched for by an employer or two and you have the money to pay for it, you should be in no matter who – unless you're clearly on – like a freaky, you know, person – although I don't know who's supposed to be the judge of that. . . . I think that's probably – a good thing, probably.

Some White co-op residents understand their sense of safety and notion of living with similar people is produced by and produces a kind of "laissez-faire racism" that economic and social structures such as housing, labor and social status tend to perpetuate (Bobo, Kluegel and Smith 1997). Gary who lives in Queens told us:

Cause first of all, there's an income screen. By the time you enter a building like that, people have at least, can afford to rent and they can mortgage a million-dollar condo. Like the apartment, I bought this for six fifty. The one that's identical to this just got sold and was sold for a million two. And the person that bought it was not acceptable to the board. Then it got re-sold for approximately a million. So, by the time you're at that level, uh, you're color blind but you don't see that many colors.

When a prospective buyer is turned down by the co-op, even if the buyer already has obtained a mortgage and the seller accepts the price and the specifics of the agreement, the seller must refuse the offer and, as in the aforementioned case, might have to accept a lower offer from someone who is more acceptable to the board.

Gary who lives with his boyfriend is surprised when he realizes what he is saying when talking about who lives in his building. He then tries to distance himself from what could be perceived as a racist attitude by mentioning that he has Hispanic and Asian friends:

> Ahm . . . it is definitely based on money. I know that this apartment is twenty-three hundred a month if I was renting it or if you add my mortgage plus my maintenance it is twenty-three hundred a month. So you have to have people who have money, ahm . . . I am trying to think if I have ever seen – I don't know are . . . I would say that the majority just so happens to be White. I am just trying to think I have. I don't think I have seen. I think I have seen like Hispanic people. I don't know if I have ever seen African Americans other than the super. Ahm . . . honestly, I never thought of it until you brought it up. [He laughs.] I think it just so happens, I think, because they are really picky in the financials they wanna make sure people can afford it, ahm . . . I am not the type of person who is racist. I could be like best friend with someone who is African American or Hispanic or you know Asian that doesn't matter at all. What matters to me is that people take pride in where they are, you know. I am not really hanging out here and spending a lot of time here. You know one of my dearest friends is Asian. The person I am seeing is Hispanic. It doesn't – I don't think it bothers me, you know as long as people respect the place. It is interesting because I never thought about it until you brought it up [laughs].

A number of co-op residents commented that the only African Americans that they see in their buildings are staff members, such as doormen, supers and janitors. In one building where there is a roof garden, the co-op board passed a series of rules that only allowed shareholders to use it because they didn't want caretakers and the families of caretakers – who were mostly African Americans – to have access to this space.

Even though some residents try to distance themselves from the governance practices of the co-op – the financial vetting, lengthy application process, use of ethnic or racial stereotypes for treating "others" rudely – real estate agents also act as gatekeepers by showing apartments only to the "right kind" of people. For example, Beth, who is African American, told me about her experience at an open house with a broker who thought she was interested in his co-op listing:

> I guess he knew the board would be most concerned about whether the applicant would be able to, um, have the financials for the place. And so his concern was always with the money thing. And for some reason, he assumed that I was looking at the place. Or maybe he was confused by the way I was dressed. It was summertime and I was wearing some you know, I was like half-naked or something. Think he was a little skeptical, "Like what is this woman [laughs] in here looking at this expensive place?" And he asked me what I did. He was very, that was the most

direct kind of [pause] question that was asked in the context of an open house. And he said, "What do you do for a living?" And I said, "I'm a physician." I think that put his mind at ease. He was like "whew."

But maintaining a purified social environment also requires constant vigilance. It is not only that the residents must be similar to assure a sense of safety but also that the people around the building – such as those sitting on the front steps – reflect the same social class, age, ethnicity and values. Martha brings up a woman who she feels threatens the image of her co-op building:

> Like when you leave here you may very well see an old woman sitting outside the building as if, well, as if there was a stoop there like in the old neighborhood . . . She's much to the consternation of people on the board . . . they think it brings down the cachet (of the building). Her crew and they come and hang out and the thing is that, their thing is they don't even know if she lives in the building! She was a dear friend of another woman who has now gone into a nursing home who no longer lives in the building . . . Now that woman is gone and she still . . . and apparently she draws all of the other older people from the neighborhood who don't live here either.

Negotiating the "people like us" formula is complicated by who can be evicted for breaking the building rules. For example, one woman has a dog that bit a child and she is a renter, so technically the board could ask her to leave. But as Keith explains, the moral standing of this woman as a Holocaust survivor put her beyond the social control of the board, even though they want to be rid of the dog and also to gain access to the rent-controlled apartment to convert it to an owner-occupied unit:

> I don't know if I would be able to keep that dog if I had it, but um . . . they made her out to be like she was the evil one attacking people. Anyway, so he wears this muzzle now. And so the board tried to get her kicked out, and I think that some of that was they wanted this big, three-bedroom, rent-stabilized apartment, you know that she probably pays three hundred a month. Anyway, the mother is a Holocaust survivor, and it's really tough to kick out a Holocaust survivor. We're just not going to do it, you know. So, anyway, so she's here and she's the big pariah.

These discursive strategies of who should or should not be included as co-op residents are made up of a complicated set of financial, moral and visual codes for evaluating social worth and class.

While the financial vetting is the most relied upon, the moral and visual codes of acceptability play a secondary, boundary-maintaining role. Once in the co-op, there is the problem of becoming involved in a conflict, since, as pointed out by Keith, the board has the ability to kick you out for any transgression of the existing rules and regulations.[7] Thus, like gated community residents, a strategy of moral minimalism – that is, using the board or other outside institutions to solve any conflict and reducing social contact among neighbors – is seen as adaptive. As Larry suggests,

> I think the best way to live in a co-op in New York City is to maintain as friendly a relationship with people, with pleasantries and so forth, but live your quiet life because I don't know. What's the Italian expression, "Don't shit where you eat?" You shouldn't, you know, have a very involved life with people.

When Yul, who lives in Queens, mentions a problem with another resident, he recounts the series of steps he tried to resolve the issue, even as everyone, including the board, attempted to distance themselves from the problem: "I told my friend the captain [of the building], and she brought it to the board's attention. And they said when you catch him doing it, call the security guard, and he'll come up and stop the guy." Vanessa worries about bringing anything up with her neighbors because of how they might view her: "I think I'd probably rather have them get involved [the board], I don't want to be the one to make waves, I rather like [to] report it anonymously." While Yvonne simply says that she is always worried about getting caught doing something that does not fit the implicit social code: "I always feel like someone's watching over my shoulder, and I don't like that feeling you know, and I think this building is particularly strict." Even though residents assure themselves that they are living with "people like us," co-op interviewees still attempt to resolve conflicts by not confronting each other and resorting to indirect tactics.

The discourse of "people like us" brings together these contradictory inclusive and exclusive practices within the space of the co-op building. Compared to the Mt. Pleasant co-op members' discourse of "home and family" that serves to unify residents across class and race, "people like us" creates a sense of safety and comfort through homogeneity and, at the same time, excludes those who do not fit within this discursively constructed and materially enforced governance regime. Yet it also seems to create a sense of insecurity in the sense that the residents seem to feel they are always being surveilled and at risk of losing their status or being sanctioned. The comparison of these place discourses and their material outcomes and impact on social relations illustrates how discourse is a critical part of any spatial analysis. The two methodologies used – the sociolinguistic transcriptions and long-term participant observation of Modan (2007) and tape-recorded residential histories, field notes and maps of the New York City study – produce evidence of how residents' discursive strategies changed the meaning and sense of place in these co-op buildings.

Conclusion

The study of the relationship of language and discourse to space expands the promise of social constructivism and a language-based model of communication by enabling a more critical stance through discourse analysis. The strength of discourse is its ability to uncover meanings and power just as easily in what is spoken as in what is not said. As Modan demonstrates in her Mt. Pleasant ethnography and as I have shown in the New York City co-op study, "the way we talk about the places we live has material implications for how those places change and develop" (Modan 2007: 7) and restricts the space to those who discursively "belong."

The weakness of discourse is that meaning-making and the discursive politics of space are linguistic and cognitive modalities that can be difficult to integrate with other analyses of space and place. While this chapter has illustrated how performative aspects of discourse can have a significant impact on the built environment, the discursive power of planning practices and spatial imaginaries can effectively cover up social inequalities. Nonetheless, there remains the concern that these linguistic models depend too heavily on theories of representation that are being questioned by proponents of nonrepresentational theory discussed in the following chapter. Thus the next chapter examines another conceptual lens that also draws its foundations from social constructivism and symbolic theory, but has evolved into a robust spatial approach that includes how space is both understood and created through emotion, affect, affective atmosphere and affective climate.

Notes

1 In the Saussurean tradition semiology is the study of meaning-making, signs, symbols and meaningful communication.
2 Similar to William Labov's (1972) notion of a "speech community," where members have shared use and understandings of linguistic features. The key to the concept is that they both use language in the same way and interpret it with the same social meanings.
3 According to the American Housing Survey (USHUD 2005), 0.6 percent of all owner-occupied homes in the United States are co-ops. Only 7.3 percent of these co-ops include residents below the poverty rate, so the majority of co-ops consist of middle- and upper-income owners. Over 80 percent of U.S. co-ops are located within New York City (Schill et al 2006).
4 For a full account of her methodology, see Modan (2007)
5 The New York City Co-op study was undertaken by the Public Space Research Group of the Graduate Center of the City University of New York with the assistance of graduate student research assistants funded by the PhD programs in Environmental Psychology and Earth and Environmental Sciences. The first phase included Gregory Donovan and J. Gieseking, and the second included Owen Toews, Hillary Caldwell and Jessica Miller.
6 Both Modan and I are interested in how people use language and discourse to include and exclude others. Much of my work has been on the discourse of fear of others used by gated communities residents to rationalize having gates and a

secured entrance as described in Chapter 7. Modan, on the other hand, is concerned with how Mt. Pleasant neighbors marginalize each other by constructing and highlighting ethnic difference (2007: 206). Her analysis of co-op discourse, however, diverges from this focus on exclusionary strategies and shows how the theme of "home and family" is used across ethnic boundaries to create a tight-knit residential community.

7 These transgressions are listed in the Covenants, Conditions & Restrictions of the co-op incorporation documents that are given to residents upon application. However, the board has the power to create new rulings if passed by the board and the co-op membership at large.

Chapter 7

Emotion, affect and space

Introduction

This chapter reviews the significant contribution that the study of emotion and affect offers the ethnography of space and place. Research on emotive landscapes and emotive institutions, as well as the insight that emotions are always socially constructed and key to understanding the culturally constituted self and lived world are foundational. These ideas provide a basis for the ethnography of space and place where emotion is the sociocultural *emotion* fixing of affect in individual lives through personal experience and meaning-making. But while some contend that affect theory recapitulates the mind/body dualities that plague the study of emotion, the addition of the concepts of affect, affective atmosphere and affective climate offer more for understanding space and place. These theoretical constructs, when employed in the study of the built environment, access the transpersonal domain and allow "feeling" to affect, circulate and infect more than one person. Affective atmosphere and affective climate also provide models of how to bring together the social, linguistic and cognitive dimensions of everyday life with the material environment.

It is not that the concept of emotion is unimportant to space and place studies. To the contrary, emotion in this analysis is the labeling of sensation and the making sense of feeling in a socially constructed and communicable way. Without the concepts of emotion, emotive landscapes and emotive institutions, a critical part of what happens to people in place and how they experience and express it is lost. As James Fernandez (1986) points out, humans use emotion to make sense of who they are in the world. But current theories of emotion do not encompass how places feel or how feeling makes places except through linguistic labeling and consciousness of the individual. To move away from this constraint, the study of space and place also needs conceptualizations, such as affect, and metaphors, such as affective atmosphere and affective climate. These concepts enable greater flexibility and creativity in our thinking as we encounter spaces and environments that are designed to affect us politically and influence our deepest feelings.

This chapter takes one step in attempting to define some of these terms and develops new ideas about how this challenge can be faced.

An example of how emotion and affect constructs are useful occurred when interviewing residents in downtown Manhattan a year after the September 11, 2001, attacks on the World Trade Center towers (9/11).[1] Not surprisingly, many residents who had lived there before the attacks reported experiencing an ongoing sense of fear. A number of those who moved into the area after 9/11 also said that they emotionally responded to the fear-laden atmosphere and ruin-filled landscape. It was more intriguing to find that while 25 percent of the sixty-five residents interviewed during the summer of 2002 said that the primary impact of 9/11 was a heightened sense of fear and anxiety, by the end of 2003, 60.2 percent of the 124 interviewees mentioned these emotional changes (Low, Taplin and Lamb 2005). Even talking about 9/11 and terrorism was linked to worry over becoming a victim and being less likely to go outside (West and Orr 2005). The initial shock of the collapse of the World Trade Center towers and the iconic media representation of the crumbling towers evoked a visceral response in residents and created an intense affective atmosphere in downtown Manhattan that then continued to be interpreted and expressed in an ever-expanding litany of individually experienced emotions.

These emotions, however, should not be considered independent of the historical moment in which they occurred and were intensified by a social and political context of fear and distrust. Residents' fear and anxiety were provoked both by the initial event being constantly replayed (an affective atmosphere based on a shared event) and also by an unpopular war in Iraq, the specter of Homeland Security, and the passing of the Patriot Act that resulted in a threatening political climate (a national affective climate) that became salient nationally and locally.

Emotion and affect are key elements in the creation, interpretation and experience of space and a constitutive component of place-making. It is difficult to imagine a space or place without associated or embedded affectivity. Yet research on the relationship of emotion and affect to space and its theorization is limited in the ethnographic literature. For this reason, this chapter attempts more than just an overview of the relevant literature and ethnographies, but examines the various theoretical foundations that make up this conceptual frame. The discussion, though, focuses on understanding the relationship of emotion, affect and space in a way that distances itself from traditional analyses of emotion and place, such as place attachment (Low 1992, Low and Altman 1992), place memories and studies of how landscapes evoke feelings based on their symbolic meanings. These relationships are covered in Chapter 4 on the social construction of space.

The conceptualization addressed here is the reciprocal and ever-changing relationship of personal and collective emotions with space and place without recourse to psychological and biological reductionist models. It includes the literature on affect as well as atmosphere and climate to consider a more productive way of studying the "feel" of space and a "sense of place." The addition of emotional response, affect, affective atmosphere, emotive landscape and affective climate offer concepts that encourage a more nuanced consideration of what is meant by the feeling that a place is "happy," "safe" or "threatening." The goal is to develop a workable terminology and methodology that enables the affective and emotive aspects of spatial production and experience to be more effectively incorporated in ethnographic practice.

This theoretical exposition begins with ethnographic efforts to resolve the mind-body duality of psychological theories of emotion by discussing Catherine Lutz and Geoffrey White's path-breaking review article (Lutz and White 1986) and John Leavitt's (1996) and Kay Milton's (2005) alternative resolutions to the problem. Classic studies of emotion and the built environment (Fernandez 1984, Ross 2004, White 2006) are also considered. The next section introduces the "affective turn" of the 1990s, in cultural studies and the social sciences highlighting the work of Kathleen Stewart (2007), Nigel Thrift (2008), Ben Anderson (2006), Gregg and Seigworth (2010), Steven Pile (2010), Ruth Leys (2011) and Patricia Clough (2007; Frank, Clough and Seidman 2013). These understandings of "affect," framed by Raymond William's (1977) concept of the "structure of feeling" and Felix Guattari's (1995) and Deleuze and Guattari's (1987) theoretical explorations, then become the basis for a discussion of work on emotive landscapes, affective atmospheres and emotional and affective climate. The terms emotion, emotive landscape, affective climate and affective atmosphere are defined and provide a conceptual lens for the concluding ethnographic examples that include the "new emotions of home" in U.S. gated communities and the affect and feelings experienced in Cairo during the Midan al-Tahrir (Liberation Square) protests.

Emotions and space

The study of emotion

The social science study of emotions has struggled to resolve the mind-body dualism of psychology that views emotion as either an instinctual and unmediated bodily process or a predominately mental, i.e., perceptual-cognitive, process or assessment. The neurobiological approach developed from Darwin (1965 [1872]), who identified emotions as a set of adaptive hardwired instincts, includes Tomkins's (1962, 1963) "affect theory," Ekman's (1980, 2003) "neurocultural" facial and bodily expressions and Izard's (1990) "differential emotions theory" in which emotion is defined by neurobiological activity.

Barrett (2015), however, discredits the idea that specific emotions, bodily sensations and facial expressions are the same for all individuals or can be located in any one part of the brain. A cognitive approach, as represented by Lazarus (1991), posits instead that emotions are cognitive assessments of neurobiological phenomenon and that these mental appraisals structure and organize experience. A few psychologists have also attempted to integrate these perspectives, including James (1884) who suggests that there is an initial physical response to a stimulus that results in a subjective feeling that is mentally apprehended. The neurobiologist Damasio (1999, 2003a, b) also makes a similar distinction between "emotion" as the physical response to the stimulus and "feeling" as the perception of emotion.

In anthropology, biological versus cognitive theories have been abandoned as new ways of thinking have redirected the theoretical arguments in productive ways. Catherine Lutz and Geoffrey White (1986) examine a decade of research on emotions and the impact of the psychological research and theory on cultural and psychological anthropology. They clarify how two-stage psychological models (such as emotion to feeling, or biological response to labeling of response) overlook the role of culture in interpretation and perception, arguing that this translation process is culturally embedded and learned. Their key theoretical concept is the "culturally constituted self," positioned at the "nexus of personal and social worlds" (Lutz and White 1986: 417). Emotion emerges as a way to talk about intentions, actions and social relations, setting the stage for a discussion of its social and cultural construction (Heider 1991).

Catherine Lutz's ethnography of the Ifaluk in Micronesia explores how emotional meaning is structured by cultural systems and social practice, arguing that emotion is not precultural, but "pre*eminently* cultural" (1988: 5). Building upon Michelle Rosaldo's notion of emotion as "embodied thoughts" (1980) and Margaret Lock and Nancy Scheper-Hughes's "mindful body" (1987), she takes the position that emotion is a way of talking about something that is inherently cultural and focuses on its socially constructed nature. Lutz links cognition and emotion by asking what role reasoning and thought play in how the Ifaluk talk about emotion and relies on symbolic theory to suggest that understanding what someone is feeling is an interpretive task. Citing Clifford Geertz (1971), emotion is seen as part of the culturally constructed web of meaning made up of cultural symbols and modes of social interaction. Thus words such as "anger" or "fear" require translation from one cultural context to another.

Lila Abu-Lughod and Catherine Lutz (1990) develop the social construction of emotion approach further by suggesting that it is through discourses of emotion as social practices that emotion can be best studied and understood. Criticizing views of emotions as "things" that cultural systems must deal with or as psychic energies that must be defused (Abu-Lughod and Lutz 1990: 2–3), they argue this problem is resolved if emotional discourses are analyzed as socially situated practices within fields of power. These socially situated practices are spatialized, thus linking discourse and place as discussed in the Chapter 6.

Geoffrey White (2000b) illustrates this point by employing a prototypical scenario for the study of emotional schema (social event → emotion → action response) in the Solomon Islands. He examines the ways that "culturally defined emotions are embedded in complex understandings about identities and scenarios of action, especially concerning the sorts of events that evoke it, the relations it is appropriate to, and the responses expected to follow from it" (White 2000a: 47). This schema can be applied to a variety of settings and places to locate the interpretive discourses used to move from an event through an emotion to a final response and resolution.

John Leavitt (1996) disagrees with Lutz, White and others about the centrality of social construction and discourse analysis for the study of emotion and instead returns to the mind-body problem. He focuses on emotion as bodily feeling, citing both Victor Turner's (1967) and Robert Desjarlais' (1992) characterization of emotion as more visceral or physiological than cerebral. He argues that emotions are transindividual, "learned and expressed in the body in social interactions through the mediation of signs, verbal and non-verbal" (Leavitt 1996: 526).

Kay Milton (2005), on the other hand, starts with James's and Damasio's formulations of emotion-feeling as a response to environmental stimuli. She reframes Damasio's theory into an ecological model in which emotions and feeling operate between an organism and the environment. An ecological approach locates emotion in the relationship between the individual and the social and nonhuman environment and "does not privilege the social over the non-social" (Milton 2005: 203). The ecological model offers a way to think about space and emotion-feeling since emotion is intrinsic to the person-environment interaction, but Milton thinks this relationship exists only between the individual and the environment and is not transindividual, as Leavitt and other scholars interested in social construction have argued.

Emotions and the built environment

There are a few classic works in sociology, environmental psychology, anthropology and geography that offer ways to consider space and place as producing particular kinds of feelings. Max Weber (1930) writes about the anxious spirit of capitalism and the emotional consequences of class exploitation producing anger and resentment in urban centers. Georg Simmel (1955) and Louis Wirth (1938) suggest that the emotional state of urban dwellers is shaped by the multiple stimuli of the modern city as well as by its class relations. The Chicago School proposes an ecological model in which the built environment is a component of the urban emotional and social relational landscape (Park, Burgress and McKenzie 1996).

Environmental psychologists, most notably Ralph Taylor (Wang and Taylor 2006), Jack Nasar (Nasar and Fisher 1994) and Douglas Perkins (Long and Perkins 2007), write about the impact of landscapes on a sense of fear and danger. Much of this work employs walking simulations and laboratory experiments to study people's fear and concern for their personal safety. These studies rely on an ecological theory of emotion that assumes individual feelings are elicited by specific aspects of the built environment that are measurable and predictable, but do not include the social context or locate people in naturally occurring settings (see Day 2006 for an important exception).

Anthropologists offer cultural analyses of the role of architecture and the built environment on emotional life. The best-known example is James Fernandez's concept of the "architectonic" – that is, "the feeling tones that activity in various constructed spaces evokes and that makes them places" (1984: 31). Fernandez (1984) is concerned with explaining how the architectonic evokes feeling by comparing three African groups, each living in a different ecological zone with a distinct feeling tone and culturally specific built environment. Expanding upon a theory of "emotional movement in social life," he argues that social subjects (the I's, you's, he's and they's of social life) are inchoate and that rituals and sacred spaces provide for the recurrent transformation of the inchoate into identity and meaningful experience. The emergent qualities that participants realize include feelings evoked by the space and the performance of ritual practices.

White (2006, 2000), drawing upon his earlier work on emotional discourse, schema and meaning, applies these insights to war memorials, including Pearl Harbor. He uncovers how the memorial space, the monument and the interpretive structure of movement through the memorial, as well as the films and other discursive products offered at the site, instruct visitors on how to feel – a kind of "domestication of affect" (2006: 50). There are cues that shape the feeling and the emotive landscape of a built environment such that the individual comes to the culturally appropriate emotional state not just through discourse but also through the structure of movement and the architectural and material culture details of the space.

As part of the emerging field of emotional geographies, Zembylas (2011) and Davidson, Bondi and M. Smith (2005) also locate emotions in space by emphasizing their sociality and challenging assumptions that emotions are private or individual. They derive their approach from earlier humanistic and phenomenological traditions within geography and contemporary nonrepresentational theory (Pile 2010, Thrift 2008). Emotional geographies link space to emotion through a complex set of relational and spatial circulations, including

> the complex range of emotions that emerge as a consequence of movement, that is the circulation of emotions through individuals and collective bodies (Ahmed 2004), shaping social relationships and challenging the taken-for-granted boundaries of the self; and, the strong links

between emotion and space/place, that is, the emotionally dynamic spatiality of belonging and subjectivity.

(Zembylas 2011: 152)

Zembylas (2011) claims that emotions circulate as actions and practices and identifies how negative emotional geographies are created by practices of exclusion and discrimination within a multicultural school. Although the architecture of the school remains in the background of the analysis, the objective is to materialize emotions as they produce exclusionary racial discourses that segregate schoolchildren. Emotional geographies' formulation of the relationship of emotion and space offers ethnographers a methodology focused on practice that inscribes emotion in space.

Theories of emotion and the built environment suggest fruitful avenues for the ethnographic study of space and place that emphasize thoughts, beliefs, practices and settings as the conduits of emotion from people to place and back. Each of these is useful for an ethnographer, but tend to focus more on individual rather than collective experience, leaving open the question of how the material environment transmits feeling.

Affect and space

The affective turn of the 1990s

Theories of affect offer new ground for scholars interested in how feelings influence and structure everyday life, politics and space and place. This "affective turn" has displaced much of the earlier thinking on emotion, and it offers a number of avenues for theorizing the space/emotion/affect interface, even though proponents continue to struggle with the same mind-body dualism of psychological theories. According to Leys,

> The claim is that we human beings are corporeal creatures imbued with subliminal affective intensities and resonances that so decisively influence or condition our political and other beliefs that we ignore those affective intensities and resonances at our peril.

(2011: 436)

Affects are considered by theorists as occurring prior to ideology and described as presubjective, prepersonal visceral intensities that influence our thinking and feelings. Ben Anderson offers the definition of "a transpersonal *capacity* which a body has to be affected (through an affection) and to affect (as the result of modification)" (2006: 735).

Most reviews of affect theory identify two major trajectories that utilize neurobiological research to bolster their arguments (Leys 2011, Gregg and Seigworth 2010). The first is best known through the work of Eve Kosofsky

Sedgwick (2003) and Daniel Lord Smail (2008). Sedgwick draws upon Tomkins's and Ekman's findings because they provide evidence for a "nonintentional, corporeal account of the emotion" (Leys 2011: 439). For Sedgwick and Smail, affects are innate and hardwired, triggered by the brain-body and functioning outside of consciousness without cognitive intervention. The second approach is influenced by the monistic ideas of Spinoza (1985 [1679]), James (1884) and Deleuze and Guattari (1987) and "locates affect in the midst of things and relations (in immanence) and, then, in the complex assemblages that come to compose bodies and worlds simultaneously" (Gregg and Seigworth 2010: 6). This view of affect is found in the work of Massumi (2002), Thrift (2008), Stewart (2007) and many others.

Both approaches separate affect and emotion, emphasizing the transcorporal, inhuman and contagious aspects of affect and its capacity to affect and to be affected as resolving the conceptual limitations of emotion as an individual and personal experience or feeling. Some scholars are only concerned with affect and subsume emotion within it through the use of Spinoza's concept of immanence (Deleuze 2001) or affect's absence of agency (Clough 2007, 2013). Deleuze and Guattari (1987) define all things human and nonhuman by their affects and intensities.

Anderson (2006) offers a three-layer model made up of the deepest noncognitive layer of affect, the precognitive layer of feelings that lie between affects and emotion and the cognitive layer of emotions that are conscious and experienced. Others retain the term emotion for the articulation of affect and ideology (Grossberg 2010) or the sociolinguistic labeling of personal experience within a social and cultural world (Anderson 2006). As Massumi suggests,

> an emotion is a subjective content, the sociolinguistic fixing of the quality of an experience which is from that point onward defined as personal. Emotion is qualified intensity, the conventional, consensual point of insertion of intensity into semantically and semiotically formed progressions, into narrativizable action-reaction circuits, into function and meaning. It is intensity owned and recognized.
>
> (2002: 28)

Emotion is used by these scholars as the sociocultural fixing of affect in individuals' lives through personal experience and meaning-making. Affect then refers to the corporeal intensity that has the ability to transform and move people transpersonally. Affects flow between bodies by circulation, transmission and contagion and allow for the removal of boundaries between human and nonhuman, thus enabling alternative social formations such as assemblages, knots, collections and networks of affective flows (Deleuze and Guattari 1987, Latour 2005, Amin and Thrift 2002).

The anthropologist Kathleen Stewart draws upon Deleuze and Guattari, Massumi and others to formulate her concept of "ordinary affects" – that is, the "varied, surging capacities to affect and to be affected that give everyday life the quality of a continual motion of relations, scenes, contingencies and emergencies" (2007: 2). Through personal vignettes, she identities ordinary affects as "public feelings" in broad circulation, but also the "stuff" that intimate lives are made of (Stewart 2007). Referring to Raymond Williams's structures of feeling ordinary affects work through the body as modes of knowing and relating, they create a contact zone where power, flows, circulations and connections come together.

Her description of ordinary affects as coincidentally intimate and in broad circulation captures some of the same dynamics that animate notions of affective climate and affective atmosphere that I will discuss in the next section. In both schemes, affect is that which circulates and gets incorporated into bodies and expressed through cultural and historical codes and labels. The terms "emotion" and "feeling" are used for the interpretation of sensation at the scale of the individual, home environment or neighborhood where social construction and cultural practices give it meaning.

Another way that affect is produced is through the ruination and deterioration of the built environment. For example, "ruins" are an ethnographic means for understanding the spatial melancholy induced by living in the houses of the ethnic other after the Greek and Turkish exchange on Cyprus (Navaro-Yashin 2009). Yael Navaro-Yashin (2009) describes Turkish-Cypriots who moved to North Cyprus after 1974 as experiencing the emotive energies discharged by the property and objects appropriated from members of the enemy community. This property of the objects creates a pervasive atmosphere of "*maraz*," a kind of deep sadness and depression. Ruins also play an affective role in Bahla, an Omani town, in this case, evoking nostalgia for past histories and the emerging power of the modern nation-state (Limbert 2008).

Another ethnographic approach to space and affect is through an interrogation of the intertwining of ideology and affect such that political and spatial projects operate on both affective and ideological levels. William Mazzarella (2009) argues that affect opens the way to study public communications and their emotional impact. The resulting two levels of communication (affective and ideological) can be contradictory, thus offering a strategy for understanding ambiguous reactions to a space or environment.

Affective and emotive landscape of the city

The cityscape has been described as provoking a wide range of feelings, affects and desires through its ever-expanding opportunities for work, play, fantasy and danger or through its architectural grandeur, dazzling street life and deteriorated ruins. Further, urban spaces have always included performative components that guide public and private emotional responses, including monuments, parades, street theater and art. The relationship of the urban environment, however, is not just that the built environment produces affect and feeling but also that affect in part produces the built environment.

For example, Ana Ramos-Zayas's (2012) ethnography of Newark, New Jersey, describes how the historical background of the migrant communities (Brazilians and Puerto Ricans) and the racial projects of both the United States and their countries of origin frame responses to the urban landscape of Newark, New Jersey. She highlights that it is the affective aspects of sociability and social interaction rather than the cultural politics or emotional quality of individuals that become a means of configuring experience. Further, there is a neoliberal shaping of emotional lives through cultural norms of what constitutes "proper" public behavior embedded in the "emotive landscape" (Ramos-Zayas 2012: 6). This landscape is most effective when targeting marginal urban populations and generates new kinds of exclusion through the measurement of individuals' attractiveness and "marketability" as defined by White employers. These "materially grounded affects" (2012: 9) are experienced through an urban environment produced by the White supremacy ideology of racial relations. For instance, the slum clearance policies of the 1950s–1960s when Black neighborhoods were replaced with housing projects and the recent Newark Renaissance of fortress-like corporate towers and transportation centers that bypass the street create such emotive landscapes. She concludes that "urban developments that privilege real estate, commercial and touristic interests, require that cities are associated with a right (middle-class or neoliberal-friendly) emotional style for their success" (2012: 51).

Zenzele Isoke (2011) views the affective consequences of the destruction and redevelopment of Newark quite differently. Based on her ethnographic work, she argues that Black women's home-making in Newark resists these devastating changes through the building of enduring positive affective relationships to the physical environment (Isoke 2011). Black home-making, she argues, has created "an affective space in the community for remembering modes of black freedom struggles" (2011: 119) rather than the racism that Ramos-Zayas finds in the urban core. Thus Black women's home-making supports a politically progressive and emotionally positive urban environment.

Affective responses can be designed into urban spaces as a "form of landscape engineering that is gradually pulling itself into existence, producing new forms of power as it goes" (Thrift 2008: 187). The current ability to program the city through lighting, design, images and signs using integrated mobile technologies and Internet websites is pervasive and pernicious. Nigel Thrift identifies corporate and state institutions as formulating this knowledge of affective states and "regimes of feeling" that influence and, in some cases, constitute political practices (2008: 188). Ultimately, he is concerned that the ability of the state to manipulate the affective dimension of the city has dangerous political consequences and must be understood to withstand the seductive lure of state-programmed regimes of feeling and retain spaces for alternative affective forms and experiences. The idea that the state controls the affective realm is developed further in the following discussion of emotional climate and atmosphere.

Emotional and affective climate and atmosphere

Emotional climate and atmosphere

Social psychology studies employ a cognitive approach to emotion to understand its production and circulation. They offer a template for dealing with the different emotional and political scales of emotionality that include the impact of events and places. Most of this research focuses on the impact of terrorist attacks, violence and conflict. Susana Conejero and Itziar Etxebarria (2007), for example, study the aftermath of the March 11, 2004, terrorist attack in Madrid that resulted in 191 deaths and 1,500 injuries. They identify the interaction of personal emotions, emotional climate and emotional atmosphere by defining "who" experiences or perceive the emotion:

> *Personal emotions* refer to the emotions felt or experienced by individuals; *emotional atmosphere* alludes to the emotions that arise when members of a group focus their attention on a specific event that affects them as a group (de Rivera 1992). Such an atmosphere appears when those who identify with a group celebrate a collective success, lament a tragedy, or suffer a common threat. *Emotional climate* refers to the set of emotions perceived in society that are relevant to its sociopolitical situation. Thus, in times of political repression, people are afraid to express their ideas in public; in times of ethnic tension, there is hate and/ or fear toward other groups, and so on.
>
> (Conejero and Etxebarria 2007: 274)

Their questionnaire-based study of 1,807 people found that personal emotions are correlated closely with emotional atmosphere and a little less so with emotional climate that appears to be more stable and not as reactive.

Joseph de Rivera, also a social psychologist, claims that societies have "emotional climates that affect how people feel and act in public situations" (de Rivera 1992; de Rivera, Kurrien and Olsen 2007: 255). He argues that emotional climate is a collective response to the social, political and economic context expressed in collective emotions and modal feelings. Emotional climate is again distinguished from atmosphere, or "sentience," which occurs when a group responds to the same situation or event. An emotional climate instead is regarded as "an emotional field that both affects and is affected by relationships between members of a society at a given point in their history" (de Rivera, Kurrien and Olsen 2007: 256). This definition shares some commonality with affect theory and the notion of an emotional field seems promising. But the use of psychological scales and questionnaires asking about how people feel – that is, to make a cognitive assessment about their political situation – does not speak to broader and more diffuse built environment and spatial concerns.

Affective atmosphere

The concept of affective atmosphere seems more suitable for the ethnography of space and place than the psychological construct of emotional atmosphere because it does not rely on culturally specific linguistic labeling of emotions nor is it limited to experience and perception by an individual or group. Affective atmosphere does not require an event or social movement to exist, though events can trigger an atmosphere, whether positive (e.g., Woodstock, VE day) or negative (9/11, the shooting of Martin Luther King Jr.). Affective atmosphere as a theoretical concept has the advantage of being located, circulated and transmitted spatially as well as through other mediums such as talk, silence, poetry, music, songs, radio broadcasts, tweets, images, movies and the built and natural environment.

For example, Anderson (2009) draws his concept of affective atmosphere from the "material imaginary of air as movement and lightness" and from Marx's metaphorical use of a "revolutionary atmosphere" of crisis, danger and hope (2009: 77). He is intrigued by the way the term is used in everyday speech and aesthetic discourse, as in the atmosphere of a room, a city, an epoch, a street, a painting, a scene or a time of day – anything that surrounds, envelops or presses upon the person. He suggests that affective atmospheres are

> a class of experience that occur *before* and *alongside* the formation of subjectivity, *across* human and non-human materialities, and *in-between* subject/object distinctions . . . atmospheres are the shared ground from which subjective states and their attendant feelings and emotions emerge.
>
> (Anderson 2009: 78)

Most importantly, he locates atmospheres spatially and as properties of objects and subjects, reducible to bodies affecting other bodies, but at the same time exceeding those bodies (Anderson 2009).

Stewart concurs that affect, as "the commonplace, labor-intensive process of sensing modes of living," depends on the feel of an atmosphere (2010: 340). In her version, spaces of all kinds become inhabited through the work of attunement to atmosphere, what she calls "worlding," the activity of sensual world making (2011). She considers these atmospheric

Ambient
Rhetoric

attunements as shifts in attending to what's happening and sensing new and old possibilities.

> An atmosphere is not an inert context but a force field in which people find themselves. It is not an effect of other forces but a lived affect – a capacity to affect and to be affected that pushes a present into a composition, an expressivity, the sense of potentiality and event. It is an attunement of the senses, of labors, and imaginaries to potential ways of living in or living through things.
>
> (Stewart 2011: 452)

Brian Massumi (2010) illustrates the all-pervasive nature and political power of affective atmospheres by offering a compelling case of how an atmosphere of threat reconfigures reality. Citing George W. Bush's defense of invading Iraq, even without finding "weapons of mass destruction," Massumi points out

> the invasion was right because *in the past there was a future threat*. You cannot erase a "fact" like that. Just because the menace potential never became clear and present danger doesn't mean that it wasn't there, all the more real for being nonexistent . . . It will have been real because it was *felt* to be real.
>
> (2010:53)

For Massumi (2010), threat has a mode of existence, and fear is its foreshadowing. The felt reality of threat can be experienced individually (emotionally) and collectively as "fear." Fear is the affective fact of the presence of an atmosphere of ongoing threat, a lingering feeling created by the nation that contributed to Bush's re-election.

Massumi (2010) draws upon C. S. Peirce's analysis of indexes, signs, that are indicators and immediately performative to explain how an atmosphere of threat comes into being. He suggests that performatives, such as a person yelling "fire" or "look out," are self-executing commands and argues that even when there is no fire, the body activation of "fire" or "look out" cannot be undone. In the same way, an affective atmosphere of threat can be triggered and transmitted by a discourse of weapons of mass destruction, even if they are never found, and this activation is the same as when a threatening event actually happens. Further, the action of the indexical sign and the accompanying body activation extend to the environment. Thus Massumi offers a way to understand how space is permeated with affect and then rendered legible through sociocultural and political cues (Ghannam 2012), media and other forms of circulating images (Masco 2008), personal histories and propensities (Stewart 2011) and translated into sociolinguistic categories of emotion or other bodily feelings (Massumi 2002).

Anthropologist Joseph Masco (2008) traces the historical construction of such threats and the accompanying negative affect from the mass circulation of images of a nuclear-bombed United States since 1945. Nuclear fear and an apocalyptic vision of the future are a central focus for nation-building beginning with Cold War civil defense and continuing with the "War on Terror." Masco argues persuasively that the public drills of what to do in the face of an impending nuclear blast psychologically reprogrammed individuals, while the Cold War globally reengineered everyday life. He finds

> that the production and management of negative affect remains a central tool of the national security state, and demonstrates the primary role the atomic bomb plays in the United States as a means of militarizing everyday life and justifying war.
>
> (Masco 2008: 390)

Juan Orrantia (2012) also describes how the aftermath of terror creates a negative atmosphere in places of violence such as the massacre in Nueva Venecia, a small town on the Caribbean coast of Colombia. A Catholic mass is held commemorating the dead each year, but otherwise there is no visible sign of collective memory. Orrantia (2012) argues that the residue of terror is found in what Colombians call "heaviness" expressed as "*el ambiente se siente pesado*" (the place feels heavy) and locate this feeling of heaviness in the air or environment. He considers "heaviness" to be a dense and foreboding atmosphere of fear both from the massacre and the threat of continuing violence from the Colombian regime.

It is conceptually useful following Conejero's and Etxebarria's work (2007) to define atmosphere as event based and spatially anchored and to retain affective climate for more diffuse and structurally produced phenomena. For example, the fear and anxiety of downtown Manhattan residents mentioned in the introduction can be thought of as produced by the affective atmosphere of living near the World Trade Center site and reactivated each year on September 11 through the emotion-laden media images of the falling towers (Low, Taplin and Lamb 2005, Smithsimon 2011, Greenspan 2013). The concept of a broader, politically induced affective climate is helpful for explaining how a national level of fear and insecurity promotes and sustains the security state (Masco 2008, Sorkin 2008). The notion of an affective climate defined in this way corresponds in many ways to Raymond Williams's (1977) structure of feeling that many scholars use to describe the relationship of structural forces to broad-based affective states. In the ethnographic examples that follow, both terms – the structure of feeling and affective climate – are employed to refer to national and statewide resonances and feelings, and affective atmosphere is used for the denser and spatially located feelings that suffuse an event, place or environment.

Ethnographic examples

The ethnographic study of gated communities

To illustrate how emotion and affect constitute and are constituted by space and place, I turn to the production of an affective climate and affective atmosphere that has transformed how some middle-class Americans experience their homes. These residents are made up of mostly suburban and urban families who feel their everyday environments are dangerous or threatening and have moved to gated communities in an effort to feel safe and secure. This ethnographic example is based on fieldwork with residents of a number of gated communities and is used to highlight how racial fears, fear of illegal immigrants and a post-9/11 state-promulgated affective climate of threat contribute to residents' feelings of fear and insecurity in their secured homes and neighborhoods.

The search for safety and security has a long history in the United States, beginning in the early 1900s when working families began fleeing the dirt and immigrant tenements of Manhattan and other large cities and the so-called White flight to burgeoning suburbs in the 1960s and 1970s. The more recent retreat to gated and other forms of private communities began in the 1980s and by 2010 made up 10 percent of all housing.[2] Gated community residents' fear of "crime" and "others" is partly a race and class-based discourse that rationalizes living behind gates or leaving a cherished neighborhood that is "changing." It reiterates post-1980s neoliberal urban policies that put the responsibility to protect oneself from crime or other misfortune on the individual rather than government services. But it is also visceral fear that I could feel in response to living in the fortress-like spaces. Children are afraid to go outside the gates to play, as they know it is "dangerous" and "people could grab them," while their parents worry whether they are wrong to feel safe inside the gates since "others" (Mexicans, Blacks, immigrants, laborers, workers) might enter at any time.

While residents' desire for a safe and secure home is best understood in the context of racial segregation and exclusionary housing practices, they are increasingly concerned with national security. Especially post-9/11, the "people who commit crimes" are imagined and even called "terrorists." This displacement of fear from mundane domestic criminals to international terrorists suggests that other factors are involved in producing these feelings, such as the melding of home with the security apparatus of Homeland Security and the implementation of the Patriot Act that sanctions stop and search for "suspicious people." Even the locally popular Secure Communities program,[3] which identifies illegal immigrants and deports them, reminds gated residents of their own sense of fear that illegal aliens are entering their homes as domestic workers, nannies and repair persons.

The impact of the political, economic and media production of an inse-cure affective climate can be seen in the microcosm of a ten-year compara-tive study of gated community residents in New York City, Long Island, New York, and San Antonio, Texas (Figure 7.1 Map of United States with New York City, Nassau County, New York, and San Antonio, Texas). For most residents, their fear and insecurity began with the economic restructuring and deployment of neoliberal urban strategies that changed their previ-ous neighborhoods, physically, ethnically and racially. Their fears post-9/11 resonated with a national security climate that reinforced prejudice and paranoia.

This ethnographic example presents only three aspects of this fear. The first is the "fear of crime and others" that developed in reaction to the changing racial composition of the residential area and deterioration of the local urban environment. The second is "fear of others" expressed by residents as a concern with porous physical and social boundaries attrib-uted to increasing numbers of illegal immigrants locally and the overall "browning of America." And the third is "fear of others and terrorists" that emerged in response to the attack on the World Trade Center towers on September 11, 2001, and the U.S. government's unrelenting production of fear and anxiety through the subsequent "war on terror."

A "gated community" is a residential development surrounded by walls, fences or earth banks covered with bushes and shrubs, with a secured entrance. In some cases, protection is provided by inaccessible land such as a nature reserve and in a few cases, by a guarded bridge (Frantz 2000–2001). The houses, streets, sidewalks and other amenities are physically enclosed within these barriers, and a guard, key or electronic identity card operate the entrance gates. Inside the development, there is often a neighborhood watch organization or professional security personnel who patrol on foot and by automobile.

The research began with gaining entry into upper-middle and middle-income gated subdivisions in 1994 and 1995: one in Nassau County on Long Island and three in the northern suburbs of San Antonio, Texas. Middle-income and middle to lower-middle income communities were added in 2000 and 2005 to answer questions about race, class and cultural differences that arose later in the project (Photo 7.1 Gated suburban master-planned development and Photo 7.2 Gated townhouse community).

Each gated community was initially mapped using the site plans of the architect or developer. These maps recorded circulation, activities, physi-cal traces and design and landscape differences for each house. The plans for the house models were collected and used to determine the cost of each house and its exact location on the site plan. Photographs were taken to illustrate each plan and, of course, photographs of the homes of interview-ees were taken to record any physical or aesthetic details missed during the interviews. Later in the fieldwork, emotional maps based on "mapping

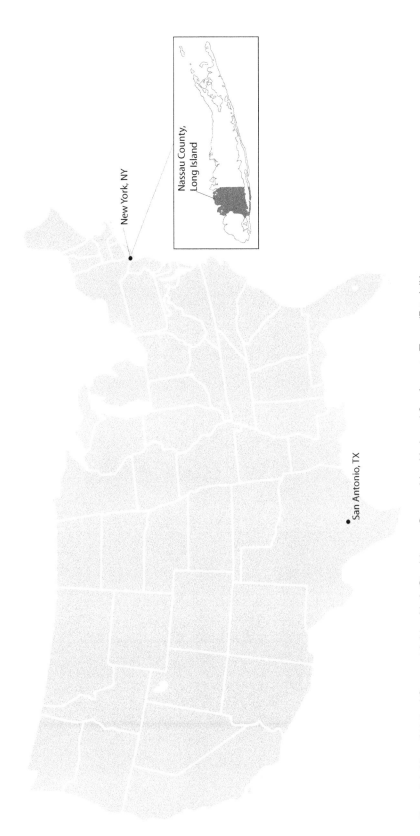

Figure 7.1 Map of United States with New York City, Nassau County, New York, and San Antonio, Texas (Erin Lilli)

Photo 7.1 Gated suburban master-planned development (Setha Low)

Photo 7.2 Gated townhouse community (Setha Low)

feeling" were attempted based on the interviews, participant observation and our own feelings and perceptions. Developers, marketing staff and architects were interviewed about the design and financial history of the development, including their perspectives on why residents wanted to live in secured housing complexes. Tax maps, visits to the town assessor, visits to the municipal or town planning office and reading the local newspapers were all part of the data collection process.

After completing the initial mapping and establishing entry to the site, a team of researchers began interviewing, using an opportunity sample of people contacted through the sales and marketing staff, family members, neighbors or local friends.[4] The one- to two-hour resident interview was organized around a semistructured residential history conducted in the home with the wife or single woman, husband or husband and wife together. The majority of the interviewees were European Americans and native born; however, four interviews were conducted in households in which one spouse was from Latin America, West Africa, Asia or the Middle East. Interviewees were eighteen through seventy-five. This absence of minority residents, particularly Hispanics in San Antonio, was indicative of the middle- and upper-middle-class composition of the interviewee sample and the gated communities that they lived in. It was also not surprising, based on the predominantly middle to high socioeconomic status of the opportunity sample, that the men interviewed were mostly professionals such as doctors, lawyers and teachers; working in industry as businessmen, managers and foremen; or retired from these same pursuits. The majority of women were either stay-at-home mothers or wives who sometimes worked part time nearby, while the husband commuted to work in the city. Of the three single, widowed or divorced women in the sample, however, two worked full time and one was retired from full-time employment.

Participant observation was ongoing in the gated communities and in the shopping, transportation and recreational areas near each development. Some communities have amenities such as tennis courts, gyms and a swimming pool complex, while even the smallest has walking paths and hiking trails, so it was possible to spend time meeting people as they walked their dogs, exercised or strolled in the evening.

The participant-observation field notes focused on identifying evidence of changes in the local environment. Further, it produced data on naturally occurring conversations and everyday observations that provided a test of ecological validity for the interviews. For example, a new shopping center was being constructed behind one of the San Antonio communities with stores backing up to the perimeter wall of the development. This change in the bucolic context increased the amount of fear of others expressed by members in their daily conversations and resulted in the perimeter wall being raised from six to eight feet. Also, increased traffic was discussed, with a proposal presented to redesign the public streets and add a traffic light so that residents can exit their gated development more easily in both San Antonio and Long Island, New York.

As has been evident in the previous fieldwork examples, the ethnographic methods used were fairly traditional and included participant observation, resident interviews, expert interviews, mapping and photography. What was different in this ethnography, and rather unexpected, was the amount of talk about fear of crime and others used to characterize the community spaces, streets, houses and walls and gates both inside and outside the gated communities. It was on the basis of a critical discourse analysis of this "fear talk" in conjunction with the recording of news events and media stories that many of the ideas presented about the emotional tone and affective atmosphere of gated communities emerged and were spatially located.

Fear of crime and others

Most gated community residents say that they moved because of their fear of crime and concern that their neighborhood was changing. But when listening closely, one can hear that they are also expressing a pervasive sense of insecurity with life in the United States. Policing, video surveillance, gating, walls and guards do not assuage the fear because they do not address the affective climate and neighborhood atmosphere that produces it. For example, Cynthia was concerned about staying in her old neighborhood.

CYNTHIA: And then I have a lot of friends who live in [my old] neighborhood in Queens, and there's been more than forty-eight robberies there in the last year and a half. And I said to myself those are homes with security and dogs and this and that.
SETHA: And are they gated?
CYNTHIA: No, they're not gated. They had alarms, and they were getting robbed because they were cutting the alarms, the phone wires outside. So I'm saying to myself, all this is in my mind, and I'm saying I can get robbed. That's why I moved.

Cynthia goes on to explain that she needed something more secure, but she seems unsure of the guards and still feels afraid at night.

During the day it's great with James [the guard] who you've met. But at night, it's like anything else [she worries]. I feel ok because if I had a problem I could call the gated community guardhouse. I remember the first night I stayed here by myself. I said if something goes wrong, who am I going to call? I don't know what to do.

Sharon was willing to "give up community convenience for safety." She said that increased neighborhood deterioration left her feeling uncomfortable in the house where she had lived for over twenty-five years. Even though she knew everyone in her old neighborhood and enjoyed walking to the corner store, "when Bloomingdale's moved out and Kmart moved in, it just brought in a different group of people, and it wasn't the safe place that it was." "Crime" and "different group of people" in these contexts is a coded reference to race or ethnicity. Residents were more comfortable talking about crime and others than confronting their own racial fears and desire to separate themselves from people of color or, in the case of Great Neck, New York, from the religion and ethnicity of Iranian Jews.

Fear of crime as a rhetorical strategy also translates into fear of poor people. This is exaggerated with gating. For example, Felicia relates her fear of crime and poor people who live outside the gates very clearly.

FELICIA: When I leave the area entirely and go downtown [little laugh], I feel quite threatened, just being out in normal urban areas, unrestricted urban areas. . . . Please let me explain. The north central part of this city, by and large, is middle-class to upper-middle-class. Period. There are very few pockets of poverty. Very few and therefore if you go to any store, you will look around and most of the clientele will be middle-class as you are yourself. So you are somewhat insulated. But if you go downtown, which is much more mixed, where everybody goes, I feel much more threatened.

SETHA: Okay.

FELICIA: My daughter feels very threatened when she sees poor people.

SETHA: How do you explain that?

FELICIA: She hasn't had enough exposure. We were driving next to a truck with some day laborers and equipment in the back, and we were parked beside them at the light. She wanted to move because she was afraid those people were going to come and get her. They looked scary to her. I explained that they were workmen, they're the "backbone of our country," they're coming from work, you know, but. . . .

In this passage, Felicia's daughter feels threatened by workers who, in the case of San Antonio, are thought to be illegal Mexican immigrants conflating the national anti-immigration climate and a local and geographical fear of "others."

Fear of others: porous physical and social boundaries

A related way that fear of others is expressed by gated residents is through their concern with the impregnability of the physical and social boundaries of their secured development. One also hears echoes of political concerns about illegal immigrants in Karen's comments.

SETHA: One thing you did say is that the workers concern you. Or is it that they are construction workers or undocumented workers?
KAREN: It's like they can slip in and slip out. Where there's no record of these guys at all. They're here today and gone tomorrow.
SETHA: I was trying to get a sense about who the people are?
KAREN LOOKS AT ME PUZZLED: Mean like now? If you asked me tomorrow if I was going to move, it would be only to a gated community.

When I probed about who she was talking about, she switched the conversation to her reasons for moving to the gated community. Following her lead, I ask her for clarification, and she returned to the discourse of the fear of crime.

SETHA: To a gated community? Why?
KAREN: I think that the security is most important; I really like knowing who is coming and going. I like knowing I'm not going to come home and find my house burglarized. Once you've been violated like that, it's really hard, I think, to continue living without one [a gate].

Metaphors of porous boundaries that "others" can penetrate also involve the racialization of space in which the representation and definition of "other" is based on racial categories. Racist fears about the "threat" of a visible minority, whether it is Blacks, Hispanics, Asians or Arabs are remarkably similar. For example, Helen highlights how race still plays a dominant role in eliciting fear that someone might be able to breach the boundary of one's home. She illustrates her point by telling me what happened to a friend who lives "in a lovely community" near Washington, DC.

HELEN: She said this fellow came to the door, and she was very intimidated because she was White, and he was Black, and you didn't get many Blacks in her neighborhood. She only bought it [what he was selling] just to hurry and quick get him away from the door, because she was scared as hell. That's terrible to be put in that situation. I like the idea of having security.
SETHA: Are you concerned about crime in your development?
HELEN: Not here, but in San Antonio. There are gangs. People are overworked, they have families, they are underpaid, the stress is out of control, and they abuse their children. The children go out because they don't like their home life. There's too much violence everywhere. It starts in the city, but then the kids get smart enough and say, "Oh, gee, I need money for

x, y or z, but it's really hot in the city, let's go out and get it someplace else." We're the natural target for it. So being in a secure area, I don't have to worry as much as another neighborhood that doesn't have security.

Another way that residents talk about porous boundaries is through their fear of kidnaping. Donna's fears of vulnerability focus on her children.

DONNA: You know, he's always so scared. . . . It has made a world of difference in him since we've been out here.
SETHA: Really?
DONNA: A world of difference. And it is that sense of security that they don't think people are roaming the neighborhoods and the streets and that there's people out there that can hurt him.
SETHA: Ah . . . that's incredible.
DONNA: . . . That's what's been most important to my husband, to get the children out here where they can feel safe, and we feel safe if they could go out in the streets and not worry that someone is going to grab them. . . . we feel so secure and maybe that's wrong too.
SETHA: In what sense?
DONNA: You know, we've got workers out here, and we still think, "Oh, they're safe out here". . . . In the other neighborhood, I never let him get out of my sight for a minute. Of course they were a little bit younger too, but I just would never, you know, think of letting them go to the next street over. It would have scared me to death, because you didn't know. There was so much traffic coming in and out, you never knew who was cruising the street and how fast they can grab a child. And I don't feel that way in our area at all ever.

Fear of others and terrorists: fear, anxiety and paranoia

The bombing of the World Trade Center on September 11, 2001, added to the repertoire of fear of others as well as a concern with porous boundaries, especially for New York residents. Linda, a single mother who lives in a house her mother bought in a gated community on Long Island, expresses her fear and its relationship to 9/11 in the following excerpt:

A couple of years before that we had something [happen here]. There were helicopters flying over . . . I don't remember specifically when, but some inmate, they were looking for someone who had escaped who had a murder record. That was quite freaky. You would look out in the back yard and there would be woods out there, and you'd wonder who is out there.

Because, you know people can come in here on foot. There's a golf course right behind us, and anyone could be wandering around on there, and decide to traipse through here. Honestly I don't know how useful the gate is.

Linda tells the following story to illustrate her point:

> One time, one of my neighbor's boys, the little one was missing. And this woman, I mean, she was white as a sheet, and she was really going to have a nervous breakdown. And we couldn't find him. He was actually in another neighbor's house with his friend, playing. I had called that house to find out, not realizing they were away, and there was a workman in the house. And these boys didn't know the workman. The workman just walked in there, went into the kid's room and started working. So she wasn't at ease [because it was so easy for the workman to walk in without any adults being home, and that her boy was there with a strange workman]. You know, we are not living in very secure times now.

SETHA: What do you mean?
LINDA: I think with the gate thing there is an increasing sense of insecurity all over the place. I think people are beginning to realize they are not really safe anywhere in Middle America. We have had so much violence and terrorism occurring. That could be part of it.

The perceived threats of crime, other people, a porous neighborhood that is easily entered and terrorism engender a defensive and insecure affective atmosphere in which residents attempt to create safe and comfortable homes. But instead reactive emotions of home – fear, insecurity, worry, paranoia and anxiety – dominate their interviews.

Most people want to feel safe and secure at home, but the strategies being used to accomplish this security – building higher walls and adding trained guards and mobile patrols to gated communities, improving home surveillance technology, adding both a private and public police presence on city streets and in neighborhood complexes, creating safe rooms, and stockpiling supplies for a terrorist attack – are producing a new level of emotional reactivity. While many Americans want home security, most do not want to live in a police state. Security enhancements do not address citizens' unarticulated concerns about the vulnerability of the state and a national climate of fear of others, including immigrants, terrorists and even the person next door.[5]

Regardless of the initiating events, increasingly new "threats" are being created and circulated. After September 11, 2001, President G. W. Bush's administration mobilized a discourse of fear and affective climate of insecurity that permitted the constriction of liberty in the United States and eventually an unpopular war in Iraq. Even though President Barack Obama's administration withdrew many of the troops, new problems in Afghanistan, Iraq, Syria, Pakistan and elsewhere throughout North Africa continue to demand military action and antiterrorist initiatives. A high incidence of fear and anxiety is reported even from the media coverage of a terrorist event (Boscarino, Figley and Adams 2003, Rothe and Muzzatti 2004, Schuster et al. 2001), especially among children (Gershoff and Aber 2004, Keinan, Sadeh and Rosen 2003, Saylor et al. 2003.)

Locally, increasing socioeconomic inequality, cultural diversity and downward mobility create the sense something is wrong and that the moorings of the middle class are shifting, reinforcing the salience of negative feelings and defensive strategies (Young 1999, Newman 1993, Ortner 1998). The perception that illegal immigrants are taking local jobs and employment opportunities and use services paid for with citizen tax dollars contribute to residents' fears and dislike of "others." Media-covered events such as high school shootings and child kidnappings combined with a national climate of insecurity and fear overwhelm feelings of home as a place where residents feel safe and secure.

Affect, space and gender in the Egyptian revolution

Another example of how emotion and affect create and change space and place is illustrated by two studies of the Egyptian Revolution and its expression in Cairo, Egypt. Farha Ghannam (2012) and Jessica Winegar (2012) are ethnographers interested in how the media coverage and personal communications of the protest that began January 25, 2011, produced local meanings, emotive spaces and political agency. Using two different methodologies, they provide evocative descriptions of how residents in other parts of Cairo experienced the uprising on Midan al-Tahrir (Liberation Square) in the center of the city (Figure 7.2 Map of Cairo, Egypt, with Tahrir Square).

While their research questions differ, they present insights into how affect and space as well as gender and class shaped feelings about the conflict. Ghannam (2012) was interested in how her long-time friends and informants were reacting to the protests downtown and was in constant contact with them by telephone and Skype. Winegar arrived in Cairo on January 28, 2011, just a few days after the protests began. She stayed at a friend's, with her son watching television and listening to the news, to answer how the revolution was experienced by women working at home. The focus on domestic environments rather than the historic downtown public space presents another example of how a national affective climate of fear and antipathy and the affective atmosphere of courage and care in al-Tahrir affected those who remained at home. These feelings were spatially mediated by the imagined space of al-Tahrir and the confined spaces of the house and neighborhood.

Ghannam (2012) suggests that the structures of feeling (Williams 1977) about the national struggle and events shaped the cultural meanings and shifting feelings of her interlocutors in al-Zawiya al-Hamra, a low-income

Figure 7.2 Map of Cairo, Egypt, with Tahrir Square (Erin Lilli)

neighborhood in Northern Cairo where she has worked for many years. She found that the views and regulation of the use of violence in the neighborhood was central to how "men and women interpreted the attacks of *baltagiyya* (thugs) on protesters in Midan al-Tahrir" (2012: 32).

At first the poorer residents of al-Zawiya al-Hamra felt unsafe and worried about their livelihoods; they had no savings, and the protests disrupted their work. But their feelings changed drastically after the violent attacks on demonstrators on February 2, 2011 (Ghannam 2012). As peaceful young people were attacked by men with clubs and guns, locals began to align with the protesters based on their own neighborhood experiences with violence. They considered the attackers "thugs" hired by governmental officials to frighten protesters. This inappropriate use of excessive force resonated with their dislike and disgust of *baltagiyya*, locally understood to use violence to impose their will on another for personal gain. Thus the ethos that regulates the proper and improper uses of violence as well as the increasing fears and worries involved in protecting their own neighborhood from *baltagiyya* who were roaming the street and the associated criminality also created an emotional identification with the protesters and their plight (Ghannam 2012). She demonstrates how

> ... thoughts and feelings, formed and emerging meanings, past and present experiences, and local and national struggles have been central to the inclusion of most Egyptians in the same political and moral project.
>
> (2012: 35)

Winegar (2012) is interested in how the revolution is experienced by women in domestic spaces, as contrasted to the iconic male revolutionary imaginary in al-Tahrir. Her perspective on the uprising is from her neighbor Mona's kitchen where she is making stuffed cabbage and watching her four-year-old son with Mona and Amal, Mona's housekeeper. With news reports of escalating violence, Amal became worried about her family's economic well-being, while Winegar and Mona worried that Mubarak might remain in power (Winegar 2012)

As the conflict continued, Winegar, Mona and various others who were not in al-Tahrir "became increasingly obsessed with al-Jazeera and al-Arabiyya television" (Winegar 2012: 63). Her friend complained of being *zahqana* (fed up) with being confined to home and unable to join the protesters while Winegar reports feeling "scared, excited, and frustrated" (2012: 63) about having to stay cooped up during the revolution. Her point is that women's work is important to managing tension and providing for children during a revolution, but that many women who wanted to participate were blocked by having child care commitments or could not get their family's permission.

Young women reported being "physically sick of TV," and their anxiety made them want the conflict to end quickly, while women with children stuck at home reflected on the risk of revolution to the maintenance of family life (Winegar 2012). Winegar points out that it was mainly un- or underemployed young men or rich and single women without family commitments who were able to go to al-Tahrir and participate in the fighting and excitement. Staying home provoked very different fears and emotions. The home affective atmosphere became one of frustration and anxiety because of the isolation and constant exposure to the media, rather than the violence, heroism and caretaking experienced by the protesters. From Winegar's vantage point, the affect and spaces of home and neighborhood reveal as much about the revolution and social transformation as events and activities documented by the news media in al-Tahrir.

Importantly, Winegar and Ghannam point out how the affective climate of Mubarak's government evoked fear of the police and the army accompanied by worry about the deterioration of the city, decreasing ability to make a living and lack of services. These concerns contributed to the wide support of Mubarak's removal from office. At the same time, they depict how those residents who were not there and not part of the ongoing struggle and jubilation experienced the affective atmosphere of Midan al-Tahrir in a different way. The euphoria of being in the square was not necessarily shared by residents, particularly women, at home who alternatively felt unsafe and worried about their livelihoods or trapped, relatively isolated and frustrated that they could not go out in the neighborhood, much less participate in the historic events occurring downtown. Both ethnographers present compelling ethnographic cases of how to study the relationship of space and affect in a very different cultural context from the U.S. residents living in gated communities.

Conclusion

This chapter reviews the significant contribution that the study of emotion and affect offers the ethnography of space and place. Some of the discussions of emotion and emotive institutions overlap with ideas presented in Chapter 4 on the social construction of space. Ethnographers concerned with emotion often draw upon social construction theories and methodologies to understand how emotion works within distinct cultural and social settings. Similar to the study of language, discourse and space presented in Chapter 6, much of the theory of emotion and emotive institutions starts with the social constructive premise that emotions are sociolinguistically fixed, learned and understood in specific cultural contexts and under certain social, historical and political conditions.

Theories of affect, on the other hand, draw more heavily on notions of embodiment and out-of-awareness systems of feeling attributed to precognitive and inchoate intensities. Ethnographic approaches to affect and space and affective atmosphere and climate resemble the phenomenological and movement analyses presented in Chapter 5. In this sense, the ideas presented in these chapters resonate with one another and reiterate similar foundational principles.

Yet one of the strengths of an emotion, affect and space methodology is that it enables the ethnographer to interrogate disparate kinds of data and social interactions. Emotional reactions to space often complicate what an informant says about a space or what the person is doing (or thinks he or she is doing) in a space. Emotional excess or emotional overload as discussed in the two ethnographic examples provides insights into how everyday assumptions about space and place can dramatically change through different avenues of emotional fixing or domestication as White (2005, 2006) suggests. Affective atmospheres and climate also offer the ethnographer theoretical and methodological tools that query the connection of local and national or global feelings and how affects generated at the national level can infiltrate the everyday spaces of home and neighborhood. Their ideas are taken up again in the next chapter's discussion of translocality in the production and experience of space.

Notes

1 See Low, Taplin and Lamb 2005 for a fuller account of the Battery Park City project.
2 The number of people estimated to be living in gated communities in the United State rapidly doubled in two years, 1995–1997, from four million to eight million (Low 2003). By 1997, there were in excess of twenty thousand gated communities with over three million housing units. Two new questions on gating and controlled access were added to the 2001 American Housing Survey, establishing that 16 million people, or 6 percent of all U.S. households, lived in gated, walled housing areas (Sanchez and Lang 2002). The most recent census figures report that closer to 10 percent of all households are located in gated communities, with the number of occupied units increasing 53 percent between 2001 and 2009 (www.security choice.com/home-security-news/ 2012).
3 Secure Communities is an American deportation program that relies on partnerships among federal, state and local law enforcement agencies. U.S. Immigration and Customs Enforcement (ICE), the immigration enforcement agency within the Department of Homeland Security, is the program manager.
4 In San Antonio, for the first five years I worked alone; however, in New York City and Long Island, graduate students joined my team. Their contributions and names are listed in the acknowledgments.
5 There are other ways that negative affective atmospheres can be produced; for example, Roger Lancaster's (2011) study of how the fear of sex offenders became a moral panic is an exaggerated version of the emotional reactions described by gated community residents. You can even go online and get a map of your neighborhood that indicates the location of all known sex offenders.

Chapter 8

Translocal space

Introduction

Translocal space encompasses the experiences and materialities of everyday lives in multiple places. In this conceptual frame, a person who lives in two or more locations often separated by national boundaries and distance has emotional, linguistic and material access to both simultaneously. Technologies that facilitate texting, messaging, instant cash transfers, talking by mobile phones and handheld computers or Skype provide an immediacy of experience and the interpenetration of one space by another.

For the individuals and collectivities that live in these circuits, life *is* translocal, inflected with the ideas, speech, smells, sounds and feelings of each place and yet limited by the structural and physical constraints of corporeality. Translocality, though, can also transcend individual bodies through affective processes and the circulation of information and communication. Thus translocal space becomes more than an individual's experience or fixed emplacement and instead part of a network of multiple localities shared by families, neighborhoods, groups and communities. This conceptual frame offers the ethnographer of space and place another lens for imagining spaces, particularly those of the future, and to explore how traditional urban spaces can be transformed into multicultural places of political possibility. This chapter reviews the ideas that led to imagining translocality as not simply moving between places, but the superposition and linking of localities through space-time compression.

At the same time that space-time compression is experienced through translocality, however, time-space expansion is also occurring, increasing the burden of poor, working and middle-class families who find it impossible to work and live in the same place (Katz 2001). Social reproduction becomes more difficult with economic restructuring that reinforces long-distance wage-labor migration to support families who reside at home. For example, highland Guatemalans from Huehuetenango move in ever-widening yearly cycles to find wage labor in lowland plantations only returning to their families for brief periods, disrupting child-rearing, marriage and care of elderly parents (Koizumi 2013).

In this chapter, the concepts of global, transnational and translocal space are considered for their utility in the ethnographic study of space and place. It posits that translocality is located in the bodies and spatiotemporal and social fields of people living in transnational circuits and not just properties of a place – an idea hinted at but not fully explicated in the work of Rouse (1991), M. Smith (2001), Kearney (1991), Brun (2001) and Andrucki and Dickinson (2015). The political importance of the concept of translocality is that it returns agency to the immigrants, refugees, laborers and travelers who live these networked and translocal spatialized lives.

One caveat, however, is necessary before embarking on the exposition of the ideas that lead to this conceptual lens. Translocality and the emergence of a translocal space occurs by degrees, experienced by a few people at home or by many people who are part of a transnational network. Public spaces like those depicted in the ethnographic examples of the Moore Street Market in New York City and the New Central Bus Station in Tel Aviv offer great potential for the kinds of encounters and activities that foster this kind of space. But there are private spaces that also cultivate conviviality where translocality can begin to be experienced and expressed.

For example, in East Hampton, New York, the Golden Pear is one of a small chain of takeout restaurants in the area where the mostly Spanish-speaking immigrants who work there have drawn an additional crowd of coffee drinkers other than the long-time locals and New York City weekend and summertime residents. English and Spanish are intermingled as people greet one another while picking up coffee, breakfast or lunch. There are several groups of older English-speaking women and men who meet most days to socialize and gossip. But there are also groups of Latino regulars who work in the area or stop by on their way to work, as well as young professionals who come to get their lattes and espressos. It is the intermingling of Spanish and English, the ritual greetings in both languages and the lively mix of Latinos, locals and part-time New Yorkers that suggests it is becoming a translocal space. Not everyone is part of a transnational network, but as personal relationships develop, family members living in Mexico or Ecuador become part of the conversations of local real estate agents and teachers, as well as lawyers and architects from Manhattan. Certainly, the customers and workers from the Dominican Republic, Colombia, Ecuador and Mexico live translocal lives, but by spending time at the Golden Pear, New Yorkers, locals and Latino immigrants are creating a contact zone where new ideas and translocal relationships are also being formed.

In the following sections, I define the concepts of global space, transnational space and translocal space and discuss how they contribute to my understanding of translocality. I use the term "translocal" to refer to both the globalization process that takes place at multiple geographical and cultural levels – the global, national and local – and to one of these levels, the translocal.

Global space

The globalization of space occurs through rapid flows of capital, labor and information that transform localities through time-space compression, creating even more fragmented, differentiated and de-territorialized spaces. Studies of globalization focus on the emergence of global cities, uneven development of regions and resources, greater flexibility of labor and wages and the marginalization of the spaces of social reproduction (Sassen 1999, Castells 1996, Harvey 1990, Katz 2001).

Eric Wolf (1982) laid the theoretical groundwork for this perspective in his landmark history of how the movement of capital and labor has transformed global relations since the 1400s, dispelling the myth that globalization is a recent phenomenon. Fran Rothstein's (2007) study of San Cosme in rural Mexico, for example, argues that "important connections have existed among different communities for thousands of years but that the connections that emerged with the rise and spread of capitalism in the late eighteenth century provide the framework for understanding the contemporary world" (2007: 4). Over fifty years ago, George Foster (1960) developed a model of how global connections were expressed in cultural terms, identifying conquest culture as a multilayered and contradictory set of beliefs, power relationships and practices. More recently, however, the question has been about how contemporary, post-1970 globalization is different from the historical flows of capital and labor associated with slavery, commodity trade routes, colonization and the rise and fall of empires. Part of the answer lies in the speed and scale of these flows and the degree of economic restructuring and capitalist penetration that has reached even remote communities and corners of the world.

Globalization during the post-colonial period has been characterized by a desire for global connections for new products and the fulfillment of universal dreams, but more often it has resulted in breakdowns and disruptions. The flow of goods, ideas and people that was imagined to proceed without interference instead has encountered *friction* "the awkward, unequal, unstable, and creative qualities of interconnection across difference" (Tsing 2005: 4). This friction between local places and capital flows is also restructuring space through uneven global development of cities and place-based struggles to retain access to local land and resources.

Many ethnographers such as Anna Tsing (2005) challenge the view that globalization is an all-encompassing process and instead examine the articulations of the global and the local at specific sites and across multiple sites and regions (Ong 1999, Mazzarella 2006, Smart and Lin 2007, Leggett 2003).[1] These studies of "glocalization" provide more nuanced and complex understandings of emerging forms of global space (Pries 2005).

Another important spatial consideration is the impact of the de-territorialization of space and place that occurs as a by-product of globalization and spatial restructuring (Sassen 1999, 2006; Susser 1996). Manuel

Castells (1996) captures this transformation in his analysis of the informational city, one in which the "space of flows" supersedes the local meaning of places. Ulf Hannerz (1989) also imagines a society based on cultural flows organized by nations, markets and movements and criticizes globalization analyses for being too simplified to reflect the complexity and fluidity of the emerging multiculturalism. For these critics, global space is conceived of as the flow of goods, people and services, as well as capital, technology and ideas across national borders and geographic regions that result in global space being increasingly detached from local places in contrast to the previously cited studies.

However, even though capital has become more mobile and thus presumably placeless, it has become more territorial in other locations as a result of processes of uneven development. Global flows bypass some poor residents without access to capital, entrapping them in disintegrating communities while entangling others. The flow and mobility of globalization is highly stratified, which results in a kind of "gated globe" that can be seen in border crossings where nations restrict the entrance of immigrants and refugees (Cunningham 2004).

Global flows of commodities and people also create new places and spatial networks, while at the same time de-territorializing them. In the seemingly displaced world of the global circulation of commerce and culture, Ted Bestor (2004) examines the reconfigurations of spatially and temporally dispersed relationships within the international seafood trade. By focusing on sushi quality tuna, Bestor is able to trace the commodity chains, trade centers and markets that make up this global space. He argues that market and place are often disconnected through the globalization of economic activity, but when reconnected, they generate spatially discontinuous hierarchies. The various dimensions of the tuna commodity chain, the social relationships of fishermen, traders and buyers, as well as the economic relationships of markets, marketplaces and distribution circuits create new forms of global space.

A different vision of global space is prompted by the restructuring of universities and the development of degree-granting university campuses at new global sites to produce "world citizens" (Looser 2012). In many ways, cities are the primary spaces of globalization, especially when the state suffers economically and must download its financial responsibilities onto urban spaces. Global cities increasingly use capital markets and compete with other municipalities for bond offerings that provide the funds to bear these costs (Looser 2012). "It is not surprising," Tom Looser argues, "that under these conditions a Special Economic Zone (SEZ) would be an attractive alternative" (2012: 100). SEZs offer a territorial prototype for the global university of English-speaking knowledge production centers that teach "world literature" and "world history" rather than topics related to the region or area where the campus is located.

These new global spaces include Songdo City, a networked urban grid planned by the LG Corporation and funded by Yonsei University just outside of Seoul and the New York University Abu Dhabi campus on Saddiyat Island envisioned as a cultural and educational center funded by the United Arab Emirates (Looser 2012). These universities fit the image of globalization as dissolving state boundaries and producing non-places, yet at the same time they remain located territories with defined borders. Thus it seems that capital is reassembling a new kind of global space, one with a "real geography, with its own sense of an area, and with at least some qualities definitive of sovereignty" (Looser 2012: 108). SEZs allow corporations to make their own rules and regulations within territorially defined urban zones.

The creation of new geographies and forms of global space is in process, whether as a tax-free island, gated globe or space of flows with fluidity of capital. A few ethnographers have offered their own formulations of what global spaces will emerge and whether they will be completely disconnected from local spaces (Looser 2012), create new circuits and relationships (Bestor 2004) or maintain a discontinuous and disruptive relationship with the local (Cunningham 2004, Tsing 2005). At this point, however, the ethnography of global spaces is underdeveloped. The majority of ethnographies of space and place instead focus on the production of transnational space, primarily through the mobility of people and culture.

Transnational spaces

Most ethnographers employ the term transnational to describe the way that people live their lives across borders and maintain their ties to home, even when their countries of origin and settlement are geographically distant (Glick Schiller, Basch and Blanc-Szanton 1992). Part of this effort is to understand the implications of the multiplicity of social relations and involvements that span borders (Mountz and Wright 1996, McHugh 2000) and to provide rich data on the gendered, classed and racialized construction of these places (Robert Smith 2006, de Genova 2005, also see Chapter 4). De Genova (2005), for example, offers another conceptualization, that of "transnational conjunctural space," to describe the Mexican community that is living in Chicago as practically and materially implicated in Mexico to capture the interaction of class formation, racialization and the transnational politics of space.

These ethnographies of transnational space add to conventional notions of borders, boundaries, nations and community redefining the relationship of the global, transnational and the local (Gardner 2008, Cunningham 2004, Smith and Guarnizo 1998). In doing so, they reformulate social and political space, supplanting static concepts of center and periphery, as well as of cultural core and difference at the margins, to imagine fluid, transnational spaces produced by people. Cultural differences found at the margins, initially interpreted solely as signs of exclusion from the center, now also refer to limitations of the nation-state to represent the whole.

Taking into consideration the instability of notions of territoriality as attached to any one place rather than as a political construction (Elden 2013), a number of ethnographers reference transnational communities as "dense networks across political borders created by immigrants in their quest for economic advancement and social recognition" (Portés 1997: 812, also see Glick Schiller 2005a and b, Levitt and Jaworsky 2007) rather than a physical space. For example, the politics of religion such as Yoruba revivalism intertwine portable cultural practices with diaspora imaginaries to form transnational notions of linkage and place (Clarke 2013). Michael Kearney (1995) refers to the Mixtec transnational community as "Oaxacalifornia" to defy previous notions of bipolar spatiality and more adequately represent them as complex migratory subjects. He suggests that this transnational community is spatially unbounded and composed of social and communications networks that include, in addition to face-to-face communication, electronic and other media" (Kearney 1995: 238).

Other conceptualizations of transnational space evoke both the diffuseness and solidarity of these sociospatial formations that are especially useful. Rouse's (1991) notion of "migrant circuits" reflects the flow of information and movement through transnational community networks. Levitt and Glick Schiller propose a social field approach and distinguish the "ways of being and ways of belonging in that field" (2004: 1002). Gina M. Pérez pays attention to the border-spanning activities of people's lives and the practices that are "embodied in specific social relations established between specific people, situated in unequivocal localities, at historically determined times" (2004: 14). She suggests that transnational networks of meaning and power intersect with the contested processes of place-making and that place-making is an important feature of transnational social fields. The idea of place-making as important for migrants and immigrants also appears prominently in the framework of "transcultural place-making" that recognizes the instability of culture and its role in the reconstitution of the city (Hou 2013).

One of the most inclusive definitions includes all these dimensions – material, mobile, symbolic, imaginary and spatial – to view transnational space as "*complex, multi-dimensional and multiply inhabited*" [italics in text] (Jackson, Crang and Dwyer 2001: 3). This formulation approaches the notion of translocality as simultaneously lived-in multiple spaces. The work of Kearney (1995) with his example of "Oaxacalifornia" as a condensed identity, Rouse's (1991) migrant circuits, Levitt's and Glick Schiller's (2004) social field approach and Pérez's transnational place-making are particularly suggestive for the development of a translocal space conceptualization.

Translocal spaces

Globalization also radically changes social relations and local places due to the intervention of electronic media and mobility and the consequent breakdown in the isomorphism of space and culture. This process of cultural globalization creates new forms of public culture and further dissolves notions of state-based territoriality, which reinforces translocal (i.e. place to place) relationships. Arjun Appadurai's (1996) framework for conceptualizing local disjunctures of global cultural flows through "ethnoscapes," "mediascapes," "technoscapes," "financescapes," and "ideoscapes" was one of the first formulations to characterize the irregularity of these landscapes. His use of ethnoscape, that is, the "landscape of persons who constitute the shifting world in which we live: tourists, immigrants, refugees, exiles, guest workers, and other moving groups and individuals" (1996: 33), focuses on how globalization affects the loyalties of groups in the diaspora, the manipulation of currencies and other forms of wealth and the strategies that alter the basis of cultural reproduction. Cultural globalization and public culture cut across conventional political and social boundaries, while cultural reproduction is occurring outside of the nation-state and stable cultural landscapes.

At the same time, Appadurai (1996) redefines "locality" as relational and contextual rather than spatial or scalar. He views locality phenomenologically as social and technological interactivity and reserves the term "neighborhood" for situated communities – virtual or spatial – as sites for social reproduction (1996: 179). Appadurai posits, "The many displaced, deterritorialized, and transient populations that constitute today's ethnoscapes are engaged in the construction of locality, as a structure of feeling, often in the face of the erosion, dispersal, and implosion of neighborhoods as coherent social formations" (1996: 199). His argument, that locality is phenomenological and separate from neighborhoods and other situated spaces, adds virtual and affective dimensions to translocality and its production.

But for many displaced people, displacement is experienced as a feeling of belonging to one place while being physically present somewhere else (Brun 2001). This paradox offers another avenue for thinking more spatially about these processes. For Catherine Brun (2001), space is "practiced place" made up of particular paths to form a "spatial grid" of memory and imagination. Her view of space as the "simultaneous coexistence of social interrelations at all spatial scales, from the most local level to the most global" (Brun 2001: 19) and place as the articulation of these relations captures the simultaneity that occurs with translocality. Most importantly, however, Brun's definition of place and space supports her claim that refugees are not "out of place" as their "place" is at the location where they are present. Refugees live in a place made up of a homeland and their physical location, and, therefore, they are not displaced at all. This assertion leads to a different kind of politics of displacement in which refugees are given more agency and seen as having some control over their lives. This simultaneity of space and place experience through a spatial grid of social relations underlies my conceptualization of translocal space.

Another way to think about translocality is through "transnational urbanism," a term that M. Smith (2005) uses to describe the distanciated yet situated possibilities of translocal connections. He singles out transnational cities as the key sites of translocality and prefers to think about the emplacement of mobile

subjects rather than a space of flows. He traces the development of the translocal space of Napa, California–El Timbinal, Guanajuato, Mexico by examining
the migrant network that contributed almost $50,000 to renovate El Timbinal's
church and town plaza, including benches inscribed with the donors' names.
M. Smith (2005) concludes that translocality is a set of relations and belong-
ings that produce a shared sense of meanings and interests that bind both the
actors and the translocal social field together through the built environment.

Translocal space as a conceptual frame draws on these authors in four
ways. The concept of translocality disengages the experience of locality and
belonging from being situated in a particular neighborhood or homeland
and instead locates it in the mobile bodies and multiplicity of spaces of
immigrant lives. It includes, however, the possibility of simultaneous social
interrelations and the integration of translocal social fields and actors occurring in the built environment, as well as virtually through digital technologies. Translocality reconnects loyalties, affects and spaces that have been
disconnected by global capital flows through the translocal reframing of
everyday life, whether it occurs in a place or through mobile communications systems. Finally, translocal space opens up the possibility of multiple
kinds of social, spatial and political formations through the shared sense of
meanings, loyalties and interests that bind people and places together.

These ideas support the contention that translocal space is a new spatial configuration that has experiential, social and material consequences in peoples'
global and local lives. Although still a work in progress, the conceptual lens of
translocal space offers a way to imagine new and different kinds of spaces that
are emerging in different parts of the world. Whether translocal spaces develop
into locations with political potential depends on many factors, including the
countervailing forces of time-space expansion that pose challenges to the ability to make connections across time and space. Clearly, this examination is only
a beginning of what is a growing area of research and theory.

This discussion highlights the development of a concept of translocal space
but is exploratory and leaves a number of unanswered questions. For example,
what constitutes an adequate ethnographic description of a translocal space?
Who identifies a space or place as translocal? Is translocality something that
people feel and talk about or is it an analytic construct used by researchers to
characterize a particular kind of place, a specific group of people or interlock-
ing set of transnational networks? Even more importantly, is translocal space
individually or collectively experienced and is it always connected to a physical, virtual or imagined space? To address these questions, two ethnographic
examples are presented in the hopes of provoking further debate.

Ethnographic examples

The first example, a REAP of the Moore Street Market, reviews research on
a Latino public market in Brooklyn, New York. The market evokes a sense
of translocality through a variety of mediums, including the daily presence

of Puerto Rican men who remain connected to their homeland, the use of colloquial Spanish, the playing of Caribbean music, the sale and consumption of Puerto Rican and Dominican specialty foods and the shops and walls decorated with Puerto Rican flags and decals of *casitas*. Vendors also produce translocality through their family origins, work trajectories and histories of relationships across continents and national boundaries. The material culture of the market, the vendors' life experiences, the presence of Latino customers, family and friends, as well as specialty products and the celebration of Latino-inflected holidays, create an affective atmosphere that recruits other Latino shoppers and workers into these established transnational networks. Latinos from Mexico, Nicaragua and Ecuador have begun to set up shops offering their own specialty foods and medicinal products, expanding the range of pan-Latin American relationships, solidarity and political, financial and emotional support.

The second example is drawn from the ethnography of Sarah Hankins (2013) and my own short-term fieldwork at Tachanah Merkazit, the New Central Bus Station in Tel Aviv, Israel. Bus stations, where the global circulation of diverse peoples taking buses, shopping and selling, waiting for and meeting friends, listening to music or sermons and stopping for coffee or a meal, offer another potential translocal space. Translocality in this context appears to be produced by the sociality of transnational networks and ethnic affiliation of groups of people who are drawn to specific forms of music that draw customers to certain shopping stalls. Gathering places such as cafés used for drinking coffee, talking and smoking; randomly located tables and chairs used for playing cards; and waiting areas with benches for weary travelers also offer spatial contexts for translocal relations to develop. The ongoing interconnection of migrants to their homelands such as the asylum seekers from South Sudan who live in the parks of Tel Aviv as well as the friendly interactions between Filipinos and Israeli citizens singing karaoke renditions of Israeli songs also suggest the possibility that a translocal space or set of spaces are evolving. Both public space examples – the market and the bus station – provide glimpses of the utility of a translocal spatial approach to the ethnography of space and place.

Moore Street Market in Brooklyn, New York

Introduction and methodology

The Moore Street Market study was an engaged anthropology project undertaken to complement a design and management assessment undertaken by the Project for Public Spaces to forestall the market's forced closing by the city. The Public Space Research Group team, made up of Babette Audant, Bree Kressler, Rodolfo Corchado and I, spent six months gathering data to make the case for the continuation of the Moore Street Market over the long term and to contribute to a revitalization plan that would be responsive to its cultural context and diverse neighborhood. To accomplish this objective, the study was organized as a REAP focused on who was served by the Moore Street Market and how the market functioned as social and cultural nexus for the community.

The REAP evolved as a collaborative process intended to promote ongoing dialogue between the community and the research team while plans were made for the continuation of the market. Not all of the stakeholders, residents and visitors agreed with any single vision of the future, thus it was vital that we interview as many groups as possible, including governmental stakeholders, Moore Street Market vendors, local street vendors, nearby business owners, residents and visitors (Puerto Rican, Mexican, Hasidic Jews, Hipsters, recent Chinese immigrants and African Americans), developers and religious and secular leaders.

The research was concentrated on two fieldwork sites: the market itself and the surrounding neighborhood. Site visits and observations generated a series of maps and field notes. Maps included physical site descriptions, behavioral maps by time of day and day of the week, circulation maps and a physical remains map of bottles, informal shelters, erosions and trash. Participant observation of community and market life produced insights into the social relations and the degree of conflict and cooperation among the groups.

Individual interviews employed a semistructured, open-ended interview covering the use of the market, its cultural and community importance, and its role in neighborhood identity and politics. The life histories of market vendors were recorded and used to obtain a deeper understanding of their migration experience and their developing sense of the market as a translocal space. Expert interviews with political, religious and community representatives were conducted, as well as archival research in the New York City Department of Agriculture and Markets archives and the New York Public Library on how the market was created and functioned during different historical periods (Audant 2013).

Field materials were organized into matrices of spaces and activities to create a schematic overview. All interviews were transcribed in the language of the interview (English, Spanish, Mandarin or French) and then translated into English. The field notes, interviews and maps were read multiple times and discussed by the research team using a reiterative process that identified theoretically and practically important themes. All data were then reanalyzed based on these themes and descriptive narratives were written to present our findings.

Urban setting and history

The Moore Street Market is one of the original enclosed food markets built in New York City from 1941 to 1948. The Department of Agriculture and Markets, with support from the Works Progress Administration, constructed nine enclosed markets in three boroughs to relocate pushcart vendors and open-air markets that were thought to be health and fire hazards. The markets were designed to move street vendors out of sight, make high-quality food available at low cost, encourage immigrants to become small merchants who pay rent and taxes and, in the process, Americanize them. Four of these enclosed markets remain, but they are no longer symbols of progress and instead are public markets whose social and cultural importance is in conflict with their economic viability (Figure 8.1 Map of Brooklyn, New York, and the Moore Street Market).

The Moore Street Market was a thriving, culturally diverse – mostly Irish, Jewish and Italian – immigrant market in its heyday. The neighborhood had a significant Puerto Rican population by 1960, but as late as the early 1970s, some of the original vendors remained. The market and the neighborhood changed during the 1970s and 1980s due New York City's financial crisis and economic deterioration. In 1995, the architectural firm of Hirsch/Danois upgraded the building, adding bright graphics and dropped-canopy ceilings. But even with the redesign, the Economic Development Corporation (EDC) announced that the market would close on June 15, 2007, to make way for affordable housing. The vendors were not given prior notice of EDC's plans and had difficulty organizing a defense.

Walking on Moore Street feels as though you have either gone back in time or left Brooklyn entirely (Photo 8.1 Moore Street Market facade). As you walk east on the street toward the market, there is Puerto Rican music playing loudly from stores on the street with store owners and employees sitting outside on folding chairs watching their goods and people pass by. Although there are several storefronts that are closed or at least never open at set times, there are places on the sidewalk where one can always be sure that there will be individuals sitting or standing. Especially in the summer, people linger in the shaded areas on the steps in front of the *Botanica* or on the makeshift bench in front of the barbershop. The two busiest places are in front of the liquor store next to the market and across from the market in front of the "Jobs" storefront. These scenes are quite different, as the liquor store attracts older Puerto Rican men who sit and drink, while the "Jobs" storefront attracts younger African American men, up to twenty at a time, sitting and only getting up to buy soda and snacks at the local *bodega*.

The contrast to Humboldt Street that runs parallel to Graham Avenue (now Avenue of Puerto Rico) is striking and feels like an entirely different neighborhood. There are very few retail establishments, and the east side of the street consists of public buildings of various sizes, including the imposing towers of public housing located just south of Moore Street. On the west side of the street opposite the public housing is a post office distribution site, the playground of the elementary school, the Moore Street Market and, just north of the market, the Bravo Grocery Store. There is little street life on Humboldt – one can walk for blocks without passing

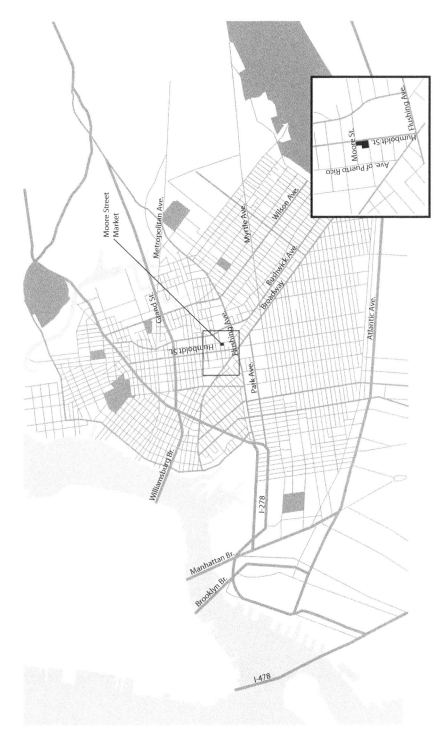

Figure 8.1 Map of Brooklyn, New York, and the Moore Street Market (Erin Lilli)

Photo 8.1 Moore Street Market facade (Babette Audant)

a single person – so that walking on Humboldt feels desolate and even dangerous to someone who is not familiar with the area.

Nostalgia and memories

As with many translocal spaces, the market has always served as an important site of Puerto Rican culture and is remembered as a space where people of all ages met and socialized. Nostalgia for this past is invoked when people reminisce about visiting the market in their youth. It's difficult to get them to stop talking as they describe how the Moore Street Market was "... a lively place everyone knows everyone ... it was fun to go ... we would see people we knew." When customers talk about their youth, they describe the large crowds during holidays that came to buy hard-to-find products like *pasteles* or cuts of meat not readily available in grocery stores. On a day-to-day basis, the market still functions as a location integral to aspects of Puerto Rican life. The market is a "second home" both to the customers who spend hours lingering in the market and to the vendors, many of whom are retirees. The market preserves a sense of community centered on another time and place and of the neighborhood more broadly, but also excludes – to some degree – those who are not part of this history.

A Puerto Rican woman in her fifties was beaming as she described parties held in the market and other events such as parades and holiday celebrations held along Graham Avenue. A Puerto Rican vendor spoke excitedly about the thick crowds shopping along Moore Street and how hard it was to cross from one side of the street to the other. A local business owner described the foods prepared in traditional Puerto Rican homes, where daughters and sons would watch their mothers' cook. There is remarkable loyalty to this neighborhood, even though most people have moved away. Many of the vendors who grew up near the Moore Street Market say that they wouldn't dream of living there today because it has changed so much. Yet the place retains its meaning and memories through the nostalgia it elicits and through the embodiment of a past that can still be experienced by being there.

The decoration of the market also announces its Puerto Rican heritage. Don Manuel's stall is adorned with multiple Puerto Rican flags and contains Puerto Rican–themed key chains, wall art and other ornaments where mountains, peasants and kitchen motifs are depicted. People peruse the cavernous interior of the store and stop when they find what they want among the hundreds of tchotchkes hanging from the racks (Andrade field-notes 2012).

The owner of Delicias Tainas, a catering and prepared foods business, said that he is "bottling nostalgia" since all his recipes are his grandmother's and are authentic dishes of the indigenous Taino people of Puerto Rico. In front of a family portrait sits a large quantity of bottled rice milk liquor, each with an identical portrait of an elderly woman's face printed on the label indicating it is "grandma's recipe." "People come from all over Brooklyn to get this drink," he says. He also has hot food for sale every day.

> There's a line out the door some days, just for these items. I can't make it all fast enough. It's really popular. My clients are a lot of Puerto Ricans, but not exclusively. My catering clients tend to be Puerto Rican, they want the traditional food for weddings and funerals and things like that. But my business here appeals to everybody.
>
> (Amanda Matles field notes 2012)

Memories of holiday events at the market, familiarity with the sounds and smells, nostalgia for an imagined past, traditional and homemade Puerto Rican foods, Puerto Rican flags and decor, as well as ongoing social relationships and everyday routines contribute to the market's sense of translocality for its regulars, shoppers, vendors and other employees (Photo 8.2 Moore Street Market customers).

Generational and transnational relationships

The shifting Latino populations living in Brooklyn and the diversity of Spanish-speaking users are considered an important element in the market's

Photo 8.2 Moore Street Market customers (Babette Audant)

social history. The Puerto Rican vendors see the arrival of Mexican vendors as a positive and desirable sign that bodes well for the market's economic viability. The Puerto Rican vendors do not see the Mexican vendors as rivals, but as complementary to the diversity of their customers. And yet, in spite of the incorporation of new vendors from various Latin American countries, the market's Latino identity is shaped mainly by the influence of immigrants from the Spanish-speaking Caribbean. This dominant Latino identity obscures and subsumes the other Latino identities of the Mexican, Nicaraguan and Ecuadorian vendors.

These differences are spatialized within the market interior. Puerto Rican vendors, all of whom are first-generation immigrants, are located in the social and economic heart of the Moore Street Market (the barbershop, beauty salon, Ramonita's café and one of the grocery stores), while the relatively new Nicaraguans and Mexican vendors are on the periphery (Figure 8.2 Interior drawing of the Moore Street Market).

This central area is also where Puerto Rican and Dominican customers do the majority of their socializing. Caribbean music adds to this particular version of Latino identity shaped by Puerto Rican and Dominican culture. Spanish is almost always spoken: it shapes market life and is used in the majority of business transactions. Puerto Rican vendors interacting with

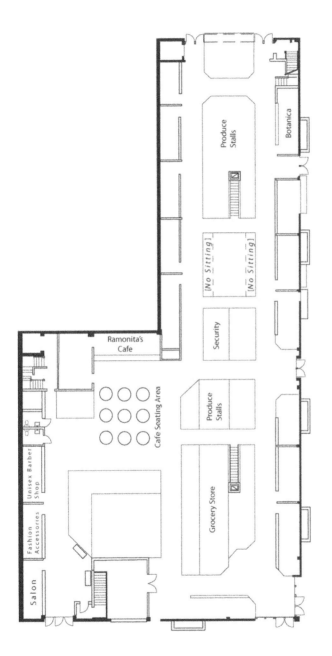

Moore St.

Varet St.

Humboldt St.

Figure 8.2 Interior drawing of the Moore Street Market (Bree Kessler, redrawn by Erin Lilli)

their customers frequently switch back and forth between English and Spanish, but some vendors, among them several Dominicans, acknowledge their lack of English proficiency.

The majority of Moore Street Market vendors came from Latin America, though they did not all come to New York City at the same time. The first wave was from Puerto Rico – from Ponce, Aguadilla and San Juan de las Sabanas. They immigrated during the 1950s and joined New York City's industrial labor force as young adults. In the 1970s, Puerto Ricans were one of the groups most adversely affected by the deindustrialization of New York's economy. The decline of employment in manufacturing, where Puerto Ricans were concentrated, resulted in high levels of poverty relative to other Latino groups. Some of the Puerto Rican vendors lost their jobs when the manufacturing industries relocated to the U.S. South.

In an interview, a Puerto Rican vendor talked about his transition from factory worker to street vendor to his current job at the market. Other vendors had been small business owners outside the market and one a former employee of the grocery store he now runs with his wife and family. Unfortunately, Moore Street Market jobs provide only subsistence wages. A female vendor complained: "I only gain an income to buy the food and pay the bills." Another worried about the rising price of food and housing, as well as declining wages, commented: "Have you seen how food prices are rising? Today it is impossible to buy a house." Others, however, have been more successful, earning enough to avoid these economic worries.

The second wave of Latino migration brought vendors who came after the immigration quota system was abolished in 1965. Immigrants continued to arrive from the traditional sending countries such as Puerto Rico, but others came from Spanish-speaking countries throughout Latin America. Vendors who belong to this second group include rural Mexicans with peasant backgrounds from the municipalities of Izucar de Matamoros and Chila de la Sal in the state of Puebla who began to migrate in the 1970s. Other Latino groups working in the market are Dominicans, Ecuadorians and Nicaraguans who came because of urban poverty, the coffee crisis in Central America and various wars and civil conflicts of the 1980s. Thus the market also acts as a transnational social field creating connections between rural and urban spaces, as well as across Latin American nations and regions.

Mexicans are among the most recent Latin American immigrants to come to New York City and the Moore Street Market. Puerto Rican vendors view them as one of the most disenfranchised groups within New York City, as they are faced with difficult working and living conditions. In the ethnically and racially segmented labor force, Mexicans fill the jobs abandoned by Puerto Ricans. One older Puerto Rican vendor observed, "Mexicans work too many hours. They do the work we don't want to do. They work harder than we do." Poverty in Mexico's rural areas is acknowledged to be one of the main factors driving Mexican migration to New York, yet Puerto Rican vendors also are aware of the poverty Mexicans face in the United States and the reason why they work under exploitative labor conditions.

The Moore Street Market has incorporated successive waves of first-generation Latino immigrants and has served as a means to social and economic mobility. This is especially evident with the second generation, as children born to first-generation immigrants often attend college and move up the ladder to white-collar jobs. A small segment of the Moore Street Market's labor force consists of men and women known as the "1.5 generation," who were brought to the United States as kids or teenagers. Some of the employees in this category work temporarily during school vacations and others are permanently employed at the market, including several Mexican vendors.

Food, music and translocal belonging

Upon entering the Moore Street Market, one sees carefully stacked displays of fresh fruit, yucca and coriander; passageways lined with cases of water and soda; and high ceilings with vestiges of the original 1940s architecture of wooden stalls, the bright panels of the 1995 redesign and ceiling fans reveal a trans-Latino world. Puerto Rican *salsa* music emanating from the video store competes with Dominican *cumbia* blaring from a radio inside the glass-enclosed counter of a narrow restaurant stall where rice, beans, *empanadas* and *arroz con pollo* glistening with oil and rubbed red spice are arrayed. The heavy smell of fried plantains fills the air as visitors gather at the round white metal tables with green umbrellas open to offer intimate places to sit and talk.

The vast majority of customers at the Moore Street Market are Puerto Rican men and women whose regular socializing is valued and prioritized over the purchase of food. In fact, for the Puerto Rican men in particular, buying food is a pretext for the socializing that takes place among the vendors and customers. Often the same men move slowly from one end of the market to the other, perching on the "no sitting" barriers and at the tables in the café area, sometimes taking a tour outside the market onto Moore or Humboldt Streets, only to return later. The Puerto Rican women, on the other hand, are almost always in motion. They often arrive in pairs, chatting as they select their vegetables. If they stop for a snack, it is often eaten leisurely, but while standing, and once their purchases are complete, they move on and out of the market. Unlike the men, the women most often shop at one stand and leave rather than making the tour of the entire space, inscribing gendered patterns of spatiotemporal movement (Photo 8.3 Moore Street Market women shopping).

It seems the food – whether fresh or prepared – appeals primarily to the Puerto Rican men and women who make up the core of its customer base,

Photo 8.3 Moore Street Market women shopping (Babette Audant)

and the younger Puerto Ricans who come on weekends to eat traditional *sancocho* and *arroz con mariscos* at Ramonita's café. Much of the produce is sold from cardboard crates and the handwritten signs may include a scrawled name along with a price such that a customer without local knowledge can not necessarily make sense of the brown, red and beige roots and tubers so important to Puerto Rican cuisine. While the produce sold is not exclusively Puerto Rican, or even Latino, the presence of foods central to a Puerto Rican diet communicates whose market it is. It is the context in which the goods are sold and the practice of exchange in an intimate, social club atmosphere that makes this space so evocative as a translocal space.

The sale of Mexican products by Mexican vendors has contributed to attracting more customers and to incorporating other Latino groups into the market's clientele. Customers from many parts of the city have welcomed the fresh cheese brought from Mexico. At the same time, Puerto Ricans and other Latinos who have adopted some of the Mexican cultural traditions such as *fiestas de quince años*, birthday parties for fifteen-year-olds, are purchasing religious figures initially bought by Mexicans. The adoption of Mexican religious practices as well as the new patterns of consumption during particular periods of the year have increased the sales in other stalls as well.

The future of the market and its translocality

Expectations about the future of the Moore Street Market are connected to its diversity and the gentrification of the neighborhood. As one merchant told us,

> In the old days, things were different. There were about fifty vendors. There were Irish, Polish, Puerto Rican *bodegas*, even people from India. The neighborhood changed as a consequence of the Puerto Rican migration. It became a Latino neighborhood; the *raza Latina* is practically the main consumer in the neighborhood. [But now] things are changing [again]; there are many Dominicans, Mexicans and Chinese.

However, most merchants feel that the market should keep its Latino identity. As one said,

> We have a lot [of] plans for the market. This is a very important and strategic place for the society in general, not only for the Puerto Ricans but for the whole society . . . The place [the market] is strategic because [it] is surrounded by the Latino population and the products that we sell here are very well bought by Latinos.

The expectation of maintaining cultural diversity accompanied by a Latino identity is creating tension and conflicts among the merchants. Some vendors support the idea of bringing new merchants to the market to increase its diversity. Yet, despite this expectation, well-established vendors are expanding their businesses into the abandoned or empty stalls instead of increasing the pool of new applicants.

The future of the Moore Street Market is still not resolved. A new fish market has been added, and both the city and market administration has changed. The neighborhood is rapidly gentrifying as Williamsburg and other parts of Brooklyn become expensive, and White hipsters and more affluent residents are buying or renting new condominiums built by local developers. These gentrifying residents support the market as a historical site and part of the neighborhood's character, similar to the role that Brixton Market plays in London (Watson 2006). But the Latino base of the neighborhood remains as do the institutions, churches and shops that draw Puerto Ricans and others back for shopping, eating and socializing.

This ethnographic example illustrates the ways in which the urban setting and built environment, material culture, sociality of the users, migration and work experience of vendors, as well as the sensory experience – music, smells, tastes, visual representations – and the affective atmosphere – nostalgia, sense of belonging and pride – work as part of the creation of a translocal space. In this sense, the translocal space at the Moore Street Market takes on a positive, agentive quality employed by the vendors to save their market and maintain a place that regulars depend on for their translocal practices and the reproduction of Latino identity and place attachment.

Tachanah Merkazit in Tel Aviv, Israel

Introduction and methodology

The second ethnographic example is based on short-term fieldwork in 2012 and 2015 and the long-term fieldwork of Sarah Hankins (2013) under-taken between 2004 and 2013. My field visits included a few interviews, participant observation, sketches of the interior, behavioral mapping and photographic and video documentation of both the exterior and interior areas. Hankins relied on "a hybrid methodology incorporating participant observation and interviews, critical analysis of audio-visual material and a speculative hermeneutics of the multiple valences of particular *ethnographic moments*" (2013: 283). She utilized techniques from media and performance studies, including the analysis of video footage of events that she attended or found on Internet recordings.

Our field observations overlap in many ways. We tracked the mobility of migrants working in Israel as well as the Israelis who commuted daily, weekly or monthly for work. Documentation through mapping of the microcircuits of the regulars and commuters within the station and the digital recording of gatherings and events were utilized to gather data about the inscription of the space through ongoing physical, social and commercial relationships. I was struck by the degree of place attachment and groupings of ethnically diverse people sitting together talking and laughing. Hankins, on the other hand, focused on the movement of regulars and visitors in relation to the cacophony of sounds and types of music that marked the local from the transnational contexts of peoples' lives.

Urban setting and history

Tachanah Merkazit is the main bus terminal in Israel located in the southern part of Tel Aviv. When it opened in 1993, it was the largest bus station in the world, with a total area of 44,000 square meters. Originally begun in 1967 and designed by Ram Karmi, it was not completed because of financial difficulties. In 1993, architects Yael Rothshild and Moti Bodek finished the station, considered a white elephant by some, and it opened with six floors for bus traffic. In practice, only four of the six floors were initially used as bus terminals, and in 1998, the first- and second-floor platforms were transferred to the newly opened seventh floor. The New Central Bus Station also houses an extensive shopping mall with numerous escalators, elevators and over a thousand shops (Figure 8.3 Map of Tel Aviv, Israel, with Tachanah Merkazit, the New Central Bus Station; Photo 8.4 New Central Bus Station interior).

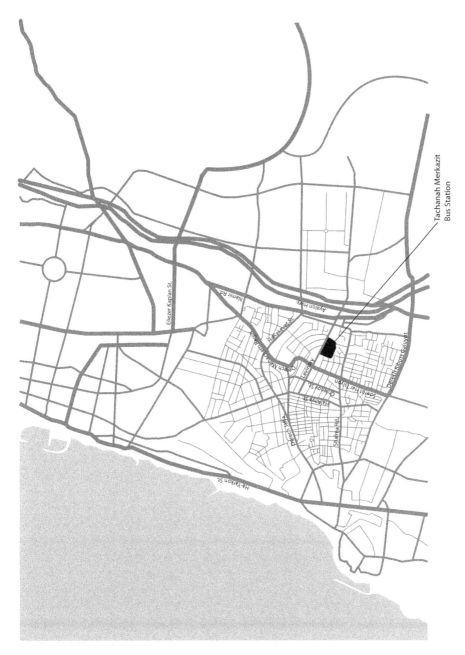

Tachanah Merkazit
Bus Station

Figure 8.3 Map of Tel Aviv, Israel, with Tachanah Merkazit, the New Central Bus Station (Erin Lilli)

Photo 8.4 New Central Bus Station interior (Joel Lefkowitz)

The bus station is a major gateway for both Jewish and Arab nationals and recent immigrants, as well as temporary workers from Asia and West Africa, refugees and asylum seekers from East African countries, tourists and members of other Israeli minority groups such as Bedouins. It suffers from a lack of maintenance and infrastructural deterioration, as it is located in one of the poorest sections of Tel Aviv with a large underserved refugee population. The neighborhood historically has been an immigrant center populated with Mizrahi, Russian and poor religious Jews. The patchwork of self-built housing and do-it-yourself renovations organized along close-knit streets with cul-de-sacs are scattered among low- to medium-height private housing complexes. Because of the diversity of users and the fragmentary and negotiated nature of Israeli citizenship and inclusiveness, it has become a hub of social networking and transcultural solidarity for many of these groups.

Finding the right entrance into the seven floors and two city blocks of the New Central Bus Station is difficult unless you know the layout of the space. Armed policepersons guard the ground-floor entrances marked by metal gates that can be closed and easily controlled. But the multiple exterior walkways and bus platforms offer many entranceways that are used by the various travelers, visitors, vendors and regulars to access this sprawling, busy transportation and shopping hub. The building accommodates numerous markets from a "gray market" of rotating vendors and stalls on the bottom two floors to permanent food stalls and cafés, clothing stores and electronics and appliance stores in the shopping mall. These stores cater to the many kinds of people who spend the day talking or reading in the cafés, shopping in the stores, resting and sleeping on the bus platform benches or walking quickly through on their way to a bus or other destination. The shops and vendor stalls offer a wide variety of ethnic and culture-specific products with cheap to expensive prices (Photo 8.5 New Central Bus Station shoppers and stalls).

Music, diversity and mobility

The diverse peoples who inhabit the bus station, as well as those who travel through, make up a complex network of social, economic and political relationships (Photo 8.6 New Central Bus Station diversity). It is considered one of the most ethnically and racially complex public spaces in Israel featuring Hebrew, oriental and globalized versions of Israeliness, as well as facilitating social interactions among recent immigrants and refugees (Hankins 2013). For Eritrean refugees, it is seen as a place where one can get anything and is important not only because it is inexpensive but also because it provides important services such as a dentist who offers cheap braces for poor refugee families (Weil 2015, personal communication). It also houses Israeli

Photo 8.5 New Central Bus Station shoppers and stalls (Joel Lefkowitz)

cultural institutions, including a Yiddish library and Miklat 209, a performance group theater. A description from Hankins (2013) captures the sense of multivocality, and I would argue the multilocality (Rodman 1992) and possible translocality of the interior of the bus station:

> The sights and sounds of "canonical" Israeliness – soldiers in uniform hurrying to catch a last bus to base, old men rattling *shesh besh* checkers atop plastic tables, shop owners *min ha'schona* ("from the old neighborhood") gossiping in a vintage Hebrew slang – are on display alongside representations of oriental Israeliness ranging from *hamsa* talisman to the strident tones of deceased *musikak mizrahit* star Zohar Argov piped through well-worn stereo speakers. And amidst this Israeli multivocality, vendors hawk their wares in Tagalog and Tigrinya; Ethiopian bridal shops blast Amharic pop music; customers dicker over prices in West Africanized French, filling the *tachanah* with a proliferation of "global" sounds undreamed of a decade ago.
>
> (Hankins 2013: 290)

Hankins' (2013) theoretical argument is that the multiple modes of sensory experience – movement, sonic dominance and sonic effect – become layered in the Tachanah Merkazit, changing it from a "nondestination" or liminal space to a place marked by nondirectional fluidity. This fluidity offers a suspension in a "transitional" space (Pellizzi 2008) better characterized as an experience of being "in between" places in the "midst of mobility" (Hankins 2013). Thus the space has components of both sedentary forms of belonging with aspects of place attachment – common language use, symbolic representation, cultural identification and social relations – and a sense of transient mobility. These contrasting aspects of the space, the mobility and the moments of being in between, produce a special kind of "place-ness" that occurs during those moments when users experience themselves at home while simultaneously being in transient or not at home or even at another home. It is this momentary kind of place attachment combined with the transient and ongoing mobility of individuals and groups within transnational networks that suggests that this public space is also a translocal one.

Hankins also explains how this sense of homeplace is produced in a public space that appears to be transient, but that promotes expressions of cultural identity through music, food, material culture and existing transnational relationships:

> On one hand, minority and non-citizen groups who make use of the *tachanah* can conceptualize it as *their* place, a home base in a city that is rife with ethnic tensions and growing anti-migrant sentiment. Because most people do not consider the *tachanah* a final destination (except, perhaps, long-term shop owners), few individuals or groups seek to

Photo 8.6 New Central Bus Station diversity (Joel Lefkowitz)

claim the *tachanah* as "Israeli" in the way that other Tel Aviv sites are frequently claimed . . . And because the *tachanah* is under-regulated by any central authority, the sonic representations of culture that minority and non-citizens produce therein may be understood as bottom-up rather than top-down, and thus as genuine expressions of identity.

(Hankins 2013: 288)

Some nonminority Israelis also experience the bus station as a transient home with ongoing social relationships and interconnections. For instance, older Israeli men often stopped to talk to some of the non-Israeli regulars, exchanging greetings or inquiring about family members. These men spend the day playing cards on deteriorated folding tables in the far reaches of the bus station space, but then join other groups of people, including recent immigrants and minority Israelis, to have coffee. Joking relationships across the various social and ethnic groups and friendly interactions suggest that some nonminority Israelis become involved in the social networks and exchanges of everyday bus station life and, like the regulars at the Golden Pear in East Hampton mentioned in the beginning of this chapter, appreciate and partake of some aspects of its translocality.

Music, shopping and belonging

Hankins found that the visitors involved in shopping "make choices of movement based on affective and cognitive distinctions between sounds" (2013: 291). Marketgoers patronize shops playing music that reminds them of home or is familiar because of their backgrounds. On the other hand, marketgoers might avoid shops playing music with song lyrics that can be interpreted as sexist or culturally disrespectful, as in the case of feminists, women and religious and conservative shoppers who are offended by sexually explicit terms and references. Sometimes the affective attraction was not so straightforward, such as the way that Russian hip-hop appeals to Russian speakers only because of hip-hop's associations with the "Afro-diasporic struggle and solidarity" (Hankins 2013).

A Filipina karaoke singer who often came to the bus station to perform is another example of the complex power of music performances in attributing meaning and establishing claims. Hankins uses the Filipina's performance of a traditional Israeli song, in which other Israelis join in, to illustrate how music performance can be used to establish one's cultural identity, while at the same time validating and asserting a sense of Israeliness. Other venues for symbolically establishing translocal and transcultural ties include purchasing items that represent one's homeland, such as specialty foods or religious items, while at the same time participating in everyday activities and social exchanges in this transitional and multifaceted cultural space.

For the bus station's regulars and marketgoers, the experience of listening to music is always accompanied by physical movement away or toward the sound in response to its representational significance. Hankins notes that as migrants move toward or away from certain sounds, gather or shop in some places rather than others, they are constructing the space and its sociality. Most importantly, she argues that it is through these sonic representations and the "sonic scape that marketgoers and bus station users are actually moving both in time and space to another section of the *tachanah* to enact their own cultural specificities" (Hankins 2013: 298). It appears that through their bodily movements, they create a temporary translocality that could be transitory or continuing depending on the stability of the social relationships, the permanence of the cultural group and the strength of their transnational networks.

Sound in this context has the power not only to affect individuals and to move their bodies but also to change their minds (Hankins 2013). This analysis of the affective and bodily power of music to create a new kind of space, one that offers ethnic solidarity and yet at the same time is used to signal a sense of Israeliness, adds another dimension to the conceptualization of translocal space. Similar to the way that the *salsa* and *cumbia* music competition at the Moore Street Market played a role in constructing Latino-ness, Hankins's sonic ethnography offers a nuanced explanation of how music can attract and repel the listeners and their circuits of movement.

The New Central Bus Station as a translocal space

The New Central Bus Station is both a transnational social field and transnational cognitive field for many of the participants, but it is also a translocal space in the sense that it embodies diverse cultural spaces simultaneously for many of the people who spend time there. The final verdict on whether the bus station is translocal, however, rests on the perceptions and experiences, as well as the embodied practices, of those who live and work there. Hankins (2013), through her analysis of the sonic environment, provides ethnographic evidence of another important thread that attachs people both to the national context and to the multiple places that they have come from simultaneously. The insight of the role that music plays in creating a translocal space adds to the findings from the Moore Street Market that food, language, material culture and social relationships are crucial to its production. The evidence from the New Central Bus Station emphasizes that the blaring *salsa* and *cumbia* music playing in the Moore Street Market was also part of the formation of its Latino solidarity.

The case of the Moore Street Market, on the other hand, emphasizes that the bodily movement of the users is implicated in its translocality. Hankins (2013) agrees that the movement of people is a part of the vitality of the New Central Bus Station, and she is particularly interested in how the music influences how people move or where they gather. The casual groupings of minority Israelis and noncitizens as well as nonminority Israelis across ethnicity, language and citizenship barriers play a significant role in the production of translocality. What is left unanswered is whether bus station regulars also help one another with job opportunities, financial support and other social and economic resources. While the role of vendors as facilitators, especially through the playing of music, selling of culturally specific items and other symbolic practices, seems apparent, it is unclear whether the different vendors in the bus station (gray market or permanent) are also part of the social networks that gather and dispense (Hankins 2013). Further research is necessary to uncover whether vendor-customer relationships play a role in the social solidarity of workers and customers at the *tachanah* in the same way that these relationships reinforce social relationships and transnational networks at the Moore Street Market.

Conclusion

This chapter has concentrated on the time-space compression qualities of globalization and the possibilities offered through translocal space. However, it is important not to assume that the forces creating translocality are benign or necessarily positive or that these forces do not include the physical destruction of places of meaning and livelihood. Many of the Nicaraguans who inhabit Parque Central in San José, Costa Rica, discussed in Chapter 3, have been forced to leave because of violence, war and economic deprivation. The space of Parque Central, like the Moore Street Market for Latinos in Brooklyn, has become a center of Nicaraguan sociality, exchange, language, nostalgia and music. Temporally and spatially, it offers a translocal space where families come together – often mediated by smartphones and texts – to remember, incorporate and live multiply located Nicaraguan lives.

The space of the New Central Bus Station similarly reflects the violence, fear, poverty and ethnic discrimination that have forced many of the refugees and asylum seekers as well as the African and Asian temporary workers to come to Israel for shelter and work. The homelike qualities and shared identities of people within the bus station and its translocal potential offer a place of respite, recognition and care. New relationships across groups emerge, even while maintaining lives at a distance within its spatial and social confines. Of course, this translocal potential can be perceived as a temporary fix for the fragmentation of these families' everyday practices and routines and the violence that has disrupted their lives. But translocal space also offers, as Brun (2001) argues in her discussion of displacement, a moment of agency and being in both worlds and is therefore placed, embodied and momentarily secure. In our increasingly globalized and fragmented world, these translocal spaces have an important role to play, not to conceal the hardships and inequities of transnational migration, but to imagine a future. Translocality and translocal space are conceptualizations that can potentially represent and facilitate the continuity of social and cultural identities, a sense of personal power and the emergence of new political practices and the expansion of the public sphere.

Note

1 Yet the "global is constructed locally just as much as the local is constructed globally" (Mazzarella 2006: 16) since capitalism depends on both spatial and symbolic resources.

Chapter 9

Conclusion

The aim of this book is to advance the study of space and place by exploring and explaining two well-established conceptual frames – social production and social construction – and four newer ones – embodied space, language and discourse, emotion and affect and translocal space. It examines how these conceptual frames work ethnographically and in relationship to one another. Another objective has been to consider the overlap of the social construction and social production of space and their points of intersection in the search for new concepts and heuristic models that might integrate them. This exploration of multiple conceptual perspectives questions the essentialism and assumed constancy and stability of any one of them and instead encourages a nuanced and multidimensional inquiry into and depiction of space and place research problems. This conclusion emphasizes how the different approaches are employed ethnographically.

The social production of space frame provides a materialist framework and theoretical scaffolding for the layering and buttressing of ethnographic data. There are many kinds of scaffolding – such as cultural history and political economy – each providing different explanatory models and ways of identifying the social, economic and political processes of social production and the power dynamics that inform and govern these processes. Contestation and resistance through political organizing and ongoing struggle in the face of imposed or unjust spatial outcomes persist as an indispensable part of any social production analysis. Various approaches to social production are discussed in Chapter 3, including the social development of the built environment, political economic analyses of space as a form of capital accumulation, spatial governance and social control strategies and space produced through everyday spatial practices and social resistance.

The ethnography of Parque Central ties many of these approaches together by interweaving narratives of the history of San José, the capital of Costa Rica, and Costa Rica's transition from a Spanish colony and a social welfare democracy to a U.S. dependent, neoliberal state. Parque Central's design, urban context and spatial form were constituted by this political economic trajectory despite attempts by citizens to resist the design changes, restrictive regulations and the subsequent policing of the contemporary era. The role of global capital, class-based forms of social control and conflicts between the municipal planners and local users played critical roles in the evolution of this social space and physical environment. Parque Central's history and development reflects colonial power relations, republican elitism and democratic impulses, as well as global restructuring and neoliberalism that have left enduring traces of these sociopolitical forces in the material environment (Stoler 2013).

The Shilin Night Market offers a different viewpoint on how space is produced by exploring informal systems of spatial appropriation by illegal street vendors, customers and the municipal police. At Shilin, there is a carefully orchestrated set of social interactions that occur between the illegal vendors and the police. The dramatic choreography of vendors going into hiding when the police arrive and almost magically reappearing when they leave generates a fluid occupancy of space that enables the market to function even when vendors are responding to the ongoing surveillance, ticketing and the issuing of fines. The collusion of the illegal street vendors, shop owners, local power brokers and the municipal police to regulate the streets and sidewalks without sacrificing the market's vitality and economic value illustrates how the social production of space also includes the material and spatial consequences of social relations, personal histories and group interactions.

The social construction of space offers a complementary meaning-based approach to the materiality of social production. Social construction underscores the strength of constructivism and semiotics for decoding the hidden power dynamics, memories and meanings in sites and spaces. If social production is the framework and scaffolding for the study of space and place, then social construction assembles and elaborates this structure through the bricks and mortar of place-making. Place-making is usually the focus of researchers who are interested in experience-near and phenomenological interpretations of space and place. A sense of belonging to a space or landscape can be established through a variety of sensory, linguistic and imaginary place-making strategies. Significant social constructions of space include the inscription of race, class and gender on the landscape and ideological transformations of space by memories, heritage claims and invented traditions.

Evidence of the social construction of space is ubiquitous, as the surface and shape of the built environment and landscape are always inscribed with indexical and referential meanings. Particularly within anthropology and sociology, the assumption that culture and cultural systems are socially constructed and reproduced through socialization and acculturation is pervasive and considered fundamental to ethnographic practice. Through ethnographic methods, such as participant observation, in-depth interviewing and other qualitative techniques, a social construction of space analysis can uncover manifest and latent elements of a group's ethos and worldview.

The erasure of African American historical sites at Independence National Historical Park in Philadelphia and the destruction of the historic downtown by Solidere in Beirut highlight the significance of historic preservation practices for place memories and cultural continuity. In both examples, gentrification processes that inscribe elite meanings and representations on the landscape destroy local residents' social constructions of place. These reinscriptions occur due to the unequal power relations of local and racialized residents and governmental decision makers. Both the decision to remove African American buildings from the National Park Service area to create a "colonial space" and the reconstruction of downtown Beirut into a more modern, international center were undertaken with little to no consideration of the people who lived there. The fragility of local meanings, settings and places is underscored when the spatial markers of local history are so easily disrupted and ignored.

The conceptual frame of embodied space is proposed in an attempt to move away from an exclusive reliance on a social constructive perspective and macroanalyses of social production. The concept of embodied space posits that bodies and their spatial and temporal fields provide a materialist approach that includes the agency of human and nonhuman bodies as well as the affects and movements of those bodies in the creation of lived space. It integrates the social production and construction of space through a focus on corporality, but also can operate as an oppositional and alternative theoretical perspective that positions bodies and embodiment at the center of a space and place analysis.

Interest in theories that include the body and embodiment as integral parts of spatial analysis respond to the need for a theoretical formulation that combines the empirical grounding of everyday experience – including affective and discursive phenomena – with a materialist model. Research and theory on mobilities, trajectories, paths and projects are included in this frame as they are useful in explaining how spatiotemporal units move through space creating nodes and places. Methodologies that include autoethnography, phenomenological description, sensory recordings, movement maps and life histories are particularly useful in capturing embodied aspects of space.

An embodied spatial analysis elucidates how body-based practices become forms of political action and political consciousness. For example, the trajectories of Critical Mass bicycle riders in both New York City and Budapest transform the city though their cycling and other bodily practices. These practices highlight citizens' "right to the city" by providing a visible metaphor of democratic political action. The ethnographic examples of the *retreta* and *corso*, while not as politically compelling, demonstrate how embodied rituals of strolling reproduce, inhabit and transform the city through walking, appropriating the space of the sidewalk and street for the strollers' own social purposes and private desires.

The social construction of space is mediated by language as a semiotic system that – directly and indirectly – connects space with personal, social, cultural and political meanings and memories. The centrality of language in place-making requires greater attention to the ways that language functions to identify, produce and transform space. Language indicates, measures and names space through place-naming and narrative, but also transforms space through metaphor, synecdoche and other forms of figurative speech. Language analysis is a crucial part of any spatial analysis because of its role in framing the experience of place, reconfiguring social relations and facilitating and constraining material outcomes.

Linguistic analyses of space and place vary from descriptive toponymy and linguistic landscapes to complex deciphering of discourse and text incorporating ambient text, nexus and discourse analyses. Critical discourse analysis is an important analytic and methodological tool because it uncovers and decodes silences and indeterminate referential language. It has the ability to probe and identify the underlying race, class and gender assumptions in spatial relations and the built environment through the examination of people's everyday conversations about living there. The comparison of the discourses of belonging for co-op residents – that of "family" or "people like us" – illustrates how language use, metaphor creation and forms of inclusion produce distinct affective atmospheres and social relations in the two apartment buildings.

Linguistics and sociolinguistics provide a plethora of methodological approaches that characterize, deconstruct, give meaning to and produce space and place. These methodologies include various forms of discourse analysis, including "big D" Discourse analysis that studies the use of language to represent and construct the world and ideology, and "small d" discourse analysis that studies the structure and organization of language. Other methodologies include conversational analysis, tracking of pronoun trajectories, analyses of turn-taking in formal and informal speech events, textual analysis and studies of movement and language. Sociolinguistics has a wealth of specialized techniques for understanding and deconstructing the underlying meanings of "everyday talk" and hegemonic language practices. The scope and sophistication of language-based studies of space and place are also extended by ethnosemantic analysis, language diffusion and Geographical Information System–based language mapping and taxonomic analyses of types of spaces and their uses.

The study of emotion and the built environment also draws upon a social constructionist point of view. Similar to language, emotion is a social practice and body experience that plays a critical role in the interpretation of and response to events and environments. Emotion is preeminently cultural, embedded in emotive landscapes and institutions that direct the sociocultural fixing of emotions in people and places. Methodologies for the study of emotion as a form of social construction of space include traditional ethnographic methods with the addition of phenomenological techniques. Asking people to keep a journal or diary, write stories about places they have been to, take a walk and audio record what is seen while walking and draw pictures or take photographs or videos are additional methods that have been employed to facilitate conversations about feelings, yearnings and sensations experienced in a particular space or place.

A spatial approach to emotion and space also includes the application of affect theory and the metaphors of affective atmosphere and affective climate. This addition opens up the possibility of studying how spaces feel and produce feeling without resorting to representational theories that utilize linguistic labeling and attributions of cognition and consciousness. The strength of nonrepresentational theory is that it directs attention to nonverbal and prepersonal modes of communication and transmission and the circulation of embodied feeling through contagion, contact and circulation. Affect is defined as an intensity or feeling that exists within bodies, groups, nonhuman and human contacts and contingencies and, most importantly for our purposes, space and place.

The methodological challenges of studying affect and space are difficult to solve without concepts such as affective atmosphere and affective climate that link everyday spatial experiences with larger sociopolitical processes. Emotive institutions and emotive landscapes also offer a way to move from emotions as described by individuals to the spatial and media contexts that produce these emotions. The metaphors of atmosphere and climate, however, provide greater flexibility and creativity in thinking through affect, emotion and space interactions and their political potential.

The ethnographic example of the fear of crime and others experienced by many Americans living in the New York region after 9/11 and by people who own homes in gated communities also identifies emotive institutions, such as the media, as one component of the production of a dystopic structure of feeling. In the New York ethnographic example, affective atmosphere and affective climate are used to examine how national threats and the desire for safe spaces are reciprocally constituted through the circulation of ideas and feelings. Affect permeates sites as intimate as the home and as expansive as the city, state and nation. Individual homeowners and neighborhood residents react to the negative affective atmosphere, locating affect – such as feelings of threat and insecurity – in their own bodies and emotional understandings. The sociolinguistic labeling of affect as fear of crime, fear of others and fear of terrorists enables individuals to identify these feelings as emotions that they can act upon. Another example is the different roles that affect played the in the domestic spaces of Cairo during the protests that centered on Tahrir Square.

The final conceptual frame examined is translocal space. Translocal space extends the concept of embodied space to people living in transnational circuits of labor and residence. For individuals and collectivities living in these circuits, life is inflected with the sensory cues, feelings and language of each place. People who live in two or more locations separated by distance, time, physical barriers and governmental borders have access to these spaces simultaneously, not just through their imaginations but also through the materiality of their embodied space. Time-space compression and mobile technologies and software programs that facilitate constant communication and social interaction through texting, messaging, video telephones, Facetime, Skype, EVO and telecommunication's immediacy of experience heighten this translocal experience of space.

Translocal space, however, can also transcend individual bodies through affective processes and the circulation of information such that it becomes more than a single person's experience and instead a spatial emplacement of multiple places shared by interrelated and socially networked families, neighborhoods, groups and communities. The intimacy of ongoing social contacts and the continuity of the social and material environment bolstered by dense networks of financial and emotional support sustain this embodied multiplicity of space. The Moore Street Market in Brooklyn and the New Central Bus Station in Tel Aviv offer complex settings that illustrate the multiple ways that people living in transnational circuits of labor and residence create places and attachments that transform local space into something more.

This radical rethinking of translocality as living simultaneously in multiple places offers a glimpse of the future and the emergence of new kinds of social spaces produced by innovative and emergent modes of living and working in a globalized world. Another new space is global or world space, a culturally and territorially disconnected, capitalist-driven corporate spatial formation organized solely for the generation of profit without the constraints of location, culture or nation-state concerns. World universities purport to be these new global spaces as do SEZs where capitalist development and exchange can proceed unhindered. Translocal space conceived as living in multiple places at the same time and global space conceived as a capitalist space untethered to any locality or culture represent new spatial formations that are being produced by the circumstances of the current sociopolitical and economic historical era and the realities of social reproduction in a globalized world.

The study of space and place that draws upon these multiple perspectives is well positioned to investigate new spatial formations and their meaning and implications for the future. The strength of the spatializing culture framework is that it is flexible, insightful, broad and multidimensional in scope but also pays careful attention to ethnographic details and nuanced explanations. This combination of breadth of theory and detailed methods of recording evidence is helpful for understanding, imagining and predicting broader social, political and economic trends.

Some of the ethnographic approaches discussed are well established with deep bodies of theory to draw upon and a wide range of methodological strategies available. The social production and social construction of space are the two conceptual frames most frequently employed utilizing traditional ethnographic methods and offering considerable explanatory power. The linguistic conceptual frame has been applied less frequently, even though language is a core component of understanding the meaning and use of a space. One of the reasons probably is that linguistic analyses can require specialized language training, professional-quality equipment for audio or video recording and experience producing annotated transcriptions. Sociolinguists who employ methodologies such as narrative analysis and discourse analysis as well as other sociolinguistic strategies undertake most discursive studies of space.

Emotion and affect studies of space and place, while rapidly increasing because of recent theoretical trends, are most often undertaken only by researchers with a background in the psychology of emotions or in cultural studies and literary theories of affect. Training in phenomenological approaches to fieldwork, autoethnographic writing as well as developing an appreciation of and sensitivity to the nuances of interviewing and social and personal context play an important role in the success of such projects.

The two most speculative of the conceptual frames are embodied space and translocal space. These approaches emerged as solutions to theoretical problems that I faced when trying to explain what I was observing in the field. Embodied space developed out of my medical anthropological research on *nervios*, a psychosocial symptom of personal and social distress that was pervasive when I was working on medical systems and child development in Guatemala and Costa Rica. Embodiment helped to theorize the relationship of physical symptoms to emotional and societal distress, now a well-worn assumption within the field of medical anthropology. This early theorizing had an impact on the way that I observed and thought about the relationship of bodies to the production and experience of spaces. As reviewed in Chapter 5, there have been many scholars interested in the relationship of the body and space, and I was able to draw upon a wide range of ethnographic examples to develop an embodied space approach. A broad range of methodologies are also available, including sensory-based and self-reflexive techniques.

Translocal space, however, is not as well substantiated nor has it been applied as frequently as the other conceptual frames. It was developed to explain what I was observing and listening to in the Moore Street Market and the New Central Bus Station. The ways people talked about, used and appropriated space evoked intense attachment and social interactions at the market site, while also evoking images, sounds, smells and behaviors from other cultural settings. The circulation of cultural specialty items, such as holiday foods and medicinal herbs and oils, as well as the circuits of the marketgoers and their family members and their ability to stay in touch through mobile phones alluded to the interpenetration of their social and spatial reality. Reviewing the global, transnational and translocal literature confirmed that it seems that immigrants are living simultaneously in multiple cultural worlds.

Based on these findings and my own ethnographic experience, I began to appreciate how important these spaces are becoming, not only for cultural identity and sociality but also for economic and political relationships and the development of new kinds of solidarities among Latino groups at the Moore Street Market; nonminority and minority Israelis and migrant workers at the New Central Bus Stations; and among locals, New York City professionals and Latino workers at the Golden Pear. These solidarities are sometimes only temporary, evoking a transitory sense of goodwill and increased intercultural knowledge, but in other cases evolve into intimate social networks that cross multiple national boundaries and socioeconomic circumstances. For this reason, I include translocal spaces in this book as an example of an emerging and new kind of spatial formation that has been on the horizon for some time. By adding the conceptual frame of translocal space, I suggest that new kinds of spatialities are occurring that ethnographic research can identify and theorize.

There are a number of conceptual frames that are also important but are not included in this discussion. The importance of mediated and virtual space is referred to in a few of the chapters, but would require another book for careful examination and illumination. Both mediated and virtual space conceptual frames are becoming critical for understanding space and place in the globalized and hypermediated world.

These conceptual frames offer professionals who are interested in the design and planning of space new ways of thinking about and approaching the human/environment interface of urban design and architecture. All of the concepts suggest methods for addressing the problem of creating socially sensitive and sustainable places. Of the approaches explored, embodied space may be the most useful in that it connects the human factors and programmatic aspects of design that determine the physical requirements needed to accommodate people and groups with social, political and symbolic meanings. Embodied space offers designers an integrated conceptual framework for understanding how users' bodies and intentions play a role in the ongoing production and construction of space. It is also a method for considering the ways that design can constrain and limit social and environmental opportunities.

Similar to Massey (2005), I view space and place as always under construction, produced by global to local interactions and constituted by multiple bodies, collectivities and trajectories. In this sense, considerations of space and place shake up the way political questions are formulated.

Many of the approaches discussed in this book accommodate an alternative vision of space and allow for a more progressive politics. As I argue in the introduction, the ethnography of space and place is particularly useful for uncovering social inequality and exclusion and other hidden power dynamics. This book offers concepts and methods for challenging the assumed transparency of space and spatial relations by probing the histories and meanings of their origin and transformation. Hopefully, this fresh perspective will facilitate a more progressive politics of space and place through the formation of new and alternative spatialities and social solidarities.

Bibliography

Abram, Simone and Gisa Weszkalnys (eds). *Elusive Promises: Planning in the Contemporary World*. New York and Oxford: Berghahn Books, 2013.

Ackerman, Bruce and James Fishkin. *Deliberation Day*. New Haven: Yale University Press, 2004.

Agnew, John. "Space: Place." In *Spaces of Geographical Thought: Deconstructing Human Geography's Binaries*. Paul Cloke and Ron Johnston (eds), 81–96. London and Thousand Oaks, CA: Sage, 2005.

Ahmed, Sara. *The Cultural Politics of Emotion*. Edinburgh: Edinburgh University Press, 2004.

Ainley, Rosa. "Watching the Detectors: Control and the Panopticon." In *New Frontiers in Space*. R. Ainley (ed.), 88–100. London: Routledge, 1998.

Alexander, H. G. (ed.). *The Leibniz-Clarke Correspondence*. Manchester: Manchester University Press, 1956.

Altheide, David L. "Notes Towards a Politics of Fear." *Journal for Crime, Conflict and the Media* 1, no. 1 (2003): 37–54.

Altman, Lawrence. "Nobel Prize in Medicine Is Awarded to Three Who Discovered Brain's Inner GPS." *New York Times*, 6 October 2014. 10/7/2014 www.nytimes.com/2014/10/07/science/nobel-prize-medicine.html?_r=.

Alvarenga, Patricia. "Passing: Nicaraguans in Costa Rica." In *The Costa Rican Reader: History, Culture, Politics*. Steven Palmer and Ivan Molina (eds), 257–263. Durham and London: Duke University Press, 2004.

Amar, Paul. *The Security Archipelago: Human-Security States, Sexuality Politics and the End of Neoliberalism*. Durham and London: Duke University Press, 2013.

Amin, Ash. "Animated Space." *Public Culture* 27, no. 2 76 (2014): 239–258.

Amin, Ash and Nigel Thrift. *Cities: Reimagining the Urban*. Cambridge: Blackwell, 2002.

Anderson, Ben. "Becoming and Being Hopeful: Towards a Theory of Affect." *Environmental and Planning D: Society and Space* 24 (2006): 733–752.

———. "Affective Atmospheres." *Emotion, Space and Society* 2 (2009): 77–81.

Anderson, Elijah. *Streetwise: Race, Class, and Change in an Urban Community*. Chicago: University of Chicago Press, 1990.

Andrucki, Max J. and Jen Dickinson. "Rethinking Centers and Margins in Geography: Bodies, Life Course, and the Performance of Transnational Space." *Annals of the Association of American Geographers* 105, no. 5 (2015): 203–218.

Appadurai, Arjun. "Introduction: Place and Voice in Anthropological Theory." *Cultural Anthropology* 3, no. 1 (1988): 16–20.

———. *Modernity at Large: Cultural Dimensions of Globalization*. Minneapolis: University of Minnesota Press, 1996.

Appleyard, Donald. "Home." *Architectural Association Quarterly* 11, no. 3 (1979): 4–19.

Arantes, Antonio. "The War of Places: Symbolic Boundaries and Liminalities in Urban Space." *Theory Culture Society* 13, no. 4 (1996): 81–92.

Ariew, Roger and Daniel Garber (trans.). *Leibniz: Philosophical Essays*. Indianapolis: Hackett Publishing Co., 1989.

Asad, Talal. "Thinking About the Secular Body, Pain, and Liberal Politics." *Cultural Anthropology* 26, no. 4 (2011): 657–675.

Ashmore, Wendy. "Site Planning and Concepts of Directionality Among the Ancient Maya." *Latin American Antiquity* 2, no. 3 (1991): 199–226.

———. *Settlement Archaeology at Quirigua, Guatemala*. Philadelphia: University of Pennsylvania Museum of Archaeology and Anthropology, 2007.

———. "Biographies of Place at Quirigua, Guatemala." In *The Archaeology of Meaningful Places*. Brenda Bowser and Maria Zedeno (eds), 15–31. Salt Lake City: University of Utah Press, 2008.

Ashmore, Wendy and Knapp A. Bernard (eds). *Archaeologies of Landscape*. Malden, MA and Oxford: Blackwell Publishers, 1999.

Ashmore, Wendy and Jeremy A. Sabloff. "Interpeting Ancient Maya Civic Plans: Reply to Smith." *Latin American Antiquity* 14, no. 2 (2003): 229–236.

Audant, Anne Babette. "From Public Market to La Marqueta: Shaping Spaces and Subjects of Food Distribution in New York City, 1930 to 2012." Graduate Center of the City University of New York, Ph.D. Dissertation, 2013.

Augé, Marc. *Non-Places: Introduction to an Anthropology of Supermodernity*. London: Verso, 1995.

Austin, J. L. *How to do Things With Words*. Oxford: Oxford University Press, 1962.

Austin, Joe. *Taking the Train: How Graffiti Art Became an Urban Crisis in New York City*. New York: Columbia University Press, 2002.

Bachelard, Gason. *The Poetics of Space*. New York: Orion Press, 1969.

Balkiz, Ghazi and Marian Smith (reports for NBC News). "TGI Fridays, Irish Pubs and Free Wi-Fi: Welcome to Edward Snowden's Airport Hideaway," 2013. Accessed 2014. Available at http://worldnews.nbcnews.com/_news/2013/06/29/19189848-tgi-fridays-irish-pubs-and-free-wi-fi-welcome-to-edward-snowdens-airport-hideaway?lite.

Banco Nacional de Costa Rica. *La Ciudad De San José, 1891–1921*. San José, Costa Rica: Antonio Lehmann, 1972.

Bank, Leslie J. *Home Spaces, Street Styles: Contesting Power and Identity in a South African City*. London, New York and Johannesburg: Pluto Press, 2011.

Barrett, Lisa Feldman. "What Emotions Are (And Aren't)." *New York Times,* 2 August 2015, sec. Week in Review, col. 1–2, p. 10.

Basso, Keith. "'Speaking with Names': Language and Landscape among the Western Apache." *Cultural Anthropology* 3, no. 2 (1988): 99–130.

———. *Western Apache Language and Culture: Essays in Linguistic Anthropology*. Tucson and London: University of Arizona Press, 1990.

————. "Wisdom Sits in Places: Notes on a Western Apache Landscape." In *Senses of Place*. Steven Feld and Keith Basso (eds), 53–90. Santa Fe: School of American Research, 1996.

Bastien, Joseph W. *The Mountain of the Condor: Metaphor and Ritual in an Andean Ayllu*. Prospect Heights: Waveland Press, 1985.

Baudrillard, Jean. *Selected Writings*. M. Poster (ed.). Palo Alto: Stanford University Press, 1988.

Baumgartner, M. P. *The Moral Order of a Suburb*. Oxford: Oxford University Press, 1988.

Beauregard, Robert A and Holcomb Briavel (eds). *Revitalizing Cities*. New York: Resource Publications in Geography, 1999.

Behar, Ruth. *Santa Maria Del Monte: The Presence of the Past in a Spanish Village*. Princeton: Princeton University Press, 1986.

Ben-Joseph, Eran. *The Code of the City: Standards and the Hidden Language of Place Making*. Cambridge and London: MIT Press, 2005.

Bender, Barbara. *Landscape: Politics and Perspectives*. Providence and Oxford: Berg, 1993.

Benjamin, Walter. *Illuminations*. New York: Schocken Books, 1968.

————. *The Arcades Project*. Cambridge and London: Belknap Press of Harvard University Press, 1999.

Berger, John and Thomas Luckmann. *The Social Construction of Reality*. Garden City, NY: Doubleday, Anchor Books, 1967.

Bernhard, S. "Out of the Ashes." *New York Times,* 2002.

Berque, Augustine. *Milieu Et Identité Humaine. Notes Pours Un Dépassement De La Modernité*. Paris: Editions Donner Lieu, 2010.

Best, Joel. "Historical Development and Defining Issues of Constructionist Inquiry." In *Handbook of Constructionist Research*. James A. Holstein and Jaber F. Gubrium (eds), 41-64. New York and London: Guilford Press, 2008.

Bestor, Theodore C. *Neighborhood Tokyo*. Stanford: Stanford University Press, 1989.

————. "Rediscovering Shitamachi: Subculture, Class, and Tokyo's 'Traditional' Urbanism." In *The Cultural Meaning of Urban Space*. Robert Rotenberg and Gary McDonogh (eds), 47–60. Westport and London: Bergin & Garvey, 1993.

————. *Tsukiji: The Fish Market at the Center of the World*. Berkeley, Los Angeles and London: University of California Press, 2004.

Billig, Michael. "The Dialogic Unconscious: Psychoanalysis, Discursive Psychology and the Nature of Repression." *British Journal of Social Psychology* 36, no. 1 (1997): 139–159.

Birdwell-Pheasant, Donna and Denise Lawrence-Zuñiga (eds). *House Life: Space, Place and Family in Europe*. London: Berg Publishers, 1999.

Birdwhistle, Ray. *Kinesics in Context: Essays on Body Motion Communication*. Philadelphia: University of Pennsylvania Press, 1970.

Bisaillon, Laura M. "Harar, Ethiopia: Dualities, Discursive Meanings and Designations." *Urbanistica PVS*, no. 54/55 (2010): 28–37.

Bissell, William Cummingham. "Engaging Colonial Nostalgia." *Cultural Anthropology* 20, no. 2 (2005): 215–248.

Blackmar, Betsy. "Re-Walking the 'Walking City': Housing and Property Relations in New York City." *Radical History Review* 21, no. 21 (1979): 131–148.

Blake, Emma. "Space, Spatiality, and Archaeology." In *A Companion to Social Archaeology*. Lynn Meskell and Robert W. Preucel (eds), 230–254. Malden, MA, and Oxford: Blackwell Publishers, 2004.

Blakely, Edward and Mary Gail Synder. *Fortress America*. Washington, DC: Brookings Institute, 1997.

Blier, Susan Preston. *The Anatomy of Architecture: Ontology and Metaphor in Batammaliba Architectural Expression*. New York: Cambridge University Press, 1987.

Blommaert, Jan James Collins and Stef Slembrouck. "Spaces of Multilingualism." *Language and Communication* 25, no. 3 (2005): 197–216.

Blu, Karen I. "'Where Do You Stay At?' Homeplace and Community Among the Lumbee." In *Senses of Place*. Steven Feld and Keith Basso (eds), 197–228. Santa Fe: School of American Research Press, 1996.

Blunt, Allison and Gillian Rose. "Women's Colonial and Postcolonial Geographers." In *Writing Women and Space*. Alison Blunt and Gillian Rose (eds), 1–14. New York: Guileford Press, 1994.

Boas, Franz. *The Central Eskimo*. Lincoln: University of Nebraska Press, 1964.

Boatright, Stephen. "Heidegger and Affect Studies: A Case Study of the Transition From Renting to Home-Ownership." *Subjectivity* 8 (2015): 25–34.

Bobo, Lawrence, James R. Kluegel and Ryan A. Smith. "Laissez-Faire Racism: The Crystallization of a Kinder, Gentler, Antiblack Ideology." In *Racial Attitudes in the 1990s: Continuity and Change*. S. A. Tuch and J. K. Martin (eds), 15–41. Westport, CT: Praeger, 1997.

Borden, Iain, Joe Kerr, Jane Rendell with Alicia Pivaro (eds). *The Unknown City: Contesting Architecture and Social Space*. Cambridge and London: MIT Press, 2001.

Bornstein, Avram. "Antiterrorist Policing in New York City after 9/11." *Human Organization* 64, no. 1 (2005): 52–61.

Boroditsky, Lera. "Lost in Translation." *Wall Street Journal*, 24 July 2010, sec. Life. Web.

Boscarino, Joseph A., Figley Charles R. and Adams Richard E. "Fear of Terrorism in New York After the September 11 Terrorist Attacks: Implications for Emergency Mental Health and Preparedness." *International Journal of Emergency Mental Health* 5, no. 4 (2003): 199–209.

Bourdieu, Perre. "The Kabyle House." In *Rules and Meanings*. M. Douglas (ed.), 98–110. Harmondsworth: Penguin Books, 1973.

———. *Outline of a Theory of Practice*. Cambridge: Cambridge University Press, 1977.

———. *Distinction*. Cambridge: Harvard University Press, 1984.

Bourgois, Phillipe. *In Search of Respect: Selling Crack in El Barrio*. Cambridge: Cambridge University Press, 1995.

Boyer, Christine. "Cities For Sale: Merchandising History at South Street Seaport." In *Variations on a Theme Park*. Michael Sorkin (ed.). New York: Noonday Press, 1992.

Boys, Jos. "Beyond Maps and Metaphors." In *New Frontiers of Space, Bodies, and Gender*. R. Ainley (ed.), 203–217. London: Routledge, 1998.

Bradbury, K. L., A. Down and K. A. Small. "Forty Theories of Urban Decline." *Urban Affairs Papers* 3, no. 2 (1981): 13–20.

Brahinsky, Josh. "Pentecostal Body Logic: Cultivating a Modern Sensorium." *Cultural Anthropology* 27, no. 2 (2012): 215–238.

Brash, Julian. *Bloomberg's New York: Class and Governance in the Luxury City.* Athens: University of Georgia Press, 2011.

Brennan, Dean and Al Zelinka. "Safe and Sound." *Planning* 64 (1997): 4–10.

Brenner, Neil and Stuart Elden. *Henri Lefebvre: Space World Selected Essays.* Minneapolis: University of Minnesota Press, 2009.

Brenner, Neil and Nik Theodore (eds). *Spaces of Neoliberalism: Urban Restructuring in North America and Western Europe.* Malden, MA and Oxford: Blackwell Publishers, 2002.

Brewer, Johanna and Paul Dourish. "Storied Spaces: Cultural Accounts of Mobility, Technology, and Environmental Knowing." *International Journal of Human-Computer Studies* 66, no. 12 (2008): 963–976.

Bridge, Gary and Sophie Watson. *The New Blackwell Companion to the City.* Malden, MA and Oxford: Wiley-Blackwell, 2011.

Briggs, Charles L. "Theorizing Modernity Conspiratorially: Science, Scale, and the Political Economy of Public Discourse in Explanations in a Cholera Epidemic." *American Ethnologist* 31, no. 2 (2004): 164–187.

———. "Mediating Infanticide: Theorizing Relations Between Narrative and Violence." *Cultural Anthropology* 22, no. 3 (2007): 315–356.

Briggs, Jean. *Never in Anger: Portrait of an Eskimo Family.* Cambridge: Harvard University Press, 1970.

Brodkin, Karen. *How Jews Became White Folks & What That Says About Race in America.* New Brunswick, NJ: Rutgers University Press, 2000.

Brown, Jacqueline Nassy. "Black Liverpool, Black America, and the Gendering of Diasporic Space." *Cultural Anthropology* 13, no. 3 (1998): 291–325.

———. *Dropping Anchor, Setting Sail: Geographies of Race in Black Liverpool.* Princeton and Oxford: Princeton University Press, 2005.

Brown, Michael P. *Closet Space: Geographies of Metaphor From the Body to the Globe.* London: Routledge, 2000.

Brown, Wendy. "American Nightmare: Neoliberalism, Neoconservatism, and De-Democratization." *Political Theory* 34, no. 6 (2006): 690–714.

Brun, Catherine. "Reterritorizing the Relationship Between People and Place in Refugee Studies." *Geografiska Annaler* 83 B, no. 1 (2001): 15–25.

Buchli, Victor. *The Anthropology of Architecture.* London: Bloomsbury, 2013.

Burawoy, Michael. "For Public Sociology." *American Sociological Review.* 70, no. 1 (February 2005): 4–28.

Burawoy, Michael, et al. *Ethnography Unbound: Power and Resistance in the Modern Metropolis.* Berkeley: University of California Press, 1991.

Burns, Ausra. "Emotion and Urban Experience: Implications for Design." *Design Issues* 16, no. 3 (2000): 67–79.

Butler, Judith. *Bodies That Matter: On the Discursive Limits of Sex.* New York and London: Routledge, 1993.

———. *Undoing Gender.* New York: Routledge, 2004.

Buttimer, Anne and David Seamon. *The Human Experience of Space and Place.* London: Croom Helm, 1980.

Caldeira, Teresa P. R. *City of Walls: Crime, Segregation, and Citizenship in São Paulo.* Berkeley: University of California Press, 2000.

————. "Imprinting and Moving Around: Vew Visibility and Configurations of Public Space in São Paulo." *Public Culture* 24, no. 2 (2012): 385–418.

Calvo Mora, Joaquin B. (comp.). *Apuntamientos Geográficos, Estadísticos e Históricos*. San José, Costa Rica: Imprenta Nacional, 1887.

Cannon, Walter. "'Voodoo' Death." *American Anthropologist* 44 (1942): 169–181.

Carleton, Don Edward. *A Crisis of Rapid Change: The Red Scare in Houston, 1945–1955*. Houston: University of Houston Press, 1978.

————. *Red Scare: Right Wing Hysteria, Fifties Fanaticism, and Their Legacy in Texas*. Austin: Texas Monthly Publications, 1985.

Carter, Rebecca Louise. "Valued Lives in Violent Places: Black Urban Placemaking at a Civil Rights Memorial in New Orleans." *City & Society* 26, no. 2 (2014): 239–261.

Cartier, Carolyn. "Symbolic City/Regions and Gendered Identity Formation in South China." *Provincial China* 8, no. 1 (2003): 60–77.

Casey, Edward. *Getting Back Into Place: Toward a Renewed Understanding of the Place-World*. Bloomington: Indiana University Press, 1993.

————. "How to Get From Space to Place in a Fairly Short Stretch of Time: Phenomenological Prolegomena." In *Senses of Place*. Steven Feld and Keith H. Basso (eds), 13–52. Santa Fe: School of American Research Press, 1996.

————. *The Fate of Place: A Philosophical History*. Berkeley: University of California Press, 1998.

————. "Between Geography and Philosophy: What Does It Mean to Be in the Place-World?" *Annals of the Association of American Geographers* 91, no. 4 (2001): 683–693.

Castells, Manuel. *The City and the Grassroots*. London and New York: Macmillan, 1983.

————. *The Rise of the Network Society*. Malden, MA: Blackwell, 1996.

Cerwonka, Allaine. *Native to the Nation: Disciplining Landscapes and Bodies in Australia*. Minneapolis and London: University of Minnesota Press, 2004.

Chambers, Iain. *Popular Culture: The Metropolitan Experience*. London: Methuen, 1986.

————. *Border Dialogues: Journeys in Postmodernity*. London: Routledge, 1990.

Chappell, Ben. "Custom Contestations: Lowriders and Urban Space." *City & Society* 22, no. 1 (2010): 25–47.

Chesluk, Benjamin. *Money Jungle: Imagining the New Times Square*. New Brunswick, NJ and London: Rutgers University Press, 2008.

Chiu, Chihsin. "Informal Management, Interactive Performance: Street Vendors and Police in a Taipei Night Market." *International Development Planning Review* 35, no. 4 (2013): 335–352.

Chudacoff, Howard P. *Major Problems in American Urban History*. Toronto: D.C. Heath and Co, 1983.

Clark, Mary A. "Transnational Alliances and Development Policy in Latin American: Non-Traditional Export Promotion in Costa Rica." *Latin American Research Review* 32, no. 2 (1997): 71–98.

————. *Gradual Economic Reform in Latin America: The Costa Rican Experience*. Albany, NY: State University of New York Press, 2001.

Clarke, Kamari. "Transnational Yoruba Revivalism and the Diasporic Politics of Heritage." *American Ethnologist* 34, no. 4 (2007): 721–734.

———. "Notes on Cultural Citizenship in the Black Atlantic World." *Cultural Anthropology* 28, no. 3 (2013): 464–474.

Clendinnen, Inga. *Aztecs*. Cambridge: Cambridge University Press, 1991.

Clifford, James. "Travelling Cultures." In *Cultural Studies*. Lawrence Grossberg, Cary Nelson and Paula A. Treichler (eds), 96–112. London: Routledge, 1992.

Cloke, Paul, Jon May and Sarah Johnsen. "Performativity and Affect in the Homeless City." *Environment and Planning D: Society and Space* 26, no. 2 (2008): 241–263.

Clough, Patricia T. *The Affective Turn: Theorizing the Social*. Durham: Duke University Press, 2007.

Colwell-Chanthaphonh, Chip and T. J. Ferguson. "Memory Pieces and Footprints: Multivocality and the Meanings of Ancient Times and Ancestral Places among the Zuni and Hopi." *American Anthropologist* 108, no. 1 (2006): 148–162.

Conejero, Susana and Itziar Etxebarria. "The Impact of Madrid Bombing on Personal Emotions, Emotional Atmosphere and Emotional Climate." *Journal of Social Issues* 63, no. 2 (2007): 273–287.

Conover, M. "The Rochdale Principles in American Cooperative Associations." *The Western Political Quarterly* 12, no. 1 (1959): 111–122.

Cooper, Matthew. "Access to the Waterfront: Transformation of Meaning on the Toronto Lakeshore." In *The Cultural Meaning of Urban Space*. Robert Rotenberg and Gary McDonogh (eds), 157–172. Westport and London: Bergin & Garvey, 1993.

———. "Spatial Discourse and Social Boundaries." *City & Society* Annual Review (1994): 92–117.

Cooper, Matthew and Margaret Rodman. "Conflicts Over Use Values in an Urban Canadian Housing Cooperative." *City & Society* 4, no. 1 (1990): 44–57.

Copjec, Joan and Michael Sorkin. *Giving Ground: The Politics of Propinquity*. New York: Verso, 1999.

Córdoba Azarate, Matilde. "Contentious Hotspots: Ecotourism and the Restructuring of Place at the Biosphere Reserve Ria Celestun (Yucatan, Mexico)." *Tourist Studies* 10, no. 2 (2010): 99–116.

Coronil, Fernando. *The Magic State: Nature, Money, and Modernity in Venezuela*. Chicago: The University of Chicago Press, 1997.

Cox, Aimee. "The Body and the City Project: Young Black Women Making Space, Community, and Love in Newark, New Jersey." *Feminist Formations* 26, no. 3 (2014): 1–28.

———. *Shapeshifters: Black Girls and the Choreography of Citizenship*. Durham: Duke University Press, 2015.

Crang, Mike and Nigel Thrift. *Thinking Space*. London and New York: Routledge, 2000.

Cresswell, Tim. "Imagining the Nomad: Mobility and the Postmodern Primitive." In *Space and Social Theory*. Georges Benko and Ulf Strohmayer (eds), 360–382. Oxford: Blackwell, 1997.

———. *Geographic Thought: A Critical Introduction*. Malden, MA: Wiley-Blackwell, 2013.

———. *Place: An Introduction*. Malden, MA and Oxford: Wiley-Blackwell, 2015.

Croft, Robin. "Folklore, Families, and Fear: Exploring the Influence of the Oral Tradition on Consumer Decision-Making." *Journal of Marketing Management* 22, no. 9–10 (2006): 1047–1070.

Csordas, Thomas J. "Embodiment and Cultural Phenomenology." In *Perspectives on Embodiment: The Intersections of Nature and Culture*. Gail Weiss and Honi Fern Haber (eds), 143–164. New York: Routledge, 1999.

Cunningham, Hilary. "Nations Rebound?: Crossing Borders in a Gated Globe." *Identities: Global Studies on Cultural and Power* 11, no. 3 (2004): 329–350.

Czeglédy, André. "Getting Around Town: Transportation and the Built Environment in Post-Apartheid South Africa." *City & Society* 16, no. 2 (2004): 63–92.

Dalakoglou, Dimitris. "The Movement and the 'Movement' of Syntagma Square-Hot Spots Cultural Anthropology Online," February 2013. Accessed 2014. Available at www.culanth.org/fieldsights/70-the-movement-and-the-movement-of-syntagma-square.

Damasio, Antonio. *The Feeling of What Happens: Body and Emotion in the Making of Consciousness*. New York: Harcourt, 1999.

———. "Feelings of Emotion and the Self." *Annals of the New York Academy of Sciences* 1001 (2003a): 253–261.

———. *Looking for Spinoza: Joy, Sorrow, and the Feeling Brain*. New York: Harcourt, 2003b.

Darwin, Charles. *The Expression of the Emotions in Man and Animals*. New York: Oxford University Press, 1872–1965.

Daveluy, Michelle and Jenanne Ferguson. "Scripted Urbanity in the Canadian North." *Journal of Linguistic Anthropology* 19, no. 1 (2009): 78–100.

Davidson, Joyce, Liz Bondi and Mick Smith. *Emotional Geographies*. Aldershot: Ashgate, 2005.

Davis, Mike. *City of Quartz: Excavating the Future in Los Angeles*. New York: Vintage Books, 1992.

———. *Ecology of Fear: Los Angeles and the Imagination of Disaster*. New York: Metropolitan Books, 1998.

———. *Dead Cities and Other Tales*. New York: W.W. Norton, 2002.

Davis, Susan G. *Parades and Power: Street Theatre in Nineteenth-Century Philadelphia*. Philadelphia: Temple University Press, 1986.

Day, Kristen. "Being Feared: Masculinity and Race in Public Space." *Environment and Planning A* 38, no. 3 (2006): 569–586.

de Certeau, Michel. *L'Invention Du Quotidien* (Practice of Everyday Life), Vol. 1, 10–18. Arts de Faire. Union Générale D'éditions, 1980.

———. *The Practices of Everyday Life*. Berkeley: University of California, 1984.

De Genova, Nicholas. *Working the Boundaries: Race, Space and "Illegality" in Mexican Chicago*. Durham and London: Duke University Press, 2005.

DeFilippis, James. *Unmaking Goliath: Community Control in the Face of Global Capital*. New York: Routledge, 2003.

Dehaene, Michiel and Lieven De Cauter (eds). *Heterotopia and the City: Public Space in a Postcivil Society*. London and New York: Routledge, 2008.

DeLanda, Manuel. *A New Philosophy of Society: Assemblage Theory and Social Complexity*. London: Continuum, 2006.

Deleuze, Gilles. *Pure Immanence: Essays on a Life*. New York: Zone Books, 2001.

———. *Two Regimes of Madness*. Paris: Semiotexte, 2006.

Deleuze, Gilles and Félix Guattari. *Nomadology: The War Machine*. New York: Semiotexte, 1986.

———. *A Thousand Plateaus: Capitalism and Schizophrenia.* Minneapolis and London: University of Minnesota Press, 1987.

de Mora, Nini. *San José: Su Desarrollo, Su Título de Ciudad. Su Rango de Capital de Costa Rica.* San José, Costa Rica: Universidad de Costa Rica, 1973.

de Rivera, J. H. "Emotional Climate: Social Structure and Emotional Dynamics." In *International Review of Studies on Emotion.* K. T. Strongman (ed.), 197–218. New York: John Wiley and Sons, 1992.

de Rivera, Joseph, Rahael Kurrien and Nina Olsen. "The Emotional Climate of Nations and Their Culture of Peace." *Journal of Social Issues* 63, no. 2 (2007): 255–272.

de Rivera, Joseph and Dario Paez. "Emotional Climate, Human Security and Cultures of Peace." *Journal of Social Issues* 63, no. 2 (2007): 233–254.

Desjarlais, Robert. *Body and Emotion: The Aesthetics of Illness and Healing in the Nepal Himalayas.* Philadelphia: University of Pennsylvania Press, 1992.

———. *Shelter Blues: Sanity and Selfhood Among the Homeless.* Philadelphia: University of Pennsylvania Press, 1997.

Diaz Cardona, Rebio N. "Ambient Text and the Urban Environment." The Graduate Center of the City University of New York. Dissertation, 2012.

———. "Ambient Text and the Becoming Space of Writing." *Environment and Planning D.: Society and Space.* (2016) February 17. Online.

Dixon, John and Kevin Durrheim. "Displacing Place-Identity: a Discursive Approach to Locating Self and Other." *British Journal of Social Psychology* 39, no. 1 (2000): 27–44.

Douglas, Mary. *Natural Symbols.* Harmondsworth: Penguin, 1970.

———. "Do Dogs Laugh? A Cross-Cultural Approach to Body Symbolism." *Journal of Psychosomatic Research* 15, no. 4 (1971): 387–390.

———. *Cultural Bias.* Occasional Paper No. 34 of the Royal Anthropological Institute of Great Britain and Ireland. London: Royal Anthropological Institute, 1978.

Dovey, Kim. *Becoming Places: Urbanism/Architecture/Identity/Power.* New York and London: Routledge, 2010.

Drake, St. Clair and Horace R. Cayton. *A Study of Negro Life in a Northern City.* Chicago: University of Chicago Press, 1945.

Droseltis, Orestis and Vivian L. Vignoles. "Towards an Integrative Model of Place Identification: Dimensionality and Predictors of Intrapersonal-Level Place Preferences." *Journal of Environmental Psychology* 30, no. 3 (2010): 23–34.

Duncan, James and David Ley. *Place/Culture/Representation.* London and New York: Routledge, 1993.

Duncan, Nancy. "(Re)Placings." In *BodySpace: Destabilizing Geographies of Gender and Sexuality.* Nancy Duncan (ed.), 1–10. London: Routledge, 1996.

Dunlap, David W. "Residents Suing to Stop 'Fortresslike' Plan for World Trade Center." *New York Times,* 14 November 2013, sec. National News, p. A31.

Duranti, Alessandro. "Language and Bodies in Social Space: Samoan Ceremonial Greetings." *American Anthropologist* 94, no. 3 (1992): 657–691.

Durkheim, Emile. *The Elementary Forms of the Religious Life.* New York: Free Press, 1965.

———. *The Rules of Sociological Method, and Selected Texts on Sociology and Its Method.* London: Macmillan, 1982.

Duyvendak, Jan Willem. *The Politics of Home*. New York: Palgrave Macmillan, 2011.

Economist American Survey. "Government by the Nice for the Nice." *The Economist* 324, no. 7769 (1992) 25–26.

Edelman, Marc. *Peasants Against Globalization: Rural Social Movements in Costa Rica*. Stanford: Stanford University Press, 1999.

———. "Bringing the Moral Economy Back in to the Study of 21st-Century Transnational Peasant Movements." *American Anthropologist* 107, no. 3 (2005): 331–345.

———. "Food Sovereignty: A Critical Dialogue." Conference Paper #72. New Haven: 2013.

Edelman, Marc and Joanne Kenen (eds). *The Costa Rican Reader*. New York: Grove Weidenfeld, 1989.

Ehrenfeucht, Renia. "New Geographies of Publics, Spaces and Politics. Presented at the Annual Meeting of the American Association of Geographers. 2012.

Einstein, Albert. *Ether and the Theory of Relativity*. London: Methuen, 1922.

Eisenstadt, Peter. *Rochale Village: Robert Moses, 6,000 Families, and New York City's Great Experiment in Integrated Housing*. Ithaca and London: Cornell University Press, 2010.

Ekman, Paul. *Face of Man: Universal Expression in a New Guinea Village*. New York: Garland, 1980.

———. *Emotions Revealed*. New York: Times Books, 2003.

Elden, Stuart. *The Birth of Territory*. Chicago and London: University of Chicago, 2013.

Eng, David and David Kazanjian. *Loss: The Politics of Mourning*. Berkeley: University of California Press, 2002.

Entrikin, J. Nicholas. *The Betweenness of Place: Towards a Geography of Modernity*. Baltimore: Johns Hopkins University Press, 1991.

Erikson, Erik H. *Childhood and Society*. New York: W. W. Norton, 1950.

Erickson, Frederick. *Talk and Social Theory: Ecologies of Speaking and Listening in Everyday Life*. Cambridge: Polity, 2004.

Escobar, Jesus R. "The Plaza Mayor of Madrid: Architecture and Urbanism for the Capital of Spain, 1560–1630." *Center, National Gallery of Art,* 15 (1995): 63–64.

Fainstein, Susan. *The City Builders: Property, Politics, and Planning in London and New York*. Oxford and Cambridge: Blackwell, 1994.

Fairclough, N. *Critical Discourse Analysis*. London: Longman, 1995.

Fanelli, Doris. Chief of Cultural Resources Management at Independence National Historical Park, National Park Service. Personal Communication with documentation, 2014.

Farman, Abou. "Speculative Matter: Secular Bodies, Minds, and Persons." *Cultural Anthropology* 28, no. 4 (2013): 737–759.

Fassin, Didier. "Why Ethnography Matters: An Anthropology and Its Publics." *Cultural Anthropology* 28, no. 4 (2013): 621–646.

Faubion, James and George E. Marcus. "Constructionism in Anthropology." In *Handbook of Constructionist Research*. James A. Holstein and Jaber F. Gubrium (eds), 67–84. New York and London: The Guilford Press, 2008.

Feagin, Joe R. *Free Enterprise City: Houston in a Political Economic Perspective*. New Brunswick: Rutgers University Press, 1988.

———. *The New Urban Paradigm: Critical Perspectives on the City*. New York: Rowman & Littlefield, 1998.

Feld, Steven. *Sound and Sentiment: Birds, Weeping, Poetics and Song in Kaluli Expression* (2nd edition) Philadelphia: University of Pennsylvania Press, 1990.

———. "Waterfall of Song: An Acoustemology of Place Resounding in Bosavi, Papua New Guinea." In *Senses of Place*. Steven Feld and Keith Basso (eds), 91–136. Santa Fe: School of American Research Press, 1996.

Feld, Steven and Keith Basso. "Introduction." In *Senses of Place*. Steven Feld and Keith Basso (eds), 3–12. Santa Fe: School of American Research Press, 1996.

Feldman, Roberta M. "Settlement-Identity: Psychology Bonds in a Mobile Society." *Environment and Behavior* 22, no. 2 (1990): 183–229.

Fennell, Catherine. "'Project Heat' and Sensory Politics in Redeveloping Chicago Public Housing." *Ethnography* 12, no. 1 (2011): 40–64.

Ferguson, James and Akhil Gupta. "Spatializing States: Toward an Ethnography of Neoliberal Governmentality." *American Ethnologist* 29, no. 4 (2002): 981–1002.

Fernandez, James W. "Fang Architectonics." *Working Papers in the Traditional Arts, No. 1*. Philadelphia: Institute for the Study of Human Issues, 1977.

———. "Emergence and Convergence in Some African Sacred Places." *Geoscience & Man* 24 (1984): 31–42.

———. *Persuasions and Performances: The Play of Tropes in Culture*. Bloomington: Indiana University Press, 1986.

Ferraro, Rafael. *Einstein's Space-Time: An Introduction to Special and General Relativity*. New York: Springer, 2007.

Filler, Martin. *Makers of Modern Architecture, Volume I: From Frank Lloyd Wright to Frank Gehry*. New York: New York Review of Books, 2007.

———. *Makers of Modern Architecture, Volume II: From Le Corbusier to Rem Koolhaas*. New York: New York Review of Books, 2013.

Fisher, Daniel. "Running Amok or Just Sleeping Rough: Long-Grass Camping and the Politics of Care in Northern Australia." *American Ethnologist* 39, no. 1 (2012): 171–186.

Fisher, Robert. "Urban Policy in Houston." *Urban Studies* 26, no. 1 (1989): 144–154.

Fiske, John. "Surveilling the City: Whiteness, the Black Man and Democratic Totalitarianism." *Theory Culture Society* 15, no. 2 (1998): 67–88.

Flannery, Kent V. "Process and Agency in Early State Formation." *Cambridge Archaeological Journal* 9, no. 1 (1999): 3–21.

Flusty, S. "Building Paranoia." In *Architecture of Fear*. N. Ellin (ed.), 47–60. New York: Princeton Architectural Press, 1997.

Forty, A. *Words and Buildings: A Vocabulary of Modern Architecture*. London: Thames and Hudson, 2000.

Foster, George. *Culture and Conquest: The American Spanish Heritage*. New York: Viking Fund Publications in Anthropology, 1960.

Foucault, Michel. *The Order of Things: An Archaeology of the Human Sciences*. New York: Vintage Books, 1973.

———. *Discipline and Punish: The Birth of Prison*. New York: Vintage, 1975.

———. *Language, Counter-Memory, Practice*. Ithaca: Cornell University Press, 1977.

———. "Des Espaces Autres." *Architecture, Mouvement, Continuite* 5 (1984): 46–49.

———. "Of Other Space." *Diacritics* Spring (1986): 22–27.

———. *Security, Territory, Population: Lectures at the Collège De France, 1977–1978*. New York: Palgrave, 2007.

Foucault, Michel and Paul Rabinow. *The Foucault Reader*. New York: Pantheon Books, 1984.

Fouratt, Caitlin. "A Multiply Wounded Country: The Legacies of Crisis in Nicaraguan Migration." *Anthropology News* September–October (2013): 5–6.

Frank, Alan, Patricia T. Clough and Steven Seidman (eds). *Intimacies: The New World of Relational Life*. New York and London: Routledge, 2013.

Frankenberg, Ruth. *White Women, Race Matters: The Social Construction of Whiteness*. Minneapolis: University of Minnesota Press, 1996.

———. "The Mirage of an Unmarked Whiteness." In *The Making and Unmaking of Whiteness*. Birgit Brander Rasmussen, Irene J. Nexica, Eric Klinenberg and Matt Wray (eds), 72–96. Durham: Duke University Press, 2001.

Frantz, Klaus. "Gated Communities in the USA: A New Trend in Urban Development." *Espace, Populations, Societes* 1 (2000–2001): 101–113.

Freeman, Joshua. *Working Class New York: Life and Labor Since World War II*. New York: New Press, 2002.

Freudendal-Pedersen, Malene. "Cyclists as Part of the City's Organism: Structural Stories on Cycling in Copenhagen." *City & Society* 27, no. 1 (2015): 30–50.

Fried, Marc. "Grieving for a Lost Home." In *Urban Condition*. Len Duhl (ed.), 359–379. New York: Basic Books, 1963.

———. "Continuities and Discontinuities of Place." *Journal of Environmental Psychology* 20, no. 3 (2000): 193–205.

Frieden, Bernard J. and Sagalyn Lynne B., eds. *Downtown, Inc: How America Rebuilds Cities*. Cambridge: MIT Press, 1989.

Gans, Herbert. *The Urban Villagers: Group and Class in the Life of Italian Americans*. New York: Free Press, 1962.

García Canclini, Néstor. *Consumers and Citizens: Globalization and Multicultural Conflicts*. Minneapolis: University of Minneapolis, 2001.

Gardner, Andrew M. "Strategic Transnationalism: The Indian Diasporic Elite in Contemporary Bahrain." *City & Society* 20, no. 1 (2008): 54–78.

Garland, David. *The Culture of Control: Crime and Social Order in Contemporary Society*. Chicago: University of Chicago Press, 2001.

Gee, James Paul. *Social Linguistics and Literacies: Ideology in Discourses*. London: Falmer, 1990.

Geertz, Clifford. *The Interpretation of Cultures*. New York: Basic Books, 1993.

Geller, Pamela. "Bodyscapes, Biology and Heteronormativity." *American Anthropologist* 111, no. 4 (2009): 504–516.

Gengzhi, Huang, Desheng Xue and Zhigang Li. "From Revanchism to Ambivalence: The Changing Politics of Street Vending in Guangzhou." *Antipode* 46, no. 1 (2014): 170–189.

Gerber, Brian J., David B. Cohen, Brian Cannon, Dennis Patterson and Kendra Stewart. "On the Front Line: American Cities and the Challenge of Homeland Security Preparedness." *Urban Affairs Review* 41, no. 2 (2005): 182–210.

Gershoff, Elizabeth and J. Lawrence Aber. "Assessing the Impact of September 11th, 2001 on Children, Youth, and Parents: Methodological Challenges to Research on Terrorism and Other Nonnormative Events." *Applied Developmental Science* 8, no. 3 (2004): 106–110.

Ghannam, Farha. *Remaking the Modern: Space, Relocation, and the Politics of Identity in a Global Cairo*. Berkeley, Los Angeles and London: University of California Press, 2002.

———. "Mobility, Liminality, and Embodiment in Urban Egypt." *American Ethnologist* 38, no. 4 (2011): 790–800.

———. "Meanings and Feelings: Local Interpretations of the Use of Violence in the Egyptian Revolution." *American Ethnologist* 39, no. 1 (2012): 32–36.

Gibson, J. J. *Ecological Approaches to Visual Perception*. Boston: Houghton Mifflin, 1979.

Giddens, Anthony. *The Constitution of Society*. Berkeley and Los Angeles: University of California Press, 1984.

Giedion, Sigfried. Space, Time and Architecture: The Growth of a New Tradition, *The Charles Eliot Norton Lectures 1938–1939*. Cambridge: Harvard University Press, 1941.

Gieryn, Thomas F. "A Space for Place in Sociology." *Annual Review of Sociology* 26 (2000): 463–496.

Gieseking, Jen Jack, William Mangold, Cindi Katz, Setha Low and Susan Saegert (eds). *The People, Place, and Space Reader*. New York and Oxen: Routledge, 2014.

Glassner, Barry. *The Culture of Fear*. New York: Basic Books, 1999.

Glick Schiller, Nina. "Transnationality." In *A Companion to the Anthropology of Politics*. David Nugent and Joan Vincent (eds), 448–467. Malden, MA: Blackwell, 2005a.

———. "Transnational Urbanism as a Way of Life: A Research Topic Not a Metaphor." *City & Society* 17, no. 1 (2005b): 49–64.

Glick Schiller, Nina, Linda Basch and Cristina Blanc-Szanton. *Towards a Transnational Perspective on Migration: Race, Class, Ethnicity and Nationalism Reconsidered*. New York: The New York Academy of Sciences, 1992.

Glick Schiller, Nina and Peggy Levitt. *Haven't We Heard This Somewhere Before: A Substantive View of Transnational Migration Studies by Way of a Reply to Waldinger and Fitzgerald*. Working Paper #06–01 . Princeton University, Princeton, NJ: Center for Migration and Development, 2006.

Goffman, Erving. *The Presentation of Self in Everyday Life*. Harmondsworth: Penguin, 1969.

Goldstein, Daniel M. *Outlawed: Between Security and Rights in a Bolivian City*. Durham and London: Duke University Press, 2012.

Gonzalez Viquez, Cleto. "San José y Sus Comienzos." *Obras Históricas. Vol. 1*. San José, Costa Rica: Universidad de Costa Rica, 1973.

Goode, Judith and Jeff Maskovsky (eds). *The New Poverty Studies: The Ethnography of Power, Politics and Impoverished People in the United States*. New York: New York University Press, 2001.

Goodman, L. 2000. "The Cooperative Century: A Historical View of Residential Coops." *The Cooperator: Coop & Condo Monthly*. Accessed April 16, 2007. http://cooperator.com/articles/540/1/The-Cooperative-Century/Page1.html.

Gopnik, Adam. "Stones and Bones: Visiting the 9/11 Memorial and Museum." *New Yorker*, 7 July 2014. Accessed 2014. www.newyorker.com/magazine/2014/07/07/stones and bones, pp. 1–19.

Gordillo, Gastón. *Landscapes of Death: Tensions of Place and Memory in the Argentinean Chaco*. Durham and London: Duke University Press, 2004.

Gossen, Gary. "Maya Zapatistas Move to the Ancient Future." *American Anthropologist* 98, no. 3 (1996): 528–538.

Graham, Elizabeth. "Lamanai Reloaded: Alive and Well in the Early Postclassic." In *Archaeological Investigations in the Eastern Maya Lowlands*. James John Morris and Sherilyne Jones Awe (eds), 223–241. Vol. 1. Belize: Research Reports in Belizean Archaeology, Institute of Archaeology, NICH, 2004.

———. "Due South: Learning From the Urban Experience in the Humid Tropics." In *BAR International Series 1529*. David M. Pendergast and Anthony P. Andrews (eds), 151–158. Oxford: British Archaeological Reports, 2006.

———. "Close Encounters." In *Maya Worldviews at Conquest*. Leslie G. Cecil and Timothy W. Pugh (eds), 17–38. Boulder: University of Colorado Press, 2009.

Graham, Elizabeth with contributions by Claude Belanger. *Lamanai Historic Monuments Conservation Project: Recording and Consolidation of New Church Features at Lamanai, Belize*, FAMSI (Foundation for the Advancement of Mesoamerican Studies, Inc.), 2008.

Graham, Elizabeth A., David M. Pendergast and Grant D. Jones. "On the Fringes of the Conquest: Maya-Spanish Contact in Colonial Belize." *Science* 246, no. 4935 (1989): 1254–1259.

Graham, Stephen and Simon Martin. *Splintering Urbanism: Networked Infrastructures, Technological Mobilities, and the Urban Condition*. London and New York: Routledge, 2001.

Gray, John. "Open Spaces and Dwelling Places: Being at Home on Hill Farms in the Scottish Borders." *American Ethnologist* 26, no. 2 (1999): 440–460.

———. *Domestic Mandala: Architecture of the Lifeworlds in Nepal*. Aldershot, UK and Burlington, VT: Ashgate, 2006.

Greenspan, Elizabeth. *Battle for Ground Zero: Inside the Political Struggle to Rebuild the World Trade Center*. New York: Palgrave Macmillan, 2013.

Gregg, Melissa and Gregory J. Seigworth. *The Affect Theory Reader*. Durham and London: Duke University Press, 2010.

Gregory, Steven. *Black Corona: Race and the Politics of Place in an Urban Community*. Princeton: Princeton University Press, 1998.

———. "The Radiant University: Space, Urban Redevelopment, and the Public Good." *City & Society* 25, no. 1 (2013): 47–69.

Grewal, Inderpal. "'Security Moms' in Early 21st Century USA: The Gender of Security in Neoliberalism.'" *Women's Studies Quarterly* 36, no. 1 & 2 (2006): 25–29.

Griaule, Marcel. "The Dogon." In *African Worlds*. Daryll Forde (ed.), 83–110. London: Oxford University Press, 1954.

Grossberg, Lawrence. "Affect's Future: Rediscovering the Virtual in the Actual." In *The Affect Theory Reader*. Melissa Gregg and Gregory J. Seigworth (eds), 309–338. Durham and London: Duke University Press, 2010.

Guano, Emanuela. "A Stroll Through La Boca: The Politics and Poetics of Spatial Experience in a Buenos Aires Neighborhood." *Space and Culture* 6, no. 4 (2003): 356–376.

Guattari, Felix. *Chaosophy: Texts and Interviews 1972–1977*. Los Angeles: Semiotext(e), 1995.

Gupta, Akhil. "The Song of the Nonaligned World: Transnational Identities and the Reinscription of Space in Late Capitalism." *Cultural Anthropology* 7, no. 1 (1992): 1–23.

Gupta, Akhil and James Ferguson. *Anthropological Locations: Boundaries and Grounds of a Field Science*. Berkeley: University of California, 1997a.

———. *Culture, Power, Place: Explorations in Critical Anthropology*. Durham and London: Duke University Press, 1997b.

Gustafson, Per. "Meanings of Place: Everyday Experience and Theoretical Conceptualizations." *Journal of Environmental Psychology* 21 (2001): 5–16.

Gutiérrez, Ramón. *Arquitectura y Urbanismo in Iberoamérica*. Madrid: Ediciones Cátedra, 1983.

Hall, Carolyn. *Costa Rica: A Geographical Interpretation in Historical Perspective*. Boulder: Westview, 1985.

Hall, Edward T. *The Hidden Dimension*. New York: Doubleday, 1966.

———. "Proxemics." *Current Anthropology* 9, no. 2 (1968): 83–95.

———. "Mental Health Research and Out-of-Awareness Cultural Systems." In *Cultural Illness and Health*. L. Nader and T. W. Maretzki, (eds), 97–103. Washington, D.C.: American Anthropological Association, 1973.

Hall, Thomas. "Urban Outreach and the Polyrhythmic City." In *Geographies of Rhythm: Places, Mobilities, Bodies*. Tim Edensor (ed.), 59–98 UK: Ashgate, 2010.

Hall, T. and R. Smith. "Stop and Go: A Field Study of Pedestrian Practice, Immobility and Urban Outreach Work." *Mobilities*, 8, no. 2 (2013): 272–292.

Hallowell, A. Irving. *Culture and Experience*. New York: Schocken Books, 1955.

Hankins, Sarah. "Multdimensional Israeliness and Tel Aviv's Tachanah Merkazit: Hearing Culture in a Polyphonic Transit Hub." *City & Society* 25 no. 3 (2013): 282–303.

Hannam, Kevin Mimi Sheller and John Urry. "Editorial: Mobilities, Immobilities and Moorings." *Mobilities* 1, no. 1 (2006): 1–22.

Hannerz, Ulf. *Exploring the City: Inquires Towards an Urban Anthropology*. New York: Columbia University Press, 1980.

———. "Notes on the Global Ecumene." *Public Culture* 1, no. 2 (1989): 66–75.

Hannigan, David. *Fantasy City: Pleasure and Profit in the Postmodern Metropolis*. New York: Routledge, 1998.

Hansen, KarenTranberg, Walter E. Little and B. Lynne Milgram. *Street Economies in the Urban Global South*. Santa Fe: School for Advanced Research Press, 2013.

Haraway, Donna. *Simians, Cyborgs, and Women: The Reinvention of Nature*. New York: Routledge, 1991.

Haridakis, Paul M. and Alan M. Rubin. "Third-Person Effects in the Aftermath of Terrorism." *Mass Communication and Society* 8, no. 1 (2005): 39–59.

Harms, Erik. "Beauty as Control in the New Saigon: Eviction, New Urban Zones, and Atomized Dissent in a Southeast Asian City." *American Ethnologist* 39, no. 4 (2012): 735–750.

Harris, Oliver J. T. and John Robb. "Multiple Ontologies and the Problem of the Body in History." *American Anthropologist* 114, no. 4 (2012): 668–679.

Harvey, David. *Social Justice and the City*. Baltimore: John Hopkins Press, 1973.

———. "Labor, Capital and Class Struggle around the Built Environment." *Politics and Society* 6, no. 3 (1976): 265–294.

———. *Consciousness and the Urban Experience: Studies in the History and Theory of Capitalist Urbanization*. Baltimore: John Hopkins Press, 1985.

———. *The Condition of Postmodernity: An Enquiry into the Origins of Cultural Change*. Oxford: Basil Blackwell, 1990.

———. "The Urban Face of Capitalism." In *Our Changing Cities*. J. F. Hunt (ed.), 50–56. Baltimore: Johns Hopkins University Press, 1991.

———. "The Body as an Accumulation Strategy." *Environment and Planning D: Society and Space* 16, no. 4 (1998): 4001–4421.

———. *Spaces of Hope*. Berkeley and Los Angeles: University of California Press, 2000.

———. *Paris: Capital of Modernity*. New York: Routledge, 2003.

———. *A Brief History of Neoliberalism*. Oxford: Oxford University Press, 2005.

———. *Spaces of Global Capitalism: A Theory of Uneven Geographical Development*. New York and London: Routledge, 2006.

Harvey, Robert. "Safety Begins at Home." *South Atlantic Quarterly* 107, no. 2 (2008): 331–372.

Hastings, Annette. "Discourse Analysis: What Does It Offer to Housing Studies?" *Housing, Theory and Society* 17, no. 3 (2000): 131–139.

Hayden, Dolores. *The Grand Domestic Revolution: A History of Feminist Designs for American Homes, Neighborhoods, and Cities*. Cambridge: MIT Press, 1981.

———. *The Power of Place*. Cambridge: MIT Press, 1995.

———. *Redesigning the American Dream: Gender, Housing, and Family Life*. New York and London: W.W. Norton, 2002.

———. *Building Suburbia: Green Fields and Urban Growth, 1820–2000*. New York: Pantheon, 2003.

Hayward, D. Geoffrey. "Home as an Environmental and Psychological Concept." *Landscape* 20, no. 1 (1975): 2–9.

Hedquist, Saul L., Stewart B. Koyiyumptewa, Peter Whiteley, Leigh J. Kuwanwisiwma, Kenneth C. Hill and T. J. Ferguson. "Recording Toponyms to Document Endangered Hopi Language." *American Anthropologist* 116, no. 2 (2014): 324–331.

Heidegger, Martin. "Building, Dwelling, Thinking." In *Poetry, Language and Thought*. A. Hofstadter (trans.), 141–161. New York: Harper and Row, 2001.

———. *Being and Time*. J. Stambaugh (trans). Albany, NY: State University of New York. 2010.

Heider, Karl G. *Landscapes of Emotion: Mapping Three Cultures of Emotion in Indonesia*. Cambridge and New York: Cambridge University Press, 1991.

Heiman, Rachel. *Driving After Class: Anxious Times in an American Suburb*. Oakland, California: University of California Press, 2015.

Helmreich, Stefan. "An Anthropologist Underwater: Immersive Soundscapes, Submarine Cyborgs and Transductive Ethnography." *American Ethnologist* 34, no. 4 (2007): 603–620.

Helms, Mary W. *Middle America: A Culture History of Heartland and Frontier*. Englewood Cliffs, NJ: Prentice Hall, 1975.

Herdt, Gibert. *Moral Panics*. New York: New York University Press, 2009.

Hernández, Bernardo, Ana M. Martín, Cristina Ruiz and Maria del Carmen Hidalgo. "The Role of Place Identity and Place Attachment in Breaking Environmental Protection Laws." *Journal of Environmental Psychology* 30, no. 3 (2010): 281–288.

Hernández, Carlos. *Banco Central*. San José, Costa Rica: Editorial Universidad Estatal a Distancia, 1986.

Herzfeld, Michael. *A Place in History: Social and Monumental Time in a Cretan Town*. Princeton: Princeton University Press, 1991.

———. "Pom Mahakan: Humanity and Order in the Historic Center of Bangkok." *Thailand Human Rights Journal* 1 (2003): 101–119.

———. *Evicted From Eternity: The Restructuring of Modern Rome*. Chicago: University of Chicago, 2009.

Hill, Jane. "The Voices of Don Gabriel: Responsibility and Self in a Modern Mexicano Narrative." In *The Dialogic Emergence of Culture*. Dennis Tedlock and Bruce Manneheim (eds), 108–147. Urbana: University of Ilinois Press, 1995.

———. "Language, Race, and White Public Space." *American Anthropologist* 100, no. 3 (1998): 680–689.

Hinds, J. and P. Sparks. "Engaging With the Natural Environment: The Role of Affective Connection and Identity." *Journal of Environmental Psychology* 28 (2008): 109–120.

Hirschkind, Charles. *The Ethical Soundscape: Cassette Sermons and Islamic Counterpublics*. New York: Columbia University Press, 2006.

———. "Is There a Secular Body?" *Cultural Anthropology* 26, no. 4 (2011): 633–647.

Hoffman, Katherine E. "Moving and Dwelling: Building the Ashelhi Homeland." *American Ethnologist* 29, no. 4 (2002): 928–962.

Holston, James. *The Modernist City: A Anthropological Critique of Brasilia*. Chicago: University of Chicago Press, 1989.

———. *Insurgent Citizenship: Disjunctions of Democracy and Modernity in Brazil*. Princeton and Oxford: Princeton University Press, 2008.

Holt, Elizabeth. *From the Classicists to the Impressionists: A Documentary History of Art and Architecture in the Nineteenth Century*. New York: Doubleday, 1966.

Hou, Jeffrey. *Transcultural Cities: Border-Crossing and Placemaking*. New York and London: Routledge, 2013.

Howe, Alyssa Cymene. "Queer Pilgrimage: The San Francisco Homeland and Identity Tourism." *Cultural Anthropology* 16, no. 1 (2001): 35–61.

Hubbard, Phil and Rob Kitchin. *Key Thinkers on Space and Place* (2nd edition). Los Angeles: Sage, 2011.

Hufford, Mary. *Chaseworld: Foxhunting and Storytelling in New Jersey's Pine Barrens*. Philadelphia: University of Pennsylvania Press, 1992.

Hugh-Jones, Christine. *From the Milk River: Spatial and Temporal Processes in Northwest Amazon*. Cambridge: Cambridge University Press, 1979.

Humphrey, Caroline. "Ideology in Infrastructure: Architecture and Soviet Imagination." *The Journal of the Royal Anthropological Institute* 11, no. 1 (2005): 39–58.

Hunn, Eugene. "Columbia Plateau Indian Place Names: What Can They Teach Us?" *Journal of Linguistic Anthropology* 6, no. 1 (1996): 3–26.

Huxtable, Ada Louise. *Unreal America: Architecture and Illusion*. New York: New York Press, 1997.

Hymes, Dell. "Letter." *Current Anthropology* 9, no. 2–3 (1968): 100.

Hyslop, John. *Inka Settlement Planning*. Austin: University of Texas Press, 1990.

Ingold, Tim. "Hunting and Gathering as Ways of Perceiving the Environment." In *Redefining Nature: Ecology, Culture and Domestication*. Roy Ellen and Katsuyoshi Fukui (eds), 117–155. Oxford: Berg, 1996.

———. "Culture on the Ground. The World Perceived Through the Feet." *Journal of Material Culture* 9, no. 3 (2004): 315–340.

———. *Lines: A Brief History.* London and New York: Routledge, 2007.

———. "Footprints Through the Weather-World: Walking, Breathing, Knowing." *Journal of the Royal Anthropological Institute* 16, no. 1 (2010): 121–139.

Ingold, Tim and Jo Lee Vergunst (eds). *Ways of Walking: Ethnography and Practice on Foot.* London: Ashgate, 2008.

International Cooperative Alliance (I.C.A.). "Statement on Cooperative Identity," 2006. Accessed 2009. Available at www.ica.coop/coop/principles.html.

Isoke, Zenzele. "The Politics of Homemaking: Black Feminist Transformations of a Cityscape." *Transforming Anthropology* 19, no. 2 (2011): 117–130.

Iveson, Kurt. "Graffiti, Street Art and the City: Introduction." *City* 14, no. 1–2 (2010): 25–32.

Izard, Carroll E. "Facial Expressions and the Regulations of Emotions." *Journal of Personality and Social Psychology* 58, no. 3 (1990): 487–498.

———. "Emotion Theory and Research: Highlights, Unanswered Questions, and Emerging Issues." *Annual Review of Psychology* 60 (2009): 1–25.

Jackson, John L. *Harlemworld: Doing Race and Class in Contemporary Black America.* Chicago: University of Chicago Press, 2001.

Jackson, Peter, Philip Crang and Claire Dwyer. *Transnational Spaces.* London and New York: Routledge, 2001.

Jacobs, Jane. *The Life and Death of Great American Cities.* New York: Random House, 1961.

Jacobs, Keith. "Waterfront Redevelopment: A Critical Discourse Analysis of the Policy-Making Process within the Chatham Maritime Project." *Urban Studies* 41, no. 4 (2004): 817–832.

James, William. "What is Emotion?" *Mind* 4 (1884):188–204.

Janeway, Elizabeth. *Man's World, Women's Place.* New York: Belling Publishing Company, 1971.

Jiménez, Alberto Corsín. "On Space as a Capacity." *Journal of the Royal Anthropological Institute* 9, no. 1 (2003): 137–153.

Johnson, Norris Brock. "Temple Architecture as Construction of Consciousness: A Japanese Temple and Garden." *Architecture and Behavior* 4, no. 3 (1988): 229–250.

Johnstone, Barbara, Neeta Bhasin and Denise Wittkofski. "'Dahntahn' Pittsburgh: Monophthongal/Aw/and Representations of Localness in Southwestern Pennsylvania." *American Speech* 77, no. 2 (2002): 148–166.

Jones, Grant D. *Maya Resistance to Spanish Rule: Time and History on a Colonial Frontier.* Albuquerque: University of New Mexico Press, 1989.

Jorgensen, B.C. and R. C. Stedman. "Sense of Place as an Attitude: Lakeshore Owners Attitudes Toward Their Properties." *Journal of Environmental Psychology* 21 (2001): 233–248

Kaartinen, Timo. *Songs of Travel, Stories of Place: Poetics of Absence in an Eastern Indonesian Society.* Helsinki: Academia Scientiarum Fennica, 2010.

Kahn, Miriam. "Stone Faced Ancestors: The Spatial Anchoring of Myth in Waimira, Papua New Guinea." *Ethnology* 29 (1990): 51–66.

Kant, Immanuel. *Critique of Pure Reason.* N. K. Smith (trans.). New York: MacMillan, 1781.

Kapchan, Deborah. "Talking Trash: Performing Home and Anti-Home in Austin's Salsa Culture." *American Ethnologist* 33, no. 3 (2006): 361–377.

Katz, Cindi. "On the Grounds of Globalization: A Topography for Feminist Political Engagement." *Signs* 26, no. 4 (2001): 1213–1234.

——. "Lost and Found: The Imagined Geographies of American Studies." *Prospects* 30 (2005): 17–25.

———. "Terrorism at Home." In *The Politics of Public Space*. Setha Low and Neil Smith (eds), 105–122. New York and London: Routledge, 2006.

Katz, Jack. *How Emotions Work*. Chicago: University of Chicago Press, 1999.

Kearney, Michael. "Borders and Boundaries of State and Self at the End of Empire." *Journal of Historical Sociology* 4, no. 1 (1991): 52–74.

———. "The Effects of Transnational Culture, Economy, and Migration on Mixtec Identity in Oaxacalifornia." In *The Bubbling Cauldron: Race, Ethnicity and the Urban Crisis*. Michael Peter and Joe Feagin Smith (eds), 226–243. Minneapolis and London: University of Minnesota Press, 1995.

Keever, Beverly Deepe. *News Zero: The New York Times and the Bomb*. Monroe, Maine: Common Courage Press, 2004.

Keinan, Giora, Avi Sadeh and Sefi Rosen. "Attitudes and Reactions to Media Coverage of Terrorist Acts." *Journal of Community Psychology* 31, no. 2 (2003): 149–165.

Kelly, Patty. *Lydia's Open Door: Inside Mexico's Most Modern Brothel*. Berkeley: University of California Press, 2008.

Kimmelman, Michael. "Finding Space for the Living at a Memorial." *New York Times*, 28 May 2014, sec. Arts/Design, pp. 1–3.

King, Anthony. *Colonial Urban Development: Culture, Social Power and Environment*. London: Routledge, 1976.

———. (ed.). *Buildings and Society: Essays on the Social Development of the Built Environment*. London, Boston, Melbourne and Henley: Routledge & Kegan Paul, 1980.

———. *The Bungalow: The Production of a Global Culture*. New York: Oxford University Press, 1984.

———. *Spaces of Global Culture: Architecture Urbanism Identity*. London: Routledge, 2004.

Kirby, Andrew and Karen A. Lynch. "A Ghost in Growth Machine: The Aftermath of Rapid Population Growth in Houston." *Urban Studies* 24, no. 1 (1987): 587–596.

Klein, Melanie. "On the Sense of Loneliness." In *Envy and Gratitude and Other Works, 1946–1963*, 300–313. New York: Delta, 1975.

Klein, Norman. *The History of Forgetting: Los Angeles and the Erasure of Memory*. New York: Verso, 1997.

Kleinman, Arthur. *Writing at the Margin: Discourse Between Anthropology and Medicine*. Berkeley: University of California Press, 1997.

Klotchkov, Vladimir. "Brevísima Historia de la Planificación Urbana de San José". *Ambientico* 99 (diciembre, 2001): 4–6.

Kohn, Margaret. *Radical Space: Building the House of the People*. Ithaca and London: Cornell University Press, 2003.

Kofman, Eleonore and Elizabeth Lebas. "Introduction." In *Writing on Cities*. Henri Lefebvre, E. Kofman and E. Lebas (eds). 3–62. Malden, MA: Blackwell Publishing, 2005.

Koizumi, Junji. "Mobility and Immobility in Circular Migration: A Case from Northwestern Guatemala." *Evolving Humanity, Emerging Worlds*. Conference Programme. Manchester: University of Manchester, 2013.

Koolhaas, Rem. "Junkspace." *October*, vol. 100, 175–190. Cambridge: MIT Press, 2001.

Kroeber, Alfred. *Cultural and Natural Areas of Native North America*. Berkeley: University of California Press, 1939.

Kuper, Hilda. "The Language of Sites in the Politics of Space." *American Anthropologist* 74, no. 3 (1972): 411–440.

Kyle, G., A. Graefe, and R. Manning. "Testing the Dimensionality of Place Attachment in Recreational Settings." *Environment and Behavior* 37 (2005): 153–177.

Labov, William. *Sociolinguistic Patterns*. Philadelphia: University of Pennsylvania Press, 1972.

Labov, William and Joshua Waletzky. "Narrative Analysis: Oral Versions of Personal Experience." *Journal of Narrative and Life History* 7, no. 1–4 (1967–1997): 3–38.

Lancaster, Roger. *Sex Panic and the Punitive State*. Berkeley, Los Angeles and London: University of California Press, 2011.

Larkin, Brian. *Signal and Noise: Media, Infrastructure, and Urban Culture in Nigeria*. Durham and London: Duke University Press, 2008.

———. "The Politics and Poetics of Infrastructure." *Annual Reviews in Anthropology* 42 (2013): 327–343.

Latour, Bruno. *Reassembling the Social: An Introduction to Actor-Network-Theory*. Oxford: Oxford University Press, 2005.

Lave, Jean and Etienne Wenger. *Situated Learning: Legitimate Peripheral Participation*. Cambridge: Cambridge University Press, 1991.

Lawrence, Denise and Setha M. Low. "The Built Environment and Spatial Form." *Annual Review of Anthropology* 19 (1990): 453–505.

Lawrence-Zuñiga, Denise. *Protecting Suburban America: Gentrification, Advocacy and the Historic Imaginary*. New York: Bloomsbury Academic, 2016.

Lazarus, Richard S. *Emotion and Adaptation*. Malden, MA and Oxford: Oxford University Press, 1991.

Leavitt, John. "Meaning and Feeling in the Anthropology of Emotions." *American Ethnologist* 23, no. 3 (1996): 514–539.

Lebow, Katherine A. "Revising the Politicized Landscape: Nowa Huta, 1949–1957." *City & Society* 11, no. 1 (1999): 165–187.

Leeds, Anthony. "Locality Power in Relation to Supralocal Power Institutions." In *Urban Anthropology: Cross-Cultural Studies of Urbanization*. Aidan Southall (ed.), 15–41. New York: Oxford University Press, 1973.

Leeman, Jennifer and Gabriella Modan. "Commodified Language in Chinatown: A Contextualized Approach to Linguistic Landscape." *Journal of Sociolinguistics* 13, no. 3 (2009): 332–362.

———. "Trajectories of Language: Orders of Indexical Meaning in Washington, DC's Chinatown." In *Re-Shaping Cities: How Global Mobility Transforms Architecture and Urban Form*. Michael Guggenheim and Ola Söderskröm (eds), 167–188. London: Routledge, 2010.

Lees, Loretta. "Urban Geography: Discourse Analysis and Urban Research." *Progress in Human Geography* 28, no. 1 (2004): 101–107.

Lefebvre, Henri. *La Production de L'Espace (The Production of Space)*. Paris: Anthropos, 1974.

———. *The Production of Space*. Cambridge and New York: Blackwell, 1991.

———. *The Right to the City*. Oxford: Blackwell, 1996.

———. *Writings on Cities*. Malden, MA and Oxford: Blackwell Publishing, 2005.

Leggett, William. "Terror and the Colonial Imagination at Work in the Transnational Corporate Spaces of Jakarta, Indonesia." *Identities: Global Studies in Culture and Power* 12, no. 2 (2003): 1–45.

Lerner, Jennifer S., Roxana M. Gonzalez, Deborah A. Small and Baruch Fischoff. "Effects of Fear and Anger on Perceived Risks of Terrorism: A National Field Experiment." *Psychological Science* 14, no. 2 (2003): 144–150.

Levinson, Stephen C. "Language and Space." *Annual Review in Anthropology* 25 (1996): 353–382.

Levitt, Peggy and B. Nadya Jaworsky. "Transnational Migration Studies: Part Developments and Future Trends." *Annual Review of Sociology* 33 (2007): 129–256.

Levitt, Peggy and Nina Glick Schiller. "Conceptualizing Simultaneity: A Transnational Social Field Perspective on Society." *International Migration Review* 38, no. 3 (2004): 1002–1039.

Levy, Robert. *The Tahitians: Mind and Experience in the Society Islands.* Chicago: University of Chicago Press, 1973.

Lewicka, Maria. "Place Attachment: How Far Have We Come in the Last 40 Years?" *Journal of Environmental Psychology* 31, no. 3 (2011): 207–230.

Lewis, I. M. *Ecstatic Religion: A Study of Shamanism and Spirit Possession.* London and New York: Routledge, 1971.

Leys, Ruth. "The Turn to Affect: A Critique." *Critical Inquiry* 37, no. 3 (2011): 434–472.

Liechty, Mark. "Kathmandu as Translocality: Multiple Places in a Nepali Space." In *The Geography of Identity.* Patricia Yaeger (ed.), 98–130. Ann Arbor: University of Michigan, 1996.

Light, Duncan and Craig Young. "Habit, Memory, and the Persistence of Socialist-Era Street Names in Postsocialist Bucharest, Romania." *Annals of the Association of American Geographers* 104, no. 3 (2014): 668–685.

Limbert, Mandana E. "In the Ruins of Bahla: Reconstructed Forts and Crumbling Walls in an Omani Town." *Social Text* 26, no. 2 (2008): 83–103.

Lin, Jan. "Ethnic Places, Postmodernism, and Urban Change in Houston." *The Sociological Quarterly* 36, no. 4 (1995): 629–647.

Little, Walter. "Facade to Street to Facade: Negotiating Public Spatial Legality in a World Heritage City." *City & Society* 26, no. 2 (2014): 196–216.

Logan, John R. and Harvey L. Molotch. *Urban Fortunes: The Political Economy of Place.* Berkeley: University of California Press, 1987.

Lomsky-Feder, Edna. "Life Stories, War, and Veterans: On the Social Distribution of Memories." *Ethos* 32, no. 1 (2004): 82–109.

Long, D. Adam and Douglas D. Perkins. "Community Social and Place Predictors of Sense of Community: A Multilevel and Longitudinal Analysis." *Journal of Community Psychology* 35, no. 5 (2007): 563–581.

Looser, Tom. "The Global University, Area Studies, and the World Citizen: Neoliberal Geography's Redistribution of the 'World.'" *Cultural Anthropology* 27, no. 1 (2012): 97–117.

Lorimer, H. (2011). "Tim Ingold." In *Key Thinkers on Space and Place.* Phil Hubbard and Rob Kitchin (eds), 249–56. Los Angeles: Sage.

Low, Setha. "Housing, Organization, and Social Change: A Comparison of Programs for Urban Reconstruction in Guatemala." *Human Organization* 47, no. 1 (1988): 15–24.

———. "Symbolic Ties that Bind." In *Place Attachment.* I. Altman and S. Low (eds), 165–184. New York: Plenum, 1992.

————. "Cultural Meaning of the Plaza: The History of the Spanish American Gridplan-Plaza Urban Design." In *The Cultural Meaning of Urban Space*. Robert McDonogh and Gary Rotenberg (eds), 75–94. Westport and London: Bergin & Garvey, 1993.

————. "Embodied Metaphors: Nerves as Lived Experience." In *Embodiment and Experience: The Existential Ground of Culture and Self*. Thomas J. Csordas (ed.), 139–162. Cambridge: Cambridge University Press, 1995.

————. "Spatializing Culture: The Social Production and Social Construction of Public Space." *American Ethnologist* 23, no. 4 (1996): 861–879.

————. (ed.).*Theorizing the City: The New Urban Anthropology Reader*. Brunswick, New Jersey: Rutgers Press, 1999.

————.*On the Plaza: The Politics of Public Space and Culture*. Austin: University of Texas Press, 2000.

————. *Behind the Gates: Life, Security and the Pursuit of Happiness in Fortress America*. New York and London: Routledge, 2003.

————. "The Memorialization of September 11: Dominant and Local Discourses on the Rebuilding of the World Trade Center Site." *American Ethnologist* 31, no. 3 (2004): 326–339.

————. "Towards a Theory of Urban Fragmentation: A Cross-Cultural Analysis of Fear, Privatization, and the State." *Cybergeo: Revue européenne de géographie* 349, no. 2 (October 2007).

————. "Maintaining Whiteness: The Fear of Others and Niceness." *Transforming Anthropology* 17, no. 2 (2009): 79–92.

————. "Claiming Space for Engaged Anthropology: Spatial Inequality and Social Exclusion." *American Anthropologist* 113, no. 3 (2011): 389–407.

Low, Setha and Irwin Altman. *Place Attachment*. New York and London: Plenum Press, 1992.

Low, Setha, Gabrielle Bendiner-Viani and Yvonne Hung. *Attachments to Liberty: A Special Ethnographic Study of the Statue of Liberty National Monument*. New York: Department of the Interior, National Park Service, 2005.

Low, Setha and Erve Chambers. *Housing, Culture and Design: A Comparative Perspective*. Philadelphia: University of Pennsylvania Press, 1989.

Low, Setha, Gregory Donovan and J. Geiseking. "Shoestring Democracy: Gated Communities and Market Rate Co-operatives in New York City." *Journal of Urban Affairs* 34, no. 3 (2012): 279–296.

Low, Setha and Denise Lawrence-Zuñiga. *The Anthropology of Space and Place: Locating Culture*. Oxford and New York: Blackwell, 2003.

Low, Setha and Sally Merry. "Engaged Anthropology: Diversity and Dilemmas." *Current Anthropology* 51, no. 2 (2010): 203–226.

Low, Setha and Neil Smith (eds). *The Politics of Public Space*. New York and London: Routledge, 2006.

Low, Setha, Dana Taplin and Mike Lamb. "Battery Park City: An Ethnographic Field Study of the Community Impact of 9/11." *Urban Affairs Review* 40, no. 5 (2005): 655–682.

Low, Setha, Dana Taplin and Suzanne Scheld. *Rethinking Urban Parks: Public Space and Cultural Diversity*. Austin: University of Texas, 2005.

Lubar, Harvey. "Building Orchard Beach." *Bronx County Historical Society Journal* 23, no. 2 (1986): 75–83.

Lungo, Mario. "Costa Rica: Dilemmas of Urbanization in the 1990s." In *The Urban Caribbean: Transition to the New Global Economy*. A. C. Core-Cabral and P. Landolt Portes (eds), 57–86. Baltimore: Johns Hopkins University Press, 1997.

Lussault, Michel. *The Space Man – The Social Construction of Human Space*. Paris: Editions du Seuil, 2007.

———. "Every Place Tells a Story." French Institute, Alliance Française, New York City, Thursday, February 3, 2011. 1–7.

Lutz, Catherine A. *Unnatural Emotions: Everyday Sentiments on a Micronesian Atoll and Their Challenge to Western Theory*. Chicago and London: University of Chicago Press, 1988.

Lutz, Catherine A. and Lila Abu-Lughod. *Language and the Politics of Emotion*. Cambridge and New York: Cambridge University Press, 1990.

Lutz, Catherine and Geoffrey M. White. "The Anthropology of Emotions." *Annual Review of Anthropology* 15 (1986): 405–436.

———. "Emotions, War and Cable News." *Anthropology News* February (2002): 6–7.

MacLeod, Gordon and Kevin Ward. "Spaces of Utopia and Dystopia: Landscaping the Contemporary City." *Geografiska Annaler* Series B, Human Geography 84B, no. 3–4, Special Issue: The Dialectics of Utopia (2002): 153–170.

Macleod, Murdo J. *Spanish Central America: A Socioeconomic History, 1520–1720*. Berkeley: University of California Press, 1973.

Maghraoui, Driss. "Gendering Urban Colonial Casablanca: The Case of the Quartier Reserve of Bousbir." In *Gendering Urban Space in the Middle East, South Asia, and Africa*. Martina Recker and Kamran Asdar Ali (eds), 17–44. New York: Palgrave Macmillan, 2008.

Maharawal, Manissa McCleave. "What Can We Do in Public: Occupy and Challenges in Public Space." *Progressive Planning* 191, no. 10–11 (2012).

Mahmood, Saba. "Feminist Theory, Embodiment, and the Docile Agent." *Cultural Anthropology* 16, no. 2 (2001): 202–236.

Malinowski, Bronislaw. *The Sexual Life of Savages*. New York: Harcourt, Brace and Work, 1929.

Malkki, Liisa. "National Geographic: The Rooting of Peoples and the Territorialization of National Identity among Scholars and Refugees." *Cultural Anthropology* 7, no. 1 (1997): 24–44.

Mantero, Vicente. "Density, Fear, and Terrorism: How 9/11 Affected People's Desire to Live in an Urban Area in Franklin County, Ohio." *EDRA* 37 (2006): 65–78.

Manzo, Lynne C. and Patrick Devine-Wright. *Place Attachment: Advances in Theory, Methods and Applications*. London and New York: Routledge, 2014.

Marcus, Clare Cooper. "The House as Symbol of Self." In *Environmental Psychology*. W. H. Ittelson, R. G. Rivlin and H. Proshansky (eds), 435–448. New York: Holt, Rhinehart, and Winston, 1976.

———. *House as a Mirror of Self: Exploring the Deeper Meaning of Home*. New York: Conari Press, 1997.

Marín, Gloria Violeta. "*El Parque De Antaño*." *La Nación*, 1991, p. 28.

Marris, Peter. *Family and Social Change in an African City*. Boston: Northwestern University Press, 1962.

Marston, Sallie A., John Paul Jones III and Keith Woodward. "Human Geography without Scale." *Transactions of the Institute of British Geographers* 30, no. 4 (2005): 416–432.

Martin, Emily. *The Woman in the Body: A Cultural Analysis of Reproduction*. Boston: Beacon Press, 2001.

Masco, Joseph. *The Nuclear Borderlands: The Manhattan Project in Post-Cold War New Mexico*. Princeton: Princeton University Press, 2006.

———. "The Billboard Campaign." *Public Culture* 17, no. 3 (2005): 487–496.

———. "'Survival Is Your Business': Engineering Ruins and Affect." *Cultural Anthropology* 23, no. 2 (2008): 361–398.

Maskovsky, Jeff. "A Home in the End Times," 2013 (manuscript).

Massey, Doreen. *For Space*. Los Angeles: Sage, 2005.

Massumi, Brian. *Parables for the Virtual: Movement, Affect, Sensation*. Durham: Duke University Press, 2002.

———. "The Future Birth of the Affective Fact: The Political Ontology of Threat." In *The Affect Theory Reader*. Melissa Gregg and Gregory J. Seigworth (eds), 52–70. Durham and London: Duke University Press, 2010.

Mauss, Marcel. "Les Techniques Du Corps." *Sociologie et Anthropologie*. Paris: Presses Universitaires de France, 1950.

———. *Sociology and Psychology*. London: Routledge and Kegan Paul, 1979.

Mauss, Marcel and H. Beauchat. *Seasonal Variations of the Eskimo*. London: Routledge and Kegan Paul, 1979 (Original publication 1906).

Mazzarella, William. *Shoveling Smoke: Advertising and Globalization in Contemporary India*. Durham and London: Duke University Press, 2006.

———. "Affect: 'What Is It Good For?'" In *Enchantments of Modernity: Empire, Nation, Globalization*. Saurabh Dube (ed.), 291–309. London and New York: Routledge, 2009.

———. *Censorium: Cinema and the Open Edge of Mass Publicity*. Durham: Duke University Press, 2013.

McAuliffe, Cameron. "Sites of Respect: Negotiating Moral Geographies." n.d.

McCallum, Cecilia. "Racialized Bodies, Naturalized Classes: Moving through the City of Salvador, Bahia." *American Ethnologist* 32, no. 1 (2005): 100–117.

McCann, E. J. "Livable City/Unequal City: The Politics of Policy-Making in a 'Creative' Boomtown." *Interventions Economiques* 37 (2008). Accessed 2015. http://benhur.teluq.uquebec.ca/rie/2008001/doss_2_McCann.html[benhur.teluq.uquebec.ca.

McDonogh, Gary. "Bars, Gender, and Virtue: Myth and Practice in Barcelona's *Barrio Chino*." *Anthropology Quarterly* 65, no. 1 (1992): 19–33.

———. "Discourses of the City: Policy and Response in Post-Transitional Barcelona." In *Theorizing the City: The New Urban Anthropology Reader*. Setha Low (ed.), 342–376. New Brunswick, NJ: Rutgers University Press, 1999.

McFarlane, C. "The City as Assemblage: Dwelling and Urban Space." *Environment and Planning-Part D* 29, no. 4 (2011): 649–662.

McHugh, Kevin. "Inside, Outside, Upside Down, Backward, Forward, Round and Round: A Case for Ethnographic Studies in Migration." *Progress in Human Geography* 24, no. 1 (2000): 71–89.

Meadows, William C. *Kiowas Ethnogeography*. Austin: University of Texas Press, 2008.

Mele, Christopher. "The Materiality of Urban Discourse: Rational Planning in the Restructuring of the Early Twentieth-Century Ghetto." *Urban Affairs Review* 35, no. 5 (2000): 628–648.

Merleau-Ponty, M. *Phenomenology of Perception*. London: Routledge, 1962.

Merrifield, Andrew. *Metromarxism. A Marxist Tale of the City*. London and New York: Routledge, 2002.

———. *The Politics of the Encounter: Urban Theory and Protest Under Planetary Urbanization*. Athens: University of Georgia Press, 2013.

Merry, Sally. *Urban Danger: Life in a Neighborhood of Strangers*. Philadelphia: Temple Press, 1981.

———. "Spatial Governmentality and the New Urban Social Order." *American Anthropologist* 103, no. 1 (2001): 36–45.

Merry, Sally, Kevin Davis and Benedict Kingsbury. *The Quiet Power of Indicators: Measuring Governance, Corruption, and Rule of Law*. Cambridge: Cambridge University Press, 2015.

Meskell, Lynn. *Archaeologies of Social Life*. Oxford: Blackwell Publishers, 1999.

Milgram, Lynne. "Remapping the Edge: Informality and Legality in the Harrison Road, Baguio, Philippines." *City & Society* 26, no. 2 (2014): 153–174.

Miller, Daniel. *A Theory of Shopping*. Ithaca: Cornell University Press, 1998.

Milton, Kay. "Emotion (or Life, the Universe, Everything)." *The Australian Journal of Anthropology* 16, no. 2 (2005): 198–2011.

Ministerio de Economía, Industría y Comercío. *Costa Rica: Calculo de Poblacíon por Provincia, Caton y Distrito*. San José, Costa Rica: Dirección General de Estadistica y Censos, 1992.

Minor, Tom. "Call This Home?" *Vox*, 2007.

Mitchell, Don. "The End of Public Space? People's Park, Definitions of the Public, and Democracy." *Annals of the Association of American Geographers* 85, no. 1 (1995): 108–133.

———. *The Right to the City: Social Justice and the Fight for Public Space*. New York: The Guilford Press, 2003.

———. "New Axioms for Reading the Landscape: Paying Attention to Political Economy and Social Justice." In *Political Economies of Landscape Change*. J. L. Wescoat Jr. and D. M. Johnston (eds), 29–50. New York: Springer, 2008.

Mitchell, Don and Lynn A. Staeheli. "Clean and Safe? Property Redevelopment, Public Space, and Homelessness in Downtown San Diego." In *Politics of Public Space*, S. Low and N. Smith (eds), 142–175. New York and London: Routledge, 2006.

Mitchell, Timothy. *Colonising Egypt*. Cambridge: Cambridge University Press, 1988.

———. *Carbon Democracy: Political Power in the Age of Oil*. London and New York: Verso, 2013.

Modan, Gabriella. *Turf Wars: Discourse, Diversity and the Politics of Place*. Malden, MA and Oxford: Blackwell Publishing, 2007.

———. "Mango Fufu Kimchi Yucca: The Depoliticizaiton of 'Diversity' in Washington, DC, Discourse." *City & Society* 20, no. 2 (2008): 188–221.

Moerman, Michael. *Talking Culture*. Philadephia: Univerisity of Pennsylvania Press, 1988.

Molina, Ivan and Steven Palmer. *The History of Costa Rica*. San José, Costa Rica: Editorial Universidad Costa Rica, 2007.

Monahan, Torin. "Securing the Homeland: Torture, Preparedness, and the Right to Let Die." *Social Justice* 33, no. 1 (2006a): 95–105.

———. "Electronic Fortification in Phoenix." *Urban Affairs Review* 42, no. 2 (2006b): 169–192.

———. (ed.). *Surveillance and Security: Technological Politics and Power in Everyday Life*. New York and London: Routledge, 2006.

Monroe, Kristin. "Being Mobile in Beirut." *City & Society* 23, no. 1 (2011): 91–111.

———. *The Insecure City: Space, Power, Mobility in Beirut*. New Brunswick, NJ: Rutgers University Press, 2016.

Moore, Charles. "Creating of Place" *Image*, no 4, 1966.

Moore, Charles, Gerald Allen and Donald Lyndon. *The Place of Houses*. Berkeley: University of California Press, 1974.

Moore, Donald. "Subaltern Struggles and the Politics of Place: Remapping Resistance in Zimbabwe's Eastern Highlands." *Cultural Anthropology* 13, no. 3 (1998): 344–381.

Moore, Henrietta. *Space, Text and Gender: An Anthropological Study of the Marakwet of Kenya*. Cambridge: Cambridge University Press, 1986.

Morgan, H. L. "Houses and House Life of the American Aborigines." In *Contributions to North American Ethnology*, Volume IV, published by the United States Geological Survey, 1881.

Morphy, Howard. "Landscape and the Reproduction of the Ancestral Past." In *The Anthropology of Landscape: Perspectives on Place and Space*. Eric Hirsch and Michael O'Hanlon (eds), 184–209. Oxford: Clarendon Press, 1995.

Morse, Richard. "Introduction. Urban Development in Latin America: A Special Issue." *Comparative Urban Research* 8 (1980): 5–13.

Mounin, Georges. "The Semiology of Orientation in Urban Space." *Current Anthropology* 21, no. 4 (1980): 491–501.

Mountz, Alison and Richard A. Wright. "Daily Life in the Transnational Migrant Community of San Agustin, Oaxaca and Poughkeepsie, New York." *Diaspora* 5, no. 3 (1996): 401–428.

Mullings, Leith. "Anthropology Matters." *American Anthropologist* 117, no. 1 (2015): 4–16.

Munn, Nancy. "Excluded Spaces: The Figure in the Australian Aboriginal Landscape." *Critical Inquiry* 22, no. 3 (1996): 446–465.

Muñoz Guillen, Mercedes. "The Narcotizing of Costa Rican Politics." In *The Costa Rican Reader: History, Culture, Politics*. Steven Palmer and Ivan Molina (eds), 342–343. Durham and London: Duke University Press, 2004.

Munt, Sally R. "Sisters in Exile: The Lesbian Nation." In *New Frontiers in Space, Bodies and Gender*. Rosa Ainley (ed.), 3–19. London: Routledge, 1998.

Murdock, George. "Ethnographic Atlas: A Summary." *Ethnology* 6, no. 2 (1967): 109–236.

Myers, Fred. *Pintupi Country, Pintupi Self: Sentiment, Place and Politics among Western Desert Aborigines*. Berkeley: University of California Press, 1991.

———. "Ways of Place-Making." *La Ricerca Folklorica* 45 (2002): 101–119.

Nasar, J. L. and B. Fisher. 1994. "Urban Design Aesthetics: The Evaluative Quality of Building Exteriors." *Environment and Behavior* 26 (1994): 377–401.

Navaro-Yashin, Yael. "Affective Spaces, Melancholic Objects: Ruination and the Production of Anthropological Knowledge." *Journal of the Royal Anthropological Institute* 28, no. 3 (2009): 1–18.

Newman, Andrew. "Urban Like a Jackalope: Culture, Capital, and Inner City Redevelopment in Houston, Texas." Bard College. Unpublished Undergraduate Honors Thesis.

———. *Landscape of Discontent: Urban Sustainability in Immigrant Paris*. Minneapolis: University of Minnesota Press, 2015.

Newman, Katherine S. *Declining Fortunes: The Withering of the American Dream*. New York: Basic Books, 1993.

Newton, Issac and Andrew Motte (trans.). *Philosophiae Naturalis Principia Mathematica*. London: Benjamin Motte, 1687.

New York Times Poll. "Four Years Later." *New York Times*, 11 September 2005, sec. Metro, col. 5 & 6, p. 36.

Ngin, ChorSwang. "A New Look at the Old 'Race' Language." *Explorations in Ethnic Studies* 16, no. 1 (1993): 5–18.

Nonini, Donald. "'Chinese Society,' Coffee-Shop Talk, Possessing Gods: The Politics of Public Space Among Diasporic Chinese in Malaysia." *Positions* 6, no. 2 (1998): 439–473.

Nugent, David. "Understanding Capitalism – Historically, Structurally, Spatially." In *Locating Capitalism in Time and Space*. David Nugent (ed.), 61–79. Stanford: Stanford University Press, 2002.

Olwig, Karen Fog and Kirsten Hastrup. *Siting Culture: The Shifting Anthropological Object*. London: Routledge, 1997.

O'Neil, John. *Five Bodies: The Shape of Modern Society*. Ithaca: Cornell University Press, 1985.

Ong, Aihwa. *Flexible Citizenship: The Cultural Logics of Transnationality*. Durham and London: Duke University Press, 1999.

Orrantia, Juan. "Where the Air Feels Heavy: Boredom and the Textures of the Aftermath." *Visual Anthropology Review* 28, no. 1 (2012): 50–69.

Ortner, Sherry. "Generation X: Anthropology in a Media Saturated World." *Cultural Anthropology* 13, no. 3 (1998): 414–440.

Oza, Rupal. "Contrapuntal Geographies of Threat and Security: the United States, India, and Israel." *Environment and Planning D: Society and Space* 25, no. 25 (2007): 9–32.

Palmer, Andie Diane. *Maps of Experience: The Anchoring of Land to Story in Secwepemc Discourse*. Toronto, Buffalo and London: University of Toronto Press, 2005.

Palmer, Steven and Ivan Molina (eds). *The Costa Rican Reader: History, Culture, Politics*. Durham and London: Duke University Press, 2006.

Pandolfi, Mariella. "Boundaries Inside the Body: Women's Sufferings in Southern Peasant Italy." *Culture, Medicine, and Psychiatry* 14, no. 2 (1990): 255–274.

Pandolfo, Stefania. "Detours of Life: Space and Bodies in a Moroccan Village." *American Ethnologist* 16, no. 1 (1989): 3–23.

Pandya, Vishvajit. "Movement and Space: Andamanese Cartography." *American Ethnologist* 17, no. 4 (1990): 775–797.

Pappas, Gregory. *The Magic City: Unemployment in a Working-Class Community*. Ithaca, NY: Cornell University Press, 1989.

Pardue, Derek. "Place Markers: Tracking Spatiality in Brazilian Hip-Hop and Community Radio." *American Ethnologist* 38, no. 1 (2011): 102–113.

Park, Robert E., Ernest W. Burgress and Roderick D. McKenzie. *The City*. Chicago: University of Chicago Press, 1996.

Parreñas, Rheana Juno Salazar. "Producing Affect: Transnational Volunteerism in a Malaysian Orangutan Rehabilitation Center." *American Ethnologist* 39, no. 4 (2012): 673–687.

Passell, Peter. "Economic Scene: Costa Rica's Debt Message." *New York Times,* 1 February 1989, sec. D, col. 1–4, p. 2.

Patterson, Thomas C. "The Turn to Agency: Neoliberalism, Individuality, and Subjectivity in Late Twentieth-Century Anglophone Archaeology." *Rethinking Marxism* 17, no. 3 (2005): 371–382.

Paul, Robert A. "The Sherpa Temple as a Model of the Psyche." *American Ethnologist* 3, no. 1 (1976): 131–146.

Pearson, Thomas. "Transgenic-Free Territories in Costa Rica: Networks, Place, and Politics of Life." *American Ethnologist* 39, no. 1 (2012): 90–105.

———. "'Life Is Not for Sale!': Confronting Free Trade and Intellectual Property in Costa Rica." *American Anthropologist* 115, no. 1 (2013): 58–71.

Peattie, Lisa. *The View From the Barrio*. Ann Arbor: University of Michigan Press, 1970.

Peck, Jaime and Adam Tickell. "Neoliberalizing Space." *Antipode* 34, no. 3 (2002): 380–404.

Pellizzi, Francesco. "Airports and Museums: New Frontiers of the Urban and Suburban." *RES: Anthropology and Aesthetics* 53/54 (2008): 331–344.

Pellow, Deborah. "Chinese Privacy." In *The Cultural Meaning of Urban Space*. Robert Rotenberg and Gary McDonogh (eds), 31–46. Westport and London: Bergin & Garvey, 1993.

———. *Setting Boundaries: The Anthropology of Spatial and Social Organization*. Westport and London: Bergin & Garvey, 1996.

———. *Landlords and Lodgers: Socio-Spatial Organization in an Accra Community*. Westport and London: Praeger, 2002.

Pendergast, David M. "Worlds in Collusion: The Maya/Spanish Encounter in Sixteenth and Seventeenth Century Belize." *Proceedings of the British Academy* 81 (1993): 105–143.

Pérez, Gina M. *The Near Northwest Side Story: Migration, Displacement and Puerto Rican Families*. Berkeley, Los Angeles and London: University of California Press, 2004.

Perlman, Diane. "Psychological dimensions of nuclear policies and proliferation," 1998. Accessed March 21, 2015. Available at http://nuclearfiles.org/menu/key-issues/ethics/basics/perlman_psychological-dimensions.htm.

Persson, Asha. "Intimate Immensity: Phenomenology of Place and Space in an Australia Yoga." *American Ethnologist* 34, no. 1 (2007): 44–56.

Peterson, Marina. *Sound, Space and the City*. Philadelphia: University of Pennsylvania, 2010.

Pfeiffer, Alice. "Doors." *Vox*, 2007.

Pile, Steve. "Emotions and Affect in Recent Human Geography." *Transactions of the Institute of British Geographers* 35, no. 1 (2010): 5–20.

Pitts-Taylor, Victoria. "The Plastic Brain: Neoliberalism and the Neuronal Self." *Health* 14, no. 6 (2010): 635–652.

Podmore, Julie. "(Re)Reading the Loft Living Habitus in Montreal's Inner City." *Urban Affairs Review* 34, no. 5 (1998): 283–302.

Polanco, Mieka Brand. *Historically Black: Imagining Community in a Black Historic District*. New York and London: New York University Press, 2014.

Portés, Alejandro. "Immigration Theory for a New Century: Some Problems and Opportunities." *International Migration Review* 31, no. 4 (1997): 799–825.

Pozniak, Kinga. "Reinventing a Model Socialist Steel Town in the Neoliberal Economy: The Case of Nowa Huta, Poland." *City & Society* 25, no. 1 (2013): 113–134.

Pred, A. "Structuration, Biography Formation, and Knowledge: Observations on Port Growth During the Late Mercantile Period." *Environment and Planning D. Society and Space* 2, no. 3 (1984): 251–275.

Premat, Adriana. "State Power, Private Plots and the Greening of Havana's Urban Agriculture Movement." *City & Society* 21, no. 1 (2009): 28–57.

Pries, Ludger. "Configurations of Geographic and Societal Spaces: A Sociological Proposal Between 'Methodological Nationalism' and the 'Spaces of Flows.'" *Global Networks* 5, no. 2 (2005): 167–190.

Proshansky, Harold M. "The City and Self-Identity." *Environment and Behavior* 10, no. 2 (1978): 147–169.

Proshansky, Harold M., Abbe K. Fabian and Robert Kaminoff. "Place-Identity: Physical World Socialization of the Self." *Journal of Environmental Psychology* 3, no. 1 (1983): 57–83.

Quayson, Ato. "Signs of the Times: Discourse Ecologies and Street Life on Oxford St., Accra." *City & Society* 22, no. 1 (2010): 72–96.

Quesada, Álvaro. "A Dictionary of Costa Rican Patriotism." In *The Costa Rican Reader*. S. Palmer and I. Molina (eds), 225–227. Durham: Duke University Press, 2006.

Rabinow, Paul. "Ordonnance, Discipline, Regulation: Some Reflections on Urbanism." *Humanities in Society* 5, no. 3–4 (1982): 267–278.

———. *French Modern: Norms and Forms of Missionary and Didactic Pathos*. Cambridge: MIT Press, 1989.

Rainwater, Lee. *Behind Ghetto Walls*. Harmondsworth: Penguin, 1963.

Ramos-Zayas, Ana Y. "Learning Affect, Embodying Race: Youth, Blackness and Neoliberal Emotions in Latino Newark." *Transforming Anthropology* 19, no. 2 (2011): 86–104.

———. *Street Therapists: Race, Affect, and Neoliberal Personhood in Latino Newark*. Chicago and London: University of Chicago Press, 2012.

Rapoport, Amos. *House Form and Culture* (Foundations of Cultural Geography Series). Englewood Cliffs, NJ: Prentice Hall, 1969.

Raventós, Ciska. "'My Heart Says NO': Political Experiences of the Struggle Against CAFTA-DR in Costa Rica." In *Central America in the New Millennium: Living Transition and Reimagining Democracy*. Jennifer L. and Ellen Moodie Burrell (eds), 80–95. New York and Oxford: Berghahn Books, 2013.

Raymond, Christopher M., Gregory Brown and Delene Weber. "The Measurement of Place Attachment: Personal, Community, and Environmental Connections." *Journal of Environmental Psychology* 30, no. 4 (2010): 422–434.

Rayner, Jeremy. "Vecinos, Ciudadanos Y Patriotas: Los Comités Patrióticos y el Espacio-Temporalidad de Oposición al Neoliberalismo en Costa Rica." *Revista de Ciencias Sociales [Journal of Social Sciences]* 121 (2008): 71–87.

———. "Defending, Contesting, and Transforming the 'Social State of Law': Organizing Opposition to Neoliberalism in Contemporary Costa Rica." American Ethnological Society and Society for Urban, National and Transnational Anthropology Annual Meeting, 2011.

———. "A New Way of Doing Politics: The Movement Against CAFTA in Costa Rica." CUNY Graduate Center. Dissertation, 2014a.

———. "When Participation Begins with a 'NO': How Some Costa Ricans Realized Direct Democracy by Contesting Free Trade." Etnofoor 26, no. 2 (2014b): 11–32.

Regis, Helen A. "Blackness and the Politics of Memory in the New Orleans Second Line." American Ethnologist 28, no. 4 (2001): 752–777.

Relph, Edward. Place and Placelessness. London: Pion, 1976.

———. Rational Landscapes and Humanistic Geography. New York: Barnes and Noble, 1981.

Revista de Costa Rica en el Siglo XIX. San José, Costa Rica: Tipográfica Nacional, 1902.

Rhodes, Lorna A. "Changing the Subject: Conversation in Supermax." Cultural Anthropology 20, no. 3 (2005): 388–411.

Riaño-Alcala, Pilar. "Remembering Place: Memory and Violence in Medillin, Colombia." Journal of Latin American Anthropology 7, no. 1 (2002): 276–309.

Richardson, Miles. "Being-in-the-Plaza Versus Being-in-the-Market: Material Culture and the Construction of Social Reality." American Ethnologist 9 (1982): 421–436.

———. "Place, Experience and Symbol." Geoscience and Man 24 (1984a): 1–3, 63–67.

———. "Material Culture and Being-in-Christ in Spanish America and the American South." In Built Form and Culture Conference Proceedings. Lawrence: University of Kansas, 1984b.

Ricoeur, Paul. From Text to Action: Essays in Hermeneutics II. Evanston: Northwestern University Press, 1991.

Rieker, Martina and Kamran Asfar Ali (eds). Gendering Urban Space in the Middle East, South Asia, and Africa. New York and Houndsmill, UK: Palgrave MacMillan, 2008.

Roberts, Rosemarie A. "Dancing With Social Ghosts: Performing Embodiments, Analyzing Critically." Transforming Anthropology 21, no. 1 (2013): 4–14.

Robin, Cynthia. "Outside of Houses: The Practices of Everyday Life at Chan Nóohol, Belize." Journal of Social Archaeology 2, no. 2 (2002): 245–268.

Robins, Steven. "At the Limits of Spatial Governmentality: A Message From the Tip of Africa." Third World Quarterly 23, no. 4 (2002): 665–689.

Rockefeller, Stuart. Starting From Quirpini: Place, Power and Movement. Bloomington: Indiana University Press, 2009.

Rodman, Margaret. "Moving Houses: Residential Mobility of Residents in Longana, Vanuatu." American Anthropologist 87, no. 1 (1985): 56–72.

———. "Empowering Place: Multilocality and Multivocality." American Anthropologist 94, no. 3 (1992): 640–656.

———. Houses Far From Home. Honolulu: University of Hawai'i Press, 2001.

Rodriguez, Sylvia. "Procession and Sacred Landscape in New Mexico." New Mexico Historical Review 77, no. 1 (1996): 1–56.

Rosaldo, Michelle Z. *Knowledge and Passion: Ilongot Notions of Self and Social Life*. Cambridge: Cambridge University Press, 1980.

Rose, Kenneth D. *One Nation Underground: The Fallout Shelter in American Culture*. New York and London: New York University Press, 2001.

Roseman, Marina. "Singers of the Landscape: Song, History, and Property Rights in the Malaysian Rain Forest." *American Anthropologist* 100, no. 1 (1998): 106–121.

Rosenweig, Roy. "Middle-Class Parks and Working-Class Play: The Struggle Over Recreational Space in Worcester, Massachusetts, 1870–1910." *Radical History Review* 21 (1979): 31–46.

Rose-Redwood, Reuben S. "Genealogies of the Grid: Revisiting Stanislawki's Search for the Origin of the Grid-Pattern Town." *The Geographical Review* 98, no. 1 (2008): 42–58.

Ross, Fiona. "Sense-Scapes: Senses and Emotion in the Making of Place." *Anthropology Southern Africa* 27, no. 1 & 2 (2004): 35–42.

Rotenberg, Robert. *Landscape and Power in Vienna*. Baltimore and London: The Johns Hopkins University Press, 1995.

Rotenberg, Robert and Gary McDonogh. *The Cultural Meaning of Space*. Westport and London: Bergin & Garvey, 1993.

Roth-Gordon, Jennifer. "The Language That Came Down the Hill; Slang, Crime, and Citizenship in Rio de Janeiro." *American Anthropologist* 111, no. 1 (2009): 57–68.

Rothe, Dawn and Stephen Muzzatti. "Enemies Everywhere: Terrorism, Moral Panic, and US Civil Society." *Critical Criminology* 12, no. 3 (2004): 327–350.

Rothstein, Frances Abrahamer. *Globalization in Rural Mexico: Three Decades of Change*. Austin: University of Texas, 2007.

Rouse, Roger. "Mexican Migration and the Social Space of Postmodernism." *Diaspora* 1, no. 1 (1991): 8–23.

Ruben, Matt and Jeff Maskovsky. "The Homeland Archipelago: Neoliberal Urban Governance After September 11." *Critique of Anthropology* 28, no. 2 (2008): 199–217.

Rutheiser, Charles. *Imagineering Atlanta: The Politics of Place in the City of Dreams*. London and New York: Verso, 1996.

———. "Mapping Contested Terrains: Schoolrooms and Streetcorners in Urban Belize." In *The Cultural Meaning of Urban Space*. Robert Rotenberg and Gary McDonogh (eds), 103–120. Westport and London: Bergin & Garvey, 1993.

Rutherford, Danilyn. "Commentary: What Affect Produces." *American Ethnologist* 39, no. 4 (2012): 688–691.

Sabatino, Michelangelo. "The Poetics of the Ordinary: The American Places of Charles W. Moore." *Places* 19, no. 2 (2007): 62–67.

Said, Edward W. *Orientalism*. New York: Vintage Books, 1978.

———. "Invention, Memory, and Place." *Critical Inquiry* 26, no. 2 (2000): 175–192.

Saito, Natsu Taylor. "The Costs of Homeland Security." *Radical History Review*, no. 53 (2005): 53–76.

Salamandra, Christa. *A New Old Damascus: Authenticity and Distinction in Urban Syria*. Bloomington: University of Indiana, 2004.

Sanchez Delgado, Nicolas and Carlos E. Umana Ugalde. "San José: Imagen y Estructural Urbana." *Revista Del Colegio Federado de Ingenieros y de Arquitectos de Costa Rica* 78 (1983): 20–29.

Sanchez, Thomas and Robert L. Lang. "Security vs. Status: The Two Worlds of Gated Communities." *Census Note* 2, no. 2 (2002): 2.

Sanchez, Thomas W., Robert E. Lang and Dawn M. Dhavale. "Security Versus Status? A First Look at the Census' Gated Community Data." *Journal Planning Education and Research* 24, no. 3 (2005): 281–291.

Sandoval-García, Carlos. *Threatening Others: Nicaraguans and the Formation of National Identities in Costa Rica.* Athens: Ohio University Press, 2004.

Sassen, Saskia. *Guests and Aliens.* New York: The New Press, 1999.

———. *Global Networks, Linked Cities. New York and London*: Routledge, 2002.

———. *Territory, Authority, Rights: From Medieval to Assemblages.* Princeton and Oxford: Princeton University Press, 2006.

Satterfield, Terre. "Emotional Agency and Contentious Practice: Activist Disputes in Old-Growth Forests." *Ethos* 32, no. 2 (2004): 233–256.

Savage, Mike. *Globalization and Belonging.* London and Thousand Oaks: Sage Publications, 2005.

Sawalha, Aseel. *Reconstructing Beirut: Memory and Space in a Postwar Arab City.* Austin: University of Texas Press, 2010.

Saylor, Conway F., Brian L. Cowart, Julie A. Lipovsky, Crystal Jackson and J. J. Finch Jr. "Media Exposure to September 11: Elementary School Students' Experiences and Post-Traumatic Symptoms." *American Behavioral Scientist* 46, no. 12 (2003): 1622–1632.

Sazama, Gerald. "A Brief History of Affordable Housing Cooperatives in the United States." *Economics Working Papers,* Paper 199609, 1996.

Scannell, Leila and Robert Gifford. "Defining Place Attachment: A Tripartite Organizing Framework." *Journal of Environmental Psychology* 30, no. 1 (2010): 1–10.

Schatzki, Theodore. "Practices and Actions: A Wittgensteinian Critique of Bourdieu and Giddens." *Philosophy of the Social Sciences* 27, no. 3 (1997): 283–308.

Schegloss, Emanuel A. "Notes on a Conversational Practice: Formulating Place." In *Studies in Social Interaction.* David N. Sudnow (ed.), 75–119. New York: The Free Press, MacMillan, 1972.

Scheper-Hughes, Nancy and Margaret Lock. "The Mindful Body." *Medical Anthropology* 1, no. 1 (1987): 6–41.

Schiffrin, Deborah. *Approaches to Discourse.* Cambridge and Oxford: Blackwell Publishers, 1994.

———. "Narrative as Self-Portrait." *Language in Society* 25, no. 2 (1996): 167–203.

Schill, Michael H., Ioan Voicu and Jonothan Miller. *The Condominium V. Cooperative Puzzle: An Empirical Analysis of Housing in New York City.* New York: Furman Center for Real Estate and Urban Policy, July 23, 2006.

Schmitt, Thomas. "Jemaa el Fna Square in Marrakech: Changes to a Social Space and to a UNESCO Masterpiece of the Oral and Intangible Hertitage of Humanity as a Result of Global Influences." *The Arab World Geographer* 8, no. 4 (2005): 173–195.

Schneider, Jane and Ida Susser (eds). *Wounded Cities: Destruction and Reconstruction in a Globalized World.* Oxford and New York: Oxford, 2003.

Schneider, Jane and Peter Schnieder. *Reversible Destiny: Mafia, Antimafia, and the Struggle for Palermo.* Berkeley and Los Angeles: University of California Press, 2003.

Schnitz, Ann and Robert Loeb. "More Public Parks! The First New York Environmental Movement." *Bronx County Historical Society Journal* 21, no. 2 (1984): 51–63.

Schuster, Mark A. et al. "A National Survey of Stress Reactions after the September 11, 2001 Terrorist Attacks." *New England Journal of Medicine* 345, no. 20 (2001): 1507–1512.

Schwenkel, Christina. "Post/Socialist Affect: Ruination and Reconstruction of the Nation in Urban Vietnam." *Cultural Anthropology* 2, no. 2 (2013): 252–277.

———. "Spectacular Infrastructure and Its Breakdown in Socialist Vietnam." *American Ethnologist* 42, no. 3 (2015): 520–534.

Scollon, Ron. "The Discourses of Food in the World System." *Journal of Language and Politics* 4, no. 3 (2005): 465–488.

Scollon, Ron and Suzanne Wong Scollon. *Discourses in Place: Language in the Material World*. London and New York: Routledge, 2003.

Scott, Catherine. *Images of America: City Island and Orchard Beach*. Charleston, SC: Arcadia, 1999.

Scott, Joan. *Feminism and History*. Oxford: Oxford University Press, 1996.

Seamon, David. *A Geography of the Lifeworld: Movement, Rest and Encounter*. London: Croom Helm, 1979.

———. "Place Attachment and Phenomenology: The Synergistic Dynamism of Place." In *Place Attachment: Advances in Theory, Methods and Research*. Lynne Manzo and Patrick Devine-Wright (eds), 11–22. New York: Routledge/Francis & Taylor, 2014.

Searle, J. R. *Speech Acts: An Essay in the Philosophy of Language*. Cambridge: Cambridge University Press, 1969.

———. *The Construction of Social Reality*. London: Penguin Books, 1995.

Searles, Harold F. *The Nonhuman Environment in Normal Development and in Schizophrenia*. Madison, CT: International Universities Press, 1960.

Sedgwick, Eve Kosofsky. *Touching Feeling: Affect, Pedagogy, Performativity*. Durham: Duke University Press, 2003.

Semper, Gottfried, Harry Francis Mallgrave and Michael Robinson. *Style in the Technical and Tectonics Arts, or, Practical Aesthetics*. Los Angeles: Getty Conservation Institute, 2004.

Sen, Arijit and Lisa Silverman (eds). *Making Place: Space and Embodiment in the City*. Bloomington and Indianapolis: Indiana University Press, 2014.

Sennett, Richard. *Classic Essays on the Cultures of Cities*. Englewood, NJ: Prentice Hall, 1969.

Sharp, Deen and Claire Panetta (eds). *Beyond the Square: Urbanism and the Arab Uprisings*. New York: Terreform, 2016.

Sharp, Lesley A. "The Invisible Woman: The Bioaesthetics of Engineered Bodies." *Body & Society* 17, no. 1 (2011): 1–30.

Shields, Rob. *Places on the Margin: Alternative Geographies of Modernity*. New York: Routledge, 1991.

Shiffman, Ron, Rick Bell, Lance Jay Brown and Elizabeth Lynne. *Beyond Zuccotti Park: Freedom of Assembly and the Occupation of Public Space*. Oakland, California: New Village Press, 2012.

Sieber, R. Timothy. "Public Access on the Urban Waterfront: A Question of Vision." In *The Cultural Meaning of Urban Space*. Robert Rotenberg and Gary McDonogh (eds), 173–194. Westport and London: Bergin & Garvey, 1993.

Siegler, R. and H. J. Levy. "Brief History of Cooperative Housing." *Cooperative Housing Journal of the National Association of Housing Cooperatives* (2001): 12–20.

Silver, Catherine. "Construction et Deconstruction des Identités de Genre." *Cahiers de Genre* 31 (2001): 185–201.

Silverman, Sydel. *Three Bells of Civilization: The Life of an Italian Hill Town.* New York: Columbia University Press, 1978.

Simmel, Georg. *Conflict: The Web of Group-affiliations.* New York: Free Press, 1955.

Simone, AbdouMaliq. "Urban Circulation and the Everyday Politics of African Urban Youth: The Case of Douala, Cameroon." *International Journal of Urban and Regional Research* 29, no. 3 (2005): 516–532.

———. "Pirate Towns: Reworking Social and Symbolic Infrastructures in Johannesburg and Douala." *Urban Studies* 43, no. 2 (2006): 357–370.

Smail, Daniel Lord. *On Deep History and the Brain.* Berkeley: University of California Press, 2008.

Smart, Alan. "Impeded Self-Help: Toleration and the Proscription of Housing Consolidation in Hong Kong's Squatter Areas." *Habitat International* 27, no. 2 (2003): 205–225.

Smart, Alan and George C. S. Lin. "Local Capitalism, Local Citizenship and Translocality: Rescaling From Below in the Pearl River Delta Region, China." *International Journal of Urban and Regional Research* 31, no. 2 (2007): 280–302.

Smart, Alan and Josephine Smart. "Urbanization and the Global Perspective." *Annual Review of Anthropology* 32 (2003): 263–285.

Smith, Adam and Nicholas David. "The Production of Space and the House of Xidi Sukur." *Current Anthropology* 36, no. 3 (1995): 441–471.

Smith, Andrea. "Place Replaced: Colonial Nostalgia and *Pied-Noir* Pilgrimages to Malta." *Cultural Anthropology* 18, no. 3 (2003): 329–364.

Smith, Michael E. "Form and Meaning in the Earliest Cities: A New Approach to Ancient Urban Planning." *Journal of Planning History* 6, no. 1 (2007): 3–47.

———. *Aztec City-State Capitals.* Gainesville: University Press of Florida, 2008.

Smith, Michael Peter. *Transnational Urbanism: Locating Globalization.* Malden, MA and Oxford: Blackwell Publishing, 2001.

———. "Power in Place/Places of Power: Contextualizing Transnational Research." *City & Society* 17, no. 1 (2005): 5–34.

Smith, Michael Peter and Matt Bakker. *Citizenship Across Borders: The Political Transformation of El Migrante.* Ithaca: Cornell University Press, 2008.

Smith, Michael Peter and Joe R. Feagin. *The Bubbling Cauldron: Race, Ethnicity and the Urban Crisis.* Minneapolis and London: University of Minnesota Press, 1995.

Smith, Michael Peter and Luis Eduardo Guarnizo (eds). *Transnationalism From Below.* New Brunswick, NJ: Transaction, 1998.

Smith, Neil. *Uneven Development.* Athens: University of Georgia Press, 1984.

———. *Uneven Development: Nature, Capital and the Production of Space* (3rd edition). Oxford: Blackwell, 1990.

———. *The New Urban Frontier: Gentrification and the Revanchist City.* New York and London: Routledge, 1996.

———. *Uneven Development: Nature, Capital and the Production of Space* (3rd edition). Oxford: Blackwell, 2008.

Smith, Neil and Cindi Katz. "Grounding Metaphor: Towards a Spatialized Politics." In *Place and the Politics of Identity.* Michael Keith and Steve Pile (eds), 67–83. London and New York: Routledge, 1993.

Smith, Robert Courtney. *Mexican New York: Transnational Lives of New Immigrants.* Berkeley: University of California Press, 2006.

Smithsimon, Gregory. *September 12: Community and Neighborhood Recovery at Ground Zero.* New York and London: New York University Press, 2011.

Soja, Edward. *Postmodern Geographies: The Reassertion of Space in Critical Social Theory.* New York: Verso, 1989.

———. *Seeking Spatial Justice.* Minneapolis and London: University of Minnesota Press, 2010.

Sopranzetti, Claudio. "Owners of the Map: Mobility and Mobilization Among Motorcycle Taxi Drivers in Bangkok." *City & Society* 26, no. 1 (2014): 120–143.

Sorkin, Michael (ed.). *Variations on a Theme Park: the New American City and the End of Public Space.* New York: Hill & Wang, 1992.

———. *Indefensible Space: The Architecture of the National Insecurity State.* New York and London: Routledge, 2008.

Sorkin, Michael and Sharon Zukin. *After the Trade Center.* New York and London: Routledge, 2002.

Spier, Leslie. *Yuman Tribes of the Gila River.* Chicago: University of Chicago Press, 1933.

Spinney, Justin. "A Chance to Catch a Breath: Using Mobile Video Ethnography in Cycling Research," *Mobilities* sec. 6, col. 2 (2011): 161–182.

Spinoza, Benedict de. "The Ethics." In *The Collected Works of Spinoza, 1.* Edwin Curley (ed. and trans.), 408–617. Princeton: Princeton University Press, 1985 [1679].

Starecheski, Amy. *Ours to Lose: When Squatters Became Homeowners in New York City.* Chicago: University of Chicago Press, 2016.

Stasch, Rupert. "The Poetics of Village Space When Villages Are New: Settlement Form as History-Making in West Papua." *American Ethnologist* 40, no. 3 (2013): 555–570.

Stewart, Kathleen. *Ordinary Affects.* Durham and London: Duke University Press, 2007.

———. "Afterword: Worlding Refrains." In *The Affect Theory Reader.* Melissa Gregg and Gregory J. Seigworth (eds), 339–354. Durham: Duke University Press, 2010.

———. "Atmospheric Attunements." *Environment and Planning D: Society and Space* 29, no. 3 (2011): 445–453.

Stewart, Pamela J. and Andrew Strathern. *Landscape, Memory and History: Anthropological Perspectives.* London: Pluto Press, 2003.

Stokols, D. and S. A. Shumaker. "People in Places." In *Cognition, Social Behavior and the Environment.* J. Harvey (ed.), 441–488. Hillsdale, NJ: Lawrence Erlbaum, 1981.

Stoler, Ann Laura. *Imperial Debris: On Ruins and Ruination.* Durham and London: Duke University Press, 2013.

Stoller, Paul. *The Taste of Ethnographic Things: The Senses in Anthropology.* Philadelphia: University of Pennsylvania Press, 1989.

———. *Money Has No Smell: The Africanization of New York City.* Chicago and London: University of Chicago Press, 2002.

Stone, C. "Crime in the City." In *Breaking Away: the Future of Cities.* Julia Vitullo-Martin (ed.), 98–103. New York: Twentieth-Century Fund Press, 1996.

Stone, Samuel. "Aspects of Power Distribution in Costa Rica." In *Contemporaries Cultures and Societies of Latin America.* Dwight Heath (ed.), 93–107. New York: Random House, 1974.

Straight, Bilinda. *Women on the Verge of Home*. Albany: State University of New York Press, 2005.

Striffler, Steve. "Neither Here nor There: Mexican Immigrant Workers and the Search for Home." *American Ethnologist* 34, no. 4 (2007): 674–688.

Sunstein, Cass R. "Terrorism and Probability Neglect." *Journal of Risk and Uncertainly* 26, no. 2 (2003): 121–136.

Susser, Ida. *Norman Street: Poverty and Politics in an Urban Neighborhood*. New York: Oxford University Press, 1982.

———. "The Construction of Poverty and Homelessness in U.S. Cities." *Annual Review of Anthropology* 25 (1996): 411–425.

Susser, Ida and Thomas Carl Patterson (eds). *Cultural Diversity in the United States: A Critical Reader*. New York: Blackwell, 2001.

Taplin, Dana H., Suzanne Scheld and Setha M. Low. "Rapid Ethnographic Assessment in Urban Parks: A Case Study of Independence National Historical Park." *Human Organization* 61, no. 1 (2004): 80–93.

Thomas, Philip. "The River, the Road, and the Rural-Urban Divide: A Postcolonial Moral Geography from Southeast Madagascar." *American Ethnologist* 29, no. 2 (2002): 366–391.

Thomas, Rachel. "Quand le pas fait corps et sens avec l'espace. Aspects perceptifs et expressifs de la marche en ville." *Cybergéo: Revue Européenne De Géographie* 261 (2004).

Thrift, Nigel. *Non-Representational Theory: Space/Politics/Affect*. London and New York: Routledge, 2008.

Tilley, Christopher. *A Phenomenology of Landscape: Places, Paths and Monuments*. Oxford and Providence: Berg, 1994.

Tomkins, Silvan S. *Affect Imagery Consciousness*, Volumes 1 and 2. New York: Springer, 1962–1963.

Torres Rivas, Edelberto. *History and Society in Central America*. Austin: University of Texas, 1993.

Trullás y Aulet, Ignacio. *Escenas Josefinas*. San José, Costa Rica: Libreria Espanola, 1913.

Tschumi, Bernard. "De-, Dis-, Ex-." In *Architecture and Disjunction*, 85. Cambridge: MIT Press, 1987.

Tsing, Anna Lowenhaupt. *Friction: An Ethnography of Global Connection*. Princeton and Oxford: Princeton University Press, 2005.

Tuan, Yi-Fu. *Space and Place: The Perspective of Experience*. London: Edward Arnold, 1977.

———. *Landscapes of Fear*. 1979: Minneapolis, University of Minnesota Press, 1979.

———. "Space and Place: Humanistic Perspective." In *Philosophy in Geography*. Stephen Gale and Gunnar Olsson (eds), 387–427. Dordrecht, Holland and Boston: D. Reidel, 1979.

Tucker, Ian. "Psychology as Space: Embodied Relationality." *Social and Personality Psychology Compass* 5, no. 5 (2011): 231–238.

Turner, Bryan S. *The Body and Society*. Oxford: Basil Blackwell, 1984.

Turner, Terence. "The Social Skin." In *Not Work Alone*. Jeremy Cherfas, and Roger Lewin (eds), 112–140. London: Temple Smith, 1980.

———. "Social Body and Embodied Subjects: Bodiliness, Subjectivity, and Sociality Among the Kayapo." *Cultural Anthropology* 10, no. 2 (1995): 143–170.

Turner, Victor. *The Forest of Symbols: Aspects of Ndembu Ritual*. Ithaca, NY: Cornell University Press, 1967.

——. *The Drums of Affliction: A Study of Religious Processes Among the Ndembu of Zambia*. Oxford: Clarendon, 1968.

Ucko, Peter J. "Foreword." In *Sacred Sites, Sacred Places, One World Archaeology*. David L. Carmichael, Jane Hubert, Brian Reeves and Audhild Schanche (eds), xiii–xxiii, vol. 23. London and New York: Routledge, 1994.

Udvarhelyi, Eva Tessza. "Reclaiming the Streets – Redefining Democracy." *Hungarian Studies* 23, no. 1 (2009): 121–145.

Üngür, Erdem. "Space: The Undefinable Space of Architecture: Theory for the Sake of the Theory." ARCHTHEO '11 Conference Proceedings, 132–143. Istanbul, Turkey: Dakam Publishing, 2011.

United States Census Bureau. *American Housing Survey for the United States*. Washington, DC: U. S. Government Printing Office, 2005.

Upton, Dell. "Seen, Unseen, and Scene." In *Understanding Ordinary Landscapes*. Paul Groth and Todd W. Bressi (eds), 174–179. New Haven: Yale University Press, 1997.

——. *Another City: Urban Life and Urban Spaces in the New American Republic*. Yale University Press, 2008.

Vale, Lawrence J. and Thomas J. Companella. *The Resilient City: How Modern Cities Recover From Disaster*. New York: Oxford University Press, 2005.

Valiani, Arafaat A. "Physical Training, Ethical Discipline, and Creative Violence: Zones of Self-Mastery in the Hindu Nationalist Movement." *Cultural Anthropology* 25, no. 1 (2010): 73–99.

Vega Carballo, José Luis. *San José: Antecedentes Coloniales y Formación Del Estado Nacional*. San José, Costa Rica: Instituto de Investigaciones Social, 1981.

Vergunst, Jo Lee. "Rhythms of Walking: History and Presence in a City Street." *Space and Culture* 13, no. 4 (2010): 376–388.

Vertovec, Steven. *Transnationalism*. London and New York: Routledge, 2009.

Vučinić-Nešković, Vesna. *Prostorno Ponasanje u Dubrovniku: Antropoloska Studija Grada Sa Ortogonalnom Strukturom (Spatial Behavior in Dubrovnik: An Anthropological Study of a City With Orthogonal Structure)*. Belgrade: Faculty of Philosophy, University of Belgrade, 1999.

Vučinić-Nešković, Vesna and Jelena Miloradović. "Corso as a Total Social Phenomenon: The Case of Smederevska Palanka, Serbia." *Ethnologia Balkanica* 10 (2006): 229–250.

Wacquant, Loic. *Urban Outcasts: A Comparative Sociology of Advanced Marginality*. Cambridge and Malden, MA: Polity, 2008.

Wang, Kevin and Ralph B. Taylor. "Simulated Walks Through Dangerous Alleys: Impacts of Features and Progress on Fear." *Journal of Environmental Psychology* 26, no. 4 (2006): 269–283.

Ward, Lester. Frank. "Evolution of Social Structures." *American Journal of Sociology* 10, no. 5 (1905): 589–605.

Watson, James L. "Presidential Address: Virtual Kinship, Real Estate, and Diaspora Formation – The Man Lineage Revisited." *The Journal of Asian Studies* 63, no. 4 (2004): 893–910.

Watson, Sophie. *Markets as Sites for Social Interaction: Spaces of Diversity*. York: Roundtree Foundation, 2006.

Weart, Spencer R. *Nuclear Fear: A History of Images*. Cambridge and London: Harvard University Press, 1988.

Weber, Max. *The Protestant Ethic and the Spirit of Capitalism*. London and New York: Routledge, 1930.

Weeks, John M. "Residential and Local Group Organization in the Maya Lowland of Southeastern Campeche, Mexico." In *Household and Community in the Mesoamerican Past*. Richard R. Wilk and Wendy Ashmore (eds), 73–96. Albuquerque: University of New Mexico Press, 1988.

Weiner, James. *The Empty Place: Poetry, Space and Being Among the Foi of Papua New Guinea*. Bloomington: University of Indiana Press, 1991.

Weinreb, Amelia Rosenberg and Yodan Rofe. "Mapping Feeling: An Approach to the Study of Emotional Response to the Built Environment and Landscape." *Journal of Architectural and Planning Research* 30, no. 2 (2013): 127–139.

Weir, Kirsten. "Design in Mind: Psychologists Can Help to Design Smart, Sustainable Spaces for the 21st Century." *Monitor on Psychology*, 40, no. 10 November (2013): 50–53.

Weiss, Brad. "Making Pigs Local: Discerning the Sensory Character of Place." *Cultural Anthropology* 26, no. 3 (2011): 438–461.

Werbner, Pnina. *Imagined Diasporas Among Manchester Muslims*. Oxford: James Currey, 2002.

West, Darrell and Marion Orr. "Managing Citizen Fear: Public Attitudes Toward Urban Terrorism." *Urban Affairs Review* 41, no. 1 (2005): 93–105.

White, Geoffrey M. "Emotional Remembering: The Pragmatics of National Memory." *Ethos* 27, no. 4 (2000a): 505–529.

———. "Representing Emotional Meaning: Category, Metaphor, Schema, Discourse." In *Handbook of Emotions* (2nd edition). Michael Lewis and Jeannette M. Haviland-Jones (eds), 30–44. New York and London: Guilford Press, 2000b.

———. "National Subjects: September 11 and Pearl Harbor." *American Ethnologist* 31, no. 3 (2004): 293–310.

———. "Emotive Institutions." In *A Companion to Psychological Anthropology: Modernity and Psychocultural Change*. Conerly Casey and Robert B. Edgerton (eds), 241–254. Malden, MA and Oxford: Blackwell Publishing, 2005.

———. "Landscapes of Power: National Memorials and the Domestication of Affect." *City & Society* 18, no. 1 (2006): 50–61.

Whitehead, T. L. *Ethnographic Overview and Assessment of Independence National Historical Park: A Final Report Submitted to the National Park Service*. Philadelphia: National Park Service, 2002.

Williams, Brett. *Upscaling Downtown: Stalled Gentrification in Washington D.C.* Ithaca, NY: Cornell University Press, 1988.

Williams, Drid. "'Semasiology': A Semantic Anthropologist's View of Human Movements and Actions." In *Semantic Anthropology*. David Parkin (ed.), 161–182. London: Academic Press, 1982.

Williams, Raymond. *Marxism and Literature*. Oxford: Oxford University Press, 1977.

Winegar, Jessica. "The Privilege of Revolution: Gender, Class, Space, and Affect in Egypt." *American Ethnologist* 36, no. 1 (2012): 62–65.

Winter, Greg. "Exodus of 9/11 is Thing of Past Near Tower Site." *New York Times*, 20 August 2002, p. 1.

Wirth, Louis. "Urbanism as a Way of Life." *American Journal of Sociology* 44, no. 1 (1938): 1–24.

Wolf, Eric. *Europe and the People Without History*. Berkeley and Los Angeles: University of California Press, 1982.

Wright, Gwendolyn. *Building the Dream: A Social History of Housing in America*. Cambridge: MIT Press, 1981.

Wroblewski, Michael. "Amazonian Kichwa Proper: Ethnolinguistic Domain in Pan-Indian Ecuador." *Journal of Linguistic Anthropology* 22, no. 1 (2012): 64–86.

Yeager, Patricia. "Narrating Space." In *The Geography of Identity*. Patricia Yeager (ed.), 1–38. Ann Arbor: University of Michigan Press, 1996.

Young, Iris. "The Logic of Masculinist Protection: Reflections on the Current Security State." *Signs: Journal of Women in Culture and Society* 29, no. 11 (2003): 1–25.

Young, Jock. *The Exclusive Society*. London: Sage Publications, 1999.

Young, Michael and Peter Willmott. *Family and Kinship in East London*. London: Routledge & Kegan, 1957.

YU, Shuenn-Der. "Meaning, disorder and the political economy of night markets in Taiwan." University of California, Davis, Ph.D. Dissertation, 1995.

Zembylas, Michalinos. "Investigating the Emotional Geographies of Exclusion at a Multicultural School." *Emotion, Space and Security* 4 (2011): 151–159.

Zevi, Bruno. *Architecture as Space*. New York: The Perseus Book Group: Da Capo Press, 1957.

Zhang, Li. "Contesting Spatial Modernity in Late-Socialist China." *Current Anthropology* 47, no. 3 (2006): 461–476.

———. *In Search of Paradise: Middle-Class Living in a Chinese Metropolis*. Ithaca, NY and London: Cornell University Press, 2010.

Zukin, Sharon. *Loft Living*. Los Angeles: University of California Press, 1982.

———. *Landscapes of Power: From Detroit to Disney World*. Los Angeles: University of California Press, 1991.

———. *The Cultures of Cities*. New York: Blackwell, 1996.

Index

Page numbers in *italics* refer to figures and tables.